LET THE DOG DRIVE

Elmer Holmes Bobst Award for Emerging Writers

Established in 1983, the Elmer Holmes Bobst Awards in Art and Letters are presented each year to individuals who have brought true distinction to the American literary scene. Recipients of the Awards include writers as varied as Toni Morrison, John Updike, Russell Baker, Eudora Welty, Edward Albee, Arthur Miller, Joyce Carol Oates, and James Merrill. The Awards were recently expanded to include categories devoted to emerging writers of poetry and fiction, and in 1992 the jurors selected winners in that category, David Bowman for his novel *Let the Dog Drive*, and Elizabeth Dodd for her collection of poetry, *Like Memory, Caverns*.

DAVID BOWMAN

LET THE DOG DRIVE

A NOVEL

NEW YORK UNIVERSITY PRESS

NEW YORK AND LONDON

NEW YORK UNIVERSITY PRESS
New York and London

Library of Congress Cataloging-in-Publication Data
Bowman, David, 1957–
Let the dog drive / David Bowman.
    p.   cm.
ISBN 0-8147-1205-3(cloth)
I. Title.
PS3552.08757L48   1992   92-31757
813'.54—dc20   CIP

New York University Press books are printed on acid-free paper,
and their binding materials are chosen for strength and durability.

Manufactured in the United States of America

10 9 8 7 6 5

Book design by Jennifer Dossin

This novel is for my friend, Dr. Eric Schneider,
and my wife, Chloe Wing.

Men and Women . . . they talk of Hallowed things,
aloud—and embarrass my Dog.

Emily Dickinson
August 1862

God in his day, had Emily Dickinson,
whose thrashing surrender under his unmeasurable weight
even she mistook for love.

Robert Stone
March 1984

ACKNOWLEDGMENTS

This novel came into being as the result of a long continuing dialogue with Brian Breger. I am most grateful to Kathy Daniel, Amy E. M. Kefauver, Andrew Ragan, Jonathan Valin, and Monique Vescia who encouraged and challenged me so generously. Deep thanks to Dr. Thomas Kay and Mike Bud Nolan for being earnest companions. More thanks to Meighan Gale and Rennie Childress for providing their grace. Finally, I am much indebted to the Bobst Awards judges Mark Richard and Amy Hempel, and especially to my editor, Barbara Epler.

Portions of this novel were published in Amherst, Massachusetts (*The Amherst Review*) and Queensland, Australia (*Earth Wings*).

CONTENTS

• •

)

PART ONE

. . . .

EMILY DICKINSON'S
VOLKSWAGEN, 1976

A woman stands beside the highway furiously pitching oranges into the desert. I approach her lugging fifty pounds of books. Heaven is hot and bleaches the outfield dunes to flour, the woman's skin to ivory. Her hair is stuffed beneath a blue baseball cap. Her hair is red, but shows no sign of flames . . . yet. She is wearing a halter of twin red-and-black diamondback bandanas, and her shoulders are peppered with freckles. Her pitching stance seems perfect—hands poised cupping the citrus waist-level behind her back, left leg arched and raised. Then she whips forward and hurls another orange across the grit, a pitch she'll later call a "knuckleball."

Sylvia will name all her pitches because she loves what she calls Arm Language. She'll refer to me as a lawn jockey—"stooping down the road with your left arm cocked as if you just wandered off someone's front yard."

I'll explain that I was simultaneously hitchhiking and searching for shade. ("This road has no shade," she said.)

And this is Interstate 8, the southernmost conversation between California and Arizona. I was hitching east—my back to traffic. On the opposite shoulder, heat waves rippled a red Volkswagen with the top down. The pitching woman was the driver. Did she have water? I ran across the road and discovered the highway leading to Sylvia layered with flattened roadlife. My eastbound lane had pancaked mammals, snouts pressed into grins. The divider was brown grass and black feathers. (The sky was empty.) Sylvia's lane was lizards and snakes flattened into zigzags. On the shoulder, the car's hubcaps were spotted yellow with hornets. All that this Darwinian downgrade lacked was fish—although that was due to the desert, not necessarily the highway: up beside Big Bear there's a road where trout leap onto the blacktop and sportsmen dash between cars to catch them.

My animal-death sprint lacked fish. But not language. A Mexican voice shouted from the car, his pauses punctuated by cheers. The radio was tuned to a bullfight. I would later learn Sylvia knew Spanish—she was parking and pitching until the matador did his swordwork. I knew Spanish too, and the announcer was yelling: "The picadors are getting angry! The picadors are getting angry!"

Below the radio lay another bag of oranges. Sylvia was fussing with her windup, so I planned to request a fruit after her next pitch. I braced my hands on the hood and the sun-baked metal scorched my palms. See me hopping in the dust, flapping my wrists—doing the Dog Dance—shouting my first words of greeting to Sylvia Cushman: "Shit/Motherfucker/Shit!"

•

I remember my first words, but don't remember the moment the woman introduced herself as "Sylvia Cushman." Perhaps her name came by osmosis. As I sucked an orange, noting the crisscrossed golf clubs on her cap, she studied me with seawater eyes—pupils dilated either from heat or dope. What she saw was a gangly 18–year-old Southern-Cal milkboy sporting a Prince Valiant. I saw an ageless woman with a slim body, bandanas barely covering slight breasts with skin smooth, not bony, along her sternum—she was an apricot dolphin.

When Sylvia grew bored of being visually annotated an apricot dolphin, she pitched another orange, grunting: "That's how the Bird does it."

I choked on a peel.

My immediate connection was Bird = Speckled Bird = My mother's church: the Tabernacle of the Speckled Bird.

Sylvia interpreted my stricken face as ignorance and scowled, "The 'Bird'—Mark Fidrych, dummy! Adored pitcher for the Tigers."

I turned to cough up the peel and then asked Sylvia why she was throwing oranges. She said the Arizona border patrol wouldn't let her enter the state with California produce: ". . . and I'll be damned if those fat fascists are going to confiscate my fruit."

I studied my orange. It was a Valencia and picked north, near San Citro. As I reached for another, she asked, "So what are you doing wandering in the desert like Bishop Pike with his Coke bottle?"

This time I caught her cultural reference . . . even picked up a higher gestalt. Sylvia was referring to the bishop from San Francisco who had wandered into the Sahara with only a bottle of Coca-Cola. She was ignorant of her duo reference to the Fatty Arbuckle rape scandal of 1921. After a wild party with other silent film stars in Frisco, he was arrested for rape. Worse, the fatman had used a Coca-Cola bottle. The girl died of internal wreckage. "But that fat slob was framed," my grandfather told me. "The *Chicago Tribune* sent me out to the trial. A botch-job got that girl." Arbuckle was acquitted, but his weight could never again be playful. His Hollywood career had been killed by that mythical Coke bottle, the same bottle that became my grandfather's Plymouth Rock in California. He stayed out west and sired my dad. Arbuckle died in '33 and hovered in limbo until I was conceived. After my birth in '58, my mother not only kept her weight, but swelled to a monstrous girth—Arbuckle using her body to purify the memory of his mass. A decade later, my grandfather convinced Bishop Pike to walk into the desert to exorcise the demonic aspects of that influential Coke. As I now stood beside this sizzling Volkswagen, I shouted, "Surely I am a corrupted Coke! Sylvia, be my Bishop Pike!"

I cried for redemption because the day before I had shot a man beneath a fruit tree. But you're not reading the narration of some punk sociopath! My shooting was justified and only caused injury, not death.

In any case, Sylvia gave a blank stare to my plea, so I mumbled that I should continue east now. That prompted her to yell: "East? Wrong direction, buster! Get your Horace Greeley trip together! Go west, young man, go west!"

Sylvia hopped into the Beetle, and then squealed from the sun-seared seat. She leaned forward and monkeyed with her keys. "Don't trance out for goodness sakes! Get in!"

I opened the passenger door and knelt sideways in my seat so I wouldn't burn. Sylvia gave the shift a quick reach, then spun us onto the road, bumping my jaw with her raised elbow. As we passed a convoy of gunmetal Piggly Wiggly trucks, she shot her head over her arm and bit my shoulder—hard—laughing: "Now an orange tree will grow there!" I knelt there stunned, blinking as the sun glinted off her fillings. Sylvia seriously stomped the gas and I fell into my seat as the car sped west.

At that moment, I believed Sylvia was Blind Justice returning me to the cops. To face the music. But in reality, the only thing I was facing was Sylvia Cushmanism, a concept about anything but truth or consequences. She shot our car over the divider and squealed a U-turn into the eastbound lane. I knelt in the seat rubbing my shoulder, muttering one of my grandfather's Tim Fontanel lines: "She hadn't drawn blood, but she might as well have" (*Hot Guns Don't Lie*, 1947).

•

W hen the steering wheel cooled, Sylvia leaned back and
lazily navigated with one hand. The sun still glared
and she shouted, "There's another cap here somewhere." I toed the blue Almond Joy candy wrappers spread on
the floor, and reached for the glove compartment. Sylvia shrieked,
"Don't! It's a horror story in there!"

I whipped my hand away, and shrugged. (There was nothing
peculiar in her outburst—I knew about glove compartments. In
Los Angeles, my mother's car was sitting on a pedestal, its glove
compartment guarded by two men who quoted Luke and carried
Browning M1935s. My mother told her congregation that the
face of an angel named Mupiel had appeared in the window of
our dryer one morning, and proclaimed that God's supplement
to the Bible—The Third Testament—had been placed in our
Mercury's glove compartment, and that neither were to be opened
until 1985, when the faithful would have need for the new
Scriptures.) Turning to look for the cap, I tried to read Sylvia's
Volkswagen. The backseat was piled with rustling tourist bro-
chures from borax ghost towns and Death Valley Scotty's Castle;
there were also desert-rat newspapers flapping: *The Indio Bee*,
The Panamint Observer; then a well-annotated Baja road map, a
dog-eared Aquarius Press paperback called *Hallucinogenic
Mushrooms of the Wild*; and finally a jiggling *Boy Scouts of
America: Survival in the Wilderness Handbook*. Beneath them, I
found the Tigers cap. As I flipped it on, I figured the books
meant that Sylvia, like me, read behind the wheel.

If this isn't your habit, know that reading and driving is neither difficult nor dangerous. You rest the book against the steering wheel and do a one-two eye movement between the page and the road, occasionally varying with a one-two-three between page, road, and rearview mirror. As I turned in my seat, my cap bill bumped Sylvia's mirror. I waited for her to readjust it. She didn't. Driving with a cocked mirror indicates that the driver doesn't read behind the wheel. I was disappointed and as I dealt with that, Sylvia heaved up the second sack of oranges and dropped it in my lap, saying: "Start pitching."

I reached in the bag and began throwing oranges into the hot blowing air.

"Jesusjack, you throw like a girl!" Sylvia yelled.

I stopped and racked my brain for baseball inspiration—what came was a '40s Fletcher cartoon octopus pitching ice cream. With this in mind, I pitched till my socket hurt. When the last orange was gone, I grabbed the empty bag so it wouldn't fly away. Sylvia yelled, "Put it on your head."

I automatically tried to fit the sack over my baseball cap.

Sylvia grabbed my arm, yelling, "I'm kidding! I'm kidding!"

She abruptly changed lanes and cut off a station wagon, getting us an angry smear of car horn. I reached up to adjust the mirror, but with quicker Arm Language she slapped it into a more-or-less correct position, and began her bio: she was 43. She was married to an auto executive. She loved taking lone road trips without him. They lived in Bloomfield Hills, Michigan. She was finishing her Master's in 19th-century American literature at the University of Michigan. She had two sons. The oldest had just begun attending Miles Standish College, an experimental school in Amherst, Massachusetts. Her 5-year-old was a promising kindergarten artist plagued with severe allergies.

"There's a chemical in yellow fingerpaint that causes his little fingers to swell like sausages," she yelled as we passed a string of trucks tugging meat and avocados. She waved up at one hard-faced driver—surely steering his rig with hands swelled into paws—and said, "I've never been out west before, where truck drivers spring fully grown from their mothers' wombs."

The trucker she waved at kept his rig beside us and jawed energetically into his C.B. We were soon boxed-in by trucks, each driver taking a turn to pull up and peer down at Sylvia's halter-topped steering technique. Sylvia drove oblivious to this attention even though their engines were so loud she had to shout to be heard: "You know, back home I'll experience so many moments—like I'll be golfing with the girls—and suddenly look around and feel so angry." She paused, searching for words. "And I feel like screaming, 'Why am I a freak?' " She swerved between two semis, then outdistanced the pack on a stretch of empty road. " 'Why am I such a fucking freak?' But out here," Sylvia said, still yelling and waving at a jut of craggy buttes, "out west—it's perfect. Everyone is a freak."

There was now no need to yell, so I asked in a regular tone, "You mean 'freak' as in 'doper'?"

"Oh honey!" She shook her head, still shouting. "What terms are you comfortable with? I mean 'freak' as in 'weirdo'!" She studied me again. "God, you're certainly a freak. You look like some Calvinist sprout about to tromp the wilds of the U.P. to convert lapsed Norwegians."

I didn't know that she had just made a Michigan geographical reference. Instead, I assumed Sylvia had hounded up my mother's Jesus vibe. We were silent for another ten miles until she asked—shouted—her first personal question of me: "So what does your father do?"

I paused, puzzled at such a nonfeminist question—especially since if we sat open-mouthed, our fillings would pick up my mother's voice broadcasting her radio show above the desert. But I answered Sylvia with my standard reply: "Nothing. He's dead."

Instead of sympathy or silence, she cried, "How?" and I replied with the truth: "He was killed by a hippopotamus."

Sylvia laughed, "Hey, that's a heck of a lot more interesting than cancer!"

•

Sylvia should have made sympathetic moos about my dead dad or else claimed I made up the hippo. She did neither. At first this was puzzling, but for the entire trip her requests for personal data would be erratic, her responses surreal. For example, a scar splits my lip—as if Kirk Douglas's cleft were raised two inches. Sylvia asked how this happened, and I told in a car crash, and that I'd bitten my tongue tip off too. She quipped, "Well, that explains why you talk like Charlie Chan." Then her tone turned astonishingly delicate to ask: "How did your digestive tract deal with that piece of tongue? Did you cough it up? Or swallow it and pass it later?" Then she added, "Were you able to taste things telepathically?"

I said I licked ice cream with ESP, and then insisted that she follow the real deal: I had been tooling along in my grandfather's beat-up Dodge on the trails behind his orange grove, steering and reading *Jumping the Gun*, one of the Spillanian mysteries my grandfather wrote under the pseudonym Rex Ringer in the '40s and '50s. As synchronicity, its cover was an illustration of a convertible racing away with Trixie O'Reilly, blond Girl Friday, gripping the wheel, her right wrist handcuffed to her boss, Tim Fontanel, Hollywood private eye. We peer down Trixie's bullet breasts while Fontanel, blond haggard hardcase, twists in his seat and fires his blunt automatic at whomever is pursing them, the gun spitting cartridges down the trunk. I had my own pedal to the floor until I was jarred by an endless crunch, and chomped my tongue, and whiplashed my face into the book into the steering wheel, and—to use a Fontanelism—I was kissing the pages with blood while oranges rolled down the windshield. It was this orange detail Sylvia retained miles later, saying: "Tell me again how you shot a man from a speeding car as oranges hit your roof."

It pissed me off that in the two hours we'd known each other she'd already scrambled two different stories. I told her again how I shot Shem Enouch, who had driven down to my grandfather's intending to drag me back to the Tabernacle of the Speckled

Bird in L.A. Before we left, however, he insisted we kneel and trance together on the Holy Ghost, then we'd reach into the box he brought. This box was cardboard. This box was from Vons. This box was filled with sleeping snakes, their rattles gently shaking as they dreamed. We were to grip our separate reptiles and raise them level with our foreheads—an act neither Freudian nor Californian nor a practice of my mother's church, but a presentation of faith developed in the backwaters of the Bible belt where Shem had learned to follow Paul's promise that the faithful "shall take up serpents."

My faith was honed on detective novels. I snagged Shem's Bible and my swing split the bridge of his nose. We were in the hacienda at the time, and I rushed into the kitchen to grab my grandfather's shotgun from behind the Frigidaire. I was hiding down in the orchard when Shem stooped, and searching beneath the orange trees, shouted, "You're seen, son! Prepare to get straight with your Savior!"

He began hopping the furrows swinging his Bible and Vons box. When he reached my row of trees, I raised the shotgun and blasted him—buckshot, serpents, orange juice—the recoil knocking me into a furrow, while a mist of oranges hung in the air. Shem had his hands to his face shouting, "Sweet shit-licking Jesus! Sweet shit-licking Jesus!"

His blasphemy sank me in regret. (I told Sylvia that he was not the first devotee I had caused to curse God: I once had a baby-sitter—a toothy spinster who sang in my mother's Hollywood church. One lunch time, I insisted this woman fix me tomato soup. The pantry lacked Campbells, so I was left alone while she ran to the grocery. This gave me ten precious minutes alone to scan the TV for my father. I had to keep my search secret. Watching television honored graven images. (My mother just used TV to get sinners hooked; the devoted kept their ears glued to her radio show.) At the moment I heard the babysitter's crash, I was kneeling watching the blue dot swirl up into a picture. I poked the set off, unplugged it, and hid the plug under the rug. Her car had just been slammed by a moving van at the edge of our stumpy driveway and she spent two hours with the dashboard crushing her lap, singing a nonstop howl against God with lyrics similar to Shem's. For the next three months she stayed silent until she was discharged from Hollywood Presbyterian to resume her babysitting chores. During our first lunch, she stood at the stove and suddenly threw the soup spoon across the room. She wailed that on the day of her crash, the Lord had tested her faith with pain. And she'd failed. She'd failed. No matter how much forgiveness she asked, she and God both knew that if she got diced by a dashboard again, she'd sing the same song. Then she twisted on the other burner and stuck the sleeves of her dress in the rings of flame . . .) I ended this tale telling Sylvia, "I wish I had shot Shem from a speeding car. Then I wouldn't have heard his curses. Then I wouldn't have known that I'd made another devotee curse their way from God."

I turned and saw Sylvia's eyes tearing. I reached out to steer while she wiped them.

"I remember the afternoon I was sliding this really majestic birthday cake out of a box," she sniffled. "Joe the baker had written *Happy Birthday Benny* on the top tier in baby-blue icing. Now my eldest is Ben, not Benny. I even blue-pencil Joan Didion, so I had to edit the frosting to: *Happy Birthday Ben*." Sylvia took the wheel again. "God, the kids were going crazy with their noisemakers so I hurried with the smear job and the candles, but I had the shakes—this being the year I suffered from The Queen Victoria Blues—so I took a sip of Bombay and lit a match. But it went out. My hands were shaking, so additional sipping became necessary. Then I burned my pointer with a match and knocked the bottle smack into the middle of the cake—oh, smeared sugar roses and dour Victoria flaming on the label! I remember sighing, 'Yes. I'm a bad girl.' " As Sylvia said this, she turned to me and closed her eyes and silently mouthed "bad girl." She was driving blind so I grabbed the wheel again. She started laughing, saying, "I never realized regret could feel so transcendental. It's like giving birth. I just stood there licking the frosting off my gin." Sylvia stopped talking and hunched over the wheel to do some serious lane hopping.

Surely this woman was driving the desert to forget her family and all those birthday cakes. She mixed up my orange stories because she didn't want my history jamming her amnesia.

•

That was my original assumption.

While writing this book, for various reasons, I learned about neurology—mine and others'. I learned that what you see (retinal visions) and what you imagine (holy or schizophrenic visions) travel by different nerves to the same optic lobe in the brain. Distinguishing the path is how one recognizes reality. Desert driving tends to merge the brain with the terrain and you leave your skin, your mind. Things you see and things you think about are viewed through the same windshield. Thus, while we drove through the Lechuguilla desert, there was no reason for Sylvia to keep my stories straight—I was just a dream she visioned up.

•

After she told me the cake story, she said: "The Arizona border is just cartographical theory, but this checkpoint is real," and slowed us down—squinting up the highway. "I don't recognize any of these hot dogs—it must be a new shift."

Sylvia rolled us to a stop at a toll booth. Our lane's hot dog politely asked if we were carrying any plants or produce. "Heck no, officer," Sylvia yelled. Then added, "But tell me. I don't get it—trucks can haul sausage across state lines, why can't I transport my goddamn oranges?" The hot dog said nothing and waved us through. Sylvia sighed to me, "Well, there's just something about a man in a uniform . . ."

A few blocks into town, a brown government sedan squealed up and flagged us over. Sylvia and I stood on a cracked sidewalk as her Volkswagen was searched down to the hubcaps.

"What is it, a police state out here?" Sylvia demanded, wiping the sweat off her forehead with her sleeve. "I just pray they don't find our homegrown stashed under the spare."

I cringed. Out here, sarcasm got one strip-searched—assuming she was being sarcastic. Was she sweating from heat or from a criminal nature (?)—those candy wrappers could mean Sylvia was a pothead with the munchies. What if there was a baggie of dope in the dash? My stomach bottomed out.

Then one of the cops flipped open her glove compartment and rooted around. Suddenly he said, "Oh shit."

Now it's coming . . .

But a moment later, they waved us back into the car. As we drove away, I turned around to see the cop stroking his hand in a Kleenex, the stain looking as if he really had discovered shit in the dash. Instead of wondering, "Does this woman have a glove compartment full of excrement?" I assumed it was. And it didn't smell. And it was hers.

On the outskirts of town, we passed a yellow weathered billboard in the scrub proclaiming: Do you have the courage to face THE THING?

"The Thing!" Sylvia sang. "I love it. I love it! I was born to be a Western girl." She pointed her lips to the sky, and I blanched as she nearly rear-ended a pick up ahead of us. Then she tilted her head back down and said, "I'm getting a blue-sky headache—will you drive?"

I nodded and she pulled over. We switched sides. My feet were hot, so I drove barefoot, scratching my foot on the accelerator.

We passed another yellow billboard advertising "THE THING," and she began rummaging in my knapsack. "What's this? You're walking through the desert carrying the Library of Congress?" She read the first titles aloud: *Girl in My Gunsights*, *Grip Me Hard Gunsel*, and *Brass Fists, Lead Hearts*—all written by Rex Ringer. My grandfather.

I explained my bookaholic devotion to the detective novel and genetic devotion to the 38 Tim Fontanel private-eye novels my grandfather had written between 1943 and 1959.

"For a paperback, that publisher was tops," I said as Sylvia held up a book with the red-end pages faded with age, its cover depicting Tim Fontanel in a trenchcoat slugging a nurse. The back was illustrated with the floor plan of a hospital morgue.

"All Dell paperbacks from the forties contained a 'mystery map' that showed the floor plan of the mansion the murder took place in, or the city that gangsters controlled, whatever . . ."

Yapping about Dell was making me leadfoot down the road. Sylvia yawned and said, "Okey-dokey, book-boy, just keep us below 90 and pointed east on our mystery map. I'm checking out."

With a brief exhalation of breath she closed her eyes. I edged into the fast lane so I could gaze her way without concentrating on the traffic. She shifted and raised her arms above her head. I forgot detective novels. I forgot the construction of paperback books. I forgot them all because the cups of Sylvia Cushman's underarms were as smooth as scoops in ice cream.

That vision may not seem remarkable now, but those were the Gerald Ford years. No girls shaved their legs, let alone anywhere else. Sprawling beside me was a delicious novelty, a moment of intensity that wasn't to be repeated until I first saw *Gilda* at the Thalia Theater in New York. The Thalia's floor slants abruptly down from the screen. I looked up that hill to see a Rita Hayworth of light slink across a nightclub bandstand. She wore a black strapless gown and raised both hands above her head and became Sylvia Cushman—both women revealing the joyous indentation of soft flesh, this revelation more ecstatic than a bare breast or haunch.

As I darted my eyes back between the road and this sleeping woman, I reached across her to finger the knob of the glove compartment. I was intoxicated enough by beauty and flesh to accept a trilogy of beauty, flesh, and shit—this being not the last time I would believe Sylvia's shit must be sweet as honey. But when the compartment popped open, I was hit with the sickly sweet smell of a dozen Almond Joys melted into a wet clump. With her eyes still shut, Sylvia grabbed my wrist and shoved my fist into the chocolate. I nearly swerved off the road, and had to do a one-handed yank of the wheel—my right arm still outstretched, palm inches above her lips.

I intended to lick off the chocolate myself, but Sylvia pulled my wrist to her face. For one intense instant I experienced the slip of her tongue and lips over my thumb.

With her eyes still closed, she swung my hand up to my face. I hesitated, then licked my pointer. Before I could do another digit, she yanked my hand back and slid her lips over my ring finger. She then tossed my hand back, my arm so limp I slapped my nose. I quickly licked the pinkie, but tasted no candy—that most minor of fingers was clean. I glanced down to see only the middle finger was left. Its vulgarity was exciting—this finger got Dennis Hopper shotgunned.

But Sylvia dropped my wrist and licked her lips, saying: "This candy tastes like gasoline."

•

Several miles later she said, "God! Did I go chocolate-crazy back there . . . I'm currently refraining from meat and can't handle more than one nutritional shot at longevity at a time."

I tensed the wheel.

Meat.

Sylvia asked if something was wrong, and I quoted the rant Shem gave as he showed me his snakes: "Remember Luke, boy: 'Consider the lilies, how they grow: they toil not, they spin not; and yet I say unto you that Solomon in all his glory was not arrayed like one of these.' What's that mean, huh? We should wear strings of flowers? No! That means plants are the breath of God. And men aren't. We got no roots. We don't eat soil. Men are meat. And while we're meat we're to only consume other meats . . . and a little bread. When we finally reach Glory the angels will press green leaves beneath our tongues and make us holy. And I've heard about 'vegetable people' who eat nothing but plants. Well, that's just hippie crock, boy—the Serpent's crock! And you can't count on the Christian establishment to teach this truth. No Sears Roebuck preacher with peas on his plate is going to tell you that as long as you thank the Lord for thy bounty, it's better to be a cannibal than to ever eat green plants."

I responded to Shem's words by shooting him. Sylvia responded by hooting: "Oh, I've seen the light! I'll trade my *Joy of Cooking* in for the *Donner Party Cookbook!*"

But by lunch she was a liar—sitting in the car wolfing a Cactus Burger at Little Arturo's near Gila Bend. I was elbowing my door-tray and doing a Mesa Burger over the steering wheel.

"Oh, stop looking at me like that," she said. "A little meat won't kill me." She took another bite, then ranted: "Anyway, I know how I'll die. I'll be Volks-ing out with the top down and suddenly find myself in a wet turquoise void. I'll let go of the wheel and kick up towards the firmament. There my head will be—bobbing on the surface of an Olympic-sized pool surrounded by umbrella'd beach tables. As I float out of the water, I'll behold your Raymond Chandler beneath one grinding his pipe, trying to finish typing *Poodle Springs*. I'll rise higher and see Dashiell Hammett sitting beneath his umbrella working on *Tulip*. I'll cup my hands and yell, 'If you guys are so tough, how come you died and left unfinished books about poodles and tulips?' Then I'll laugh and give them your regards, now noticing a thousand beach tables stretching to the horizon, each one occupied by pulp writers, cigarettes dangling off their lips as they slouch over typewriters pecking barking-gun visions. I could linger in your Valhalla of Hardboiled Writers, but I'll wing the hell out of there for the previous century, only pausing long enough among the more highly regarded 20th century literati to personally guide F. Scott through the Louvre, pointing out the small penises on the Greek statues. But then, I'll make tracks for the 19th century and hover above a field of Gettysburg dead. I'll yell down and ask Whitman for directions to Amherst. I won't fly there; I'll tunnel northeast and embrace the soil's most precious tenant—her jeweled soul churning the New England dirt like a worm."

Sylvia stopped talking and used a straw to work the bottom of a milk shake as thoroughly as I would later see her snort powder. Then she panted, " 'I taste a liquor never brewed, from tankards scooped in pearl.' "

I responded: "Huh?"

She said, "Emily Dickinson."

I replied: "Oh."

And that set her off: "What do you mean—'*Oh*'?" she cried, pinching my arm. " 'Oh.' I know that 'Oh.' You don't know who I'm talking about. Oh God, such a culturally deprived puppy." She raised her arm to her brow in mock melodrama: "Ignorance of Mark Fidrych was bad enough—but Emily Dickinson too? Don't they make you read anything in the Golden Bear aside from Charlie Chan novels?" I started to protest that

Earl Derr Biggers was an inferior crime writer, but Sylvia plowed on: "Emily Dickinson was a great American poet." Sylvia gave the following capsule bio with the same fervor that my mother used when she described Jesus curing lepers.

"Emily Dickinson was a frail weed. A plain woman. The only beauty among the kangaroos. She was probably agoraphobic, because she never left her father's house in Amherst, Massachusetts. She just hid out, writing and writing in secret—in her lifetime only publishing a few anonymous nuggets about God and death. She carried on a correspondence with a literary big shot named Higginson, but never got a book out of it. As the years passed, she tunneled further and further into reclusion. She went on a virginity trip and only wore a white dress. Maybe now and then she'd lighten up—bake some gingersnaps and lower them in a basket out of her second-story bedroom for the neighborhood brats. By the Civil War, her poetic repertoire expanded from God and death to include God and death and sex—(she was writing a lot about swelling worms and snakes). Then she finally did the dirty romp with a widowed judge while her married brother Austin did it with a married neighbor, Mabel Loomis Todd. All this congruent fucking created genteel New England distress in their respective households until Emily finally stopped for death. When Mabel found the lifetime of poems Emily had squirreled away, she went to Higginson—(brooding all these years that he had never made it with Emily)—and they published Emily's work posthumously—so that now almost a century later, Emily Dickinson lived, wrote, and died so she could become yet another great American that you have never heard of."

Sylvia's fingers were dug into my collarbone and she was shaking me back and forth. Then she jumped out of the car and yanked open the hood. What was wrong with the engine? The hood slammed, and she stomped around to my door, gripping a large book. The car had been literally running on literature! Then I remembered that a VW engine was back in the trunk. Sylvia slapped the book down on my tray, and then headed to the rest room. A Dewey decimal sticker was on the spine with "The University of Michigan Graduate Library" stamped on the side pages. I picked up the six-pounder—*The Collected Poems of Emily Dickinson*, edited by Andrew C. Ragan. I wiped a smear of ketchup off the plastic slipcover illustrated with a daguerreotype of Emily—you know it, the famous one taken when the poet was only 17, her plain face staring up in an image so grainy she looks Jamaican—flat nose, thick lower lip, hair parted in the simplest of buns. When I first saw this photo, it hit me how I'd gone through high school ignoring the Emily Dickinsons of Doheny State Beach. She had been one of those flat brainiac girls—the ones uncomfortable in their bikinis but willing to drop their *Advanced Chem* and take a nervous toke. In Sylvia's Volkswagen, I began jiggling my foot. If you can love Sissy Spacek, you can love Emily Dickinson. This book confirmed that my psychic compass pointed in the right direction: east. Out east the girls would be Emily Dickinsons. They would welcome me in skinny embraces. Sylvia hopped back in the car and shouted, "Come on, Orange Boy, crank up this little Kraut and eastward ho!"

•

At the end of our first day—sunset—we pulled into the Arizona Inn down the highway in Eloy. "Look, there's no reason for you to fish-up another ride," Sylvia said. "With your luck you'll get picked up by an illicit semi. We'll ride again tomorrow."

I was confused by her words. Then I felt stupid. It had never dawned on me that we would go our separate ways. I waited in the car and watched her register. I bit my lip and wiped my palms on my jeans. Where would I be expected to sleep—in the car or the room? And if I was invited into the room, would I be expected to split the cost (?)—an expense I couldn't afford. Sylvia stepped out of the office door swinging a large plastic key ring. She paused by the Coke machine glowing in the shadows. I heard her change drop. The thunk of a can. Then she stood in the machine light rubbing the cold Coke across her shoulders and belly.

I pulled Sylvia's bag out from the hood—a pigeon-gray polygonal Samsonite—and lugged it into the room. Sylvia switched on the light. I cleverly observed that the walls were the color of Pepto Bismol. "No. Calamine lotion," Sylvia said. Then she nodded at the twin paintings over the beds. One was a desert rose, and the other—a cactus.

"Guess which bed you get," she said.

"They both have Magic Fingers."

We pumped quarters into the coin boxes and watched the headboards thump the wall. "The neighbors will think you're a real jackhammer," Sylvia commented, yelling as if we were still on the road. She padded into the bathroom. I hopped to my bed and rode the jiggling mattress. The shaking made me nauseous. Sylvia began banging things and I raised my head, straining my neck. Behold: the closed bathroom door.

I then looked over at my feet—"My insteps are sunburned from driving barefoot," I called. A beat later, Sylvia strode out wearing a man's striped pajama top. "Now all we must do," she shouted, "is string a curtain down the center of the room."

I jumped up on my bouncing bed and tried to pull the curtains from the rods. Sylvia stopped me. She knelt and patiently described the plot to *It Happened One Night* as she took my ankles and leaned forward to spray Solarcaine across the tops of my feet. I was staring down her pajama top at the tips of her breasts. There was the soft curve of her stomach, the silk hyphen of her panties, but all I could think of was Jesus washing the feet of his disciples. Meanwhile, Sylvia chattered how it was chemically possible to distill a decent cocaine from Solarcaine.

She finished and my feet were numb. "Turn off the light!" she yelled, then switched on the b&w Zenith, flooding the now-dark room with blue light. She bounced onto her bed. I tentatively lay back on mine. She threw me a jumbo-pak of potato chips. We began tossing the bag back and forth while watching a rerun of *McCloud*. On the screen, a New Mexican cowboy rode his horse down the blue streets of New York. "God, I want to live there," Sylvia sighed. "Hang out with Patti Smith and Lillian Hellman."

I wasn't paying attention—I was studying the show's setup. At a commercial, I said: "The great thing about the old crime shows they made before I was born was that the detectives had real mysteries to solve. On modern shows, the criminal is revealed in the first five minutes—we spend the next fifty-five waiting for the detective to discover what we already—"

Sylvia interrupted: "Forget the construction of detective shows and tell me something interesting." She paused. I looked over. She was staring at the ceiling and following something invisible around with her eyes. Then she said, "Tell me again how you were redeemed by Richard Nixon."

•

As icons, Emily Dickinson and Nixon are obviously shouts apart: Sylvia's Emily-love was an individual interest, while her Nixon-fascination seemed typical of women of specific age and intellectual bent; a fascination I now figure involves the progression from virgin to mother corresponding with Nixon's tenure as vice president, defeat to Kennedy, and the long Monday of his rule between '69 and '74. Thus, a delight in Watergate is not just political; it's joy at the real end of the '50s —the end of Daddy's mother/whore worldview; the end of Daddy's will. And as perceptive or crackpot as this sounds, it ties in with my original assumption that Sylvia was driving the desert to forget her family.

N ow, my redemption by Nixon was actual, not figurative. He redeemed me after my gunplay. Shem had finished his "Christians should only eat meat" rap by saying: "Snakes are the meat that caused man's fall. Squeezing one tells God you accept your role in the food chain and have enough faith that Satan cannot bite you."

Shem's faith was strong, but he still got shot, and after I pulled the trigger I gripped a tree trunk and cried, my forehead beating an orange. Suddenly, I heard the thump of a helicopter. I looked up. In a patch between the orange trees, I saw Richard Nixon whirlybirding across the sky.

Nixon was a familiar traveler in my grandfather's firmament. His hacienda sat beneath the ex-president's San Clemente flight route. Back in '72, my grandfather had placed 400 rocks on a hill to spell out: *Four More Years.* Nixon saw it and ever since his pilots flew the same route. As the helicopter now began its low waltz above the grove, I saw Nixon inside eating something from a bag. I squinted and made out the bag's yellow hoops. I knew his food. Richard Nixon haloed above me eating grain and meat. I remembered the episode in Luke where Jesus is presented with a rabbi's dead daughter and Jesus whispers, "Little girl, arise." At once the child sits up, alive. Jesus then orders she be fed. Fed meat. And now Nixon flew above my head offering me the meat of life and redemption from the air.

After I finished this story, I looked over at Sylvia. Her eyes were closed, her forehead furrowed in a scowl. "Bless this sleeping girl with meat," I whispered. Sylvia gave a sudden groan and became a sleeping six-year-old.

The next morning Sylvia paid for the room. She paid for the scrambled eggs and chocolate cake I ate for breakfast. She bought sun block for my feet. She was to take basic financial responsibility for our journey, while I supplied the necessary trinkets from Stuckey's.

Later that morning, we pulled into the parking lot of "The Thing." Sylvia paid the admission, and we stood before a canoe wrapped with bandages. It was the mummy of an extraterrestrial found in the desert. Back on the road, Sylvia said she peeked— the mummy was really Amelia Earhart and part of her cockpit.

Without making a manifesto out of it, Sylvia and I were searching for the plastic heart of America. The difference between us was: this was my first trip out of California—so even the most mundane item from Stuckey's was infused with magic. Sylvia craved Stuckey's because she wanted to maintain a cartoon level of reality for as long as possible. The Volkswagen's needs revealed the thin line between kitsch and the heart of darkness. Sylvia insisted we only stop in one-of-a-kind service stations like "Broken Arrow Oil," or "Gas, Bait, and Ammo." We'd pull into semi-depraved gas holes where Sylvia found blood puddled in the bathroom while I sat in the car watching blind Hopi girls fill our tank by touch or sullen one-armed Mexicans scrape 300 miles' worth of bugs off the windshield.

•

W hile we traveled, Sylvia and I slept together apart. We curled in separate sleeping bags. We lay in double motel beds. But by Texas, I stopped yearning for her to slide beside me because we had shared a moment of intimacy more powerful than sex: Sylvia had some mushrooms she wanted to finish, we just had to find the right spot. "A power spot?" I asked. She nodded. Sylvia's power spot was an egg-shaped boulder on the outskirts of Thoreau, New Mexico. I'd tripped before, but never on mushrooms. They tasted leathery, and we washed them down with grape pop. We squatted in the shade beneath the rock and waited. An hour went by. Nothing happened. Then we simultaneously jumped to our feet and began gagging. We scrambled bent-over in opposite directions, throwing up in the bear grass. From thirty feet away, I heard the depth of her heaving—retching as intricately scored as a symphony. She was throwing up herds of horses. I was throwing up Apaches. Clutching our bellies, we shuffled back toward each other until we hunched side by side, shoulders touching, weeping with dry heaves. And in this pain we were married, stooping above a stone marked with a petroglyph of a snake swallowing a heart.

•

After that mushroom day, Sylvia's cartoon abruptly wound down.

To begin: Sylvia was driving and stopped us for morning gas in Albuquerque. Across the street on the eastbound on-ramp, a hitchhiker my age stood beside his astronaut backpack. He was taller than me. He had a barbell physique. It ate my crow that his hair was longer than mine. Sylvia watched him as our gas bell rang. When we left the station, he stuck out his thumb and I'd never seen anyone make that gesture with such virility and confidence. Sylvia swerved to the shoulder, saying: "Let's see if this joker can teach you some tricks of the road." I turned to her. Wide-eyed. Stricken. She actually raised her hand to her mouth in chagrin, then she grabbed the wheel and floored it —leaving the kid lumbering after us, an astronaut in wrong gravity.

I nixed adding another character to her cartoon, but that wasn't what ruined it. At noon, outside Morriarty, we were tailgated by two separate cars, both driven by hunching bald men. "The Khrushchev twins," I remarked. "Any minute they'll start beating their shoes on their dashboards."

Sylvia shuddered and abruptly pulled off to the shoulder. She said she didn't want to drive anymore. She spent the afternoon curled asleep on the passenger side, while I steered and read Dickinson's confettilike stanzas to God.

It took us six days of zigzags to finally reach Texas. Zigzags because Sylvia couldn't read a road map. ("So what we're lost," she shouted. "We'll sleep in the Petrified Forest." "Great," I sneered. "I always wanted to see trees turned to stone." "Fuck you, Orange Boy. That's what you get for reading instead of navigating.") Then in Texas, Sylvia's despair broke loose. We had taken a room at the Wilderado Motel Lodge. I left the room because Sylvia wanted to phone her husband. When I returned, the room was empty and the shower was running in the bathroom. Over the water, I heard Sylvia sobbing—her sobs sounding from a place deeper than the mushrooms had reached. Then I heard her fists beating the tiles. I slipped some bills from her purse and left the room again, jogging across the road to a drugstore. She had complained that the constant wind from driving had infected her right ear, so I bought eardrops. Returning to the room, I walked by the open screen of our small bathroom window. The shower was off. The room was quiet. I unlocked our door and found Sylvia asleep on the bed. She was lying on her back and she was naked.

I turned away to compose myself, then sat on the edge of the desk soaking in the sight: the white freckled skin that refused to sunburn, her sparse red wisps of hair. I was one of the elders who caught Susanna bathing. As I studied, I had to keep moving my eyes from her torso to her face to connect that, yes, this was Sylvia's body. Those were her breasts. This was her sex. But the reality of her body grew abstract. I might as well have been chewing mushrooms. Each time I considered her face—nose flared, lips slightly parted—it erased the memory of her breasts. The longer I gazed on that face, the more I forgot where I was: motel room/Texas/on the lam.

In Orange Boy fashion, askew thoughts lined up in my brain like rooming house boarders before a bathroom. I held out my arm and compared it with Sylvia's body. From my vision's perspective both were the same size. I saw Sylvia's form replacing my arm. Then I saw her nakedness tattooed on my arm. I remembered that, long before I met or shot him, Shem had a woman on his arm, but he peeled her off with a knife.

I slipped out of our room to the pool, sitting down in the row of white wire chairs. The flames of the tiki lights danced on the black water.

•

Time looped down the rim of the Wilderado Motel pool so I wasn't merely "remembering" events, but reliving them. The Texas motel became the Mohave motel where my mother and I once stayed—the Cactus Flower Motor Court: a series of bunkers where framed photos of Goldie Hawn hung in every unit. My mother had dragged me along on a ministry of desert-rat trailer courts. At the time I was a scrawny 13-year-old bookworm who just wanted to be left alone with his whodunits. But there was my mother badgering: "You're almost fourteen, boy. Old enough to be accountable for sin. Old enough to be baptized in the blood of the lamb. Don't think there's not one thousand schoolboys spending prom night in Hell." And so I stood before her, struggling to tug up my trunks while covering myself at the same time. My mother was already in her white muumuu. While I tied my suit, she marched me out to the edge of the traditional kidney-shaped pool. The glaring water seemed thick like model airplane glue. Together, we sunk down the steps into the pit.

Five years later, at the Wilderado in Texas, Sylvia suddenly wandered—dressed again—beneath flicking tiki flames. She crouched at the edge of the water. Her face shimmered in the wavy underwater light and glowed like aluminum. She yelled: "My auditory canals thank you!" Then she pointed into the pool. "What do you see?"

At that moment, my brain was projecting memory into the water, just like at a drive-in. I closed my eyes and continued the movie for Sylvia, showing how the teenage girl kicked across the Mohave pool in her white bikini—how the girl splashed us as she dove for the bottom, and my mother stared at her feet, seeing the future, seeing the girl's flesh flame as she frog-kicked to Hell.

My mother and I continued wading until the water reached my belly. My mother pawed my forehead, her grip like a mitt, and just before she dipped me, I glimpsed the girl. She had grabbed the bottom of the diving board to hang half-in/half-out of the water, staring at us, her penny nipples revealed beneath the fabric of her wet white top. My mother's arm tensed and she plunged my head backward and I was down. Heavy water. Her technique was no quick Baptist dunk. No. She pushed until I was arched backwards, my forehead lodged under her belly, nose pressing that Santa Claus slope. I struggled to pray, "Oh Jesus, let your wet light into my heart"—but kept thinking about *The Long Goodbye* which I was reading for the first time. "Did Terry Lenox really kill himself in Mexico?" I wondered. "No!"

My mother pressed my face deeper and deeper into the jelly

of her gut, and, within a myriad of underwater gurgles and pounding ear-blood, I heard a voice—faint like a neighbor's radio—coming closer and closer. And although the voice came from my mother's mass, it wasn't her voice. It was masculine. I assumed I was imagining it. But then I knew it was real. Was it Jesus?

No.

I recognized the voice of my father. And Dad was no message from Christ.

•

Before I began this book, I talked out the plot with my grandfather. He was sitting on an upside-down wheelbarrow, slicing an avocado and scowling (both at what I was saying and his knife strokes). Finally, he looked up to snort: "Kid, put the past in the bird cage. Anti-Dad Memoirs are for pussies. If you don't have the common sense to write a detective story, then shoot down to El Dos Passos or wherever and write a goddamn book about Central America." He sucked a sliver of fruit off his blade. "I mean, that's what's fashionable now days —or am I misreading the waters?"

I asked how one read water, but he was seriously devouring his avocado and didn't answer. I dropped the subject. Surely I was writing a detective novel. My father had been a private eye. My father even believed Tim Fontanel was based on him:

Fontanel peered in the mirror and grunted. He saw a handsome face with rugged features that gin-soaked blondes liked to caress.

He saw a pair of cloud-gray eyes. How kind they could be in the bedroom or while helping a lost child. Yet they could be blank as slate staring down a dirty dog who had double-crossed him.

Fontanel adjusted his Hawaiian shirt and slipped his Army-issue .45 into the waistband of his chinos. Yes, his eyes were the last thing Sven the Norwegian was going to see tonight. Sven was going to be wriggling on the rug with his guts looped in his hands, begging Fontanel for the coup de grace. Then Fontanel would lean down and grab Sven's chin and wiggle it back and forth, snarling, "Sing for it a little more, you *'wegian* pup."

Rex Ringer's comment: "Your father was the biggest pussy that ever walked the earth."

That old man raised my father to adulthood, and then drank with him—so this evaluation is as valid as anything. When I told this to Sylvia in the Wilderado, she leaned from her pool chair and asked, "So what did the alleged 'pussy' do before he started talking through your mother's belly?"

I explained that in the early '50s, my father had been a sleazy Hollywood bedroom peeper until he got goods on a Red director with a taste for jailbait. My father shook the Commie down, but not for money or power: Dad blackmailed his way to become one of Lex Barker's stand-ins—my father's lifelong desire being to one day play Tarzan. But Dad only swung the vine in two Tarzan films before he fell out of a fake baobab tree and spent a year in traction. At Hollywood Presbyterian he met my mother. I was told she was there as a candystriper, but later my grandfather claimed she'd been in for shock therapy. ("Your mother saw Jesus because of General Electric," he laughed.) Whichever was true, my father referred to my mother during this period as (1) "skinny as a plank" and (2) "a horny little mouse." They got themselves in trouble, and her father, a West Coast politician of minor importance, shotgunned a marriage.

Now a husband and no longer Tarzan, Dad resumed his career as a cheap dick and sleazed the peripheries of Hollywood until my grandfather bankrolled him in a real estate scam renting nonexistent offices in the Capitol Records building. Dad cleaned up and I was born. Mom kept her Arbuckle weight, while my father invested his money and became a successful used-car magnate, starring in his own TV commercials, and like his rival, Cal Worthington, would ride large African livestock through his car lot yelling: "Folks, just look at this gorgeous '72 Rambler . . . For those of you with black-and-white television sets, this baby is mint-green with red vinyl interior. She only has sixty-thousand miles, and I'll let her go for the steal of . . ."

My mother never watched his commercials. She believed his hippos were a reference to her.

At this, Sylvia snorted in irritation—perhaps in feminine loyalty to the concept of body despair. Sylvia then slipped off her slippers and toed the water, saying: "So Dad was a jerk. Bitch and moan, little boy. Bitch and moan." Pause. "But he was a color-ful jerk . . . A California jerk . . . Didn't he ever ride you on his hippo or inform you of the truth to be found beneath girls' bikinis?"

I resisted the urge to push Sylvia into the pool. Instead I told her that, yes, my father gave me the facts of life. At a very early age. I was probably six or seven. It was Thanksgiving morning and he waved me into the kitchen, gripped my shoulder, and shoved me to the turkey pan sitting on the counter. Dad needs help hefting the pan? No. He put his other hand on my lower arm, just above the wrist, and jammed my hand into the open slit of the uncooked bird.

"You're telling me that for no reason at all your father stuck your hand inside the Thanksgiving turkey?" Sylvia asked. I nodded and told her he used the same Arm Language she had used when she jammed my hand into her glove compartment of candy. And while my father held me in the turkey, he bleared and said, "There's your mother for you, son."

Sylvia was quiet for a moment, and then said, "Don't tell me any more stories about your father."

I complied because there were few additional stories to tell. Dad died in Pasadena wearing a golden sombrero with crimson tassels. Dad rode to the Reaper on the back of a baby hippopotamus waddling in the Rose Bowl Parade. Dad waved to the crowd and waved to the NBC cameras, and didn't notice the light lather on his hippo's back until it was too late. The marching band was blowing "Up, Up, and Away" at the moment the hippo collapsed and rolled on my father's chest. Dad's own Adam's rib pierced his lung. He lay gasping in the street, silently moving his mouth, looking as if he were on a TV with the volume turned off. A concerned clown rushed up and covered my father's face with his sombrero.

•

Two years after my father's death, my mother was baptizing me and I discovered my father in her belly—where, I theorized, he was being crushed by that hippo over and over, the way the local news replayed his tumble on TV. And as I pressed my ear into my mother, Dad was crying for help. What was surprising was that he even managed to call me "son," i.e.: "Help me, Son! Help me!"

Although you can't physically speak underwater, I had the ability of speech similar to dreams—the ability to yell, actually, to shout: "Fuck you!" Then again: "Fuck you, Dad! Fuck you." I was young enough that this was not the mindless curse you yell at a dipshit who cuts you off on the freeway—these were my first words of an angry new language. But my father shouted back: "You say that because you just remember my demons, boy. Can't you remember anything else? Can't you? . . .

"Can't you remember the afternoon I drove you up the winding road to Mount Palomar? Didn't I drive you further into the night than you had ever been? Didn't I keep you up past your bedtime so you could enter the observatory? Didn't I let you peer into that glass nozzle? And when you peeked, what did you see? The surface of the moon. A mountain of ice. And when I told you about the blue-skinned women up there, didn't you see them too? You shouted, 'Dad! Dad! I see them! They're naked.' And I never told you they were naked, did I? That was your brain speaking. But didn't I let you see them that way? And you said, 'Dad, Dad, they're beautiful.' So don't talk turkey to me, boy, because I gave you a vision of moon ice and pussy that neither your mother nor Jesus Christ can ever take away."

Under the pool I considered Dad's words. Great men have demons, but that doesn't diminish their greatness. I envisioned a white marble giant, a combination of the Lincoln Memorial and my father. Perhaps Dad had dark demons the way Abe Lincoln had dark demons. Perhaps I should become a hawk-headed Egyptian god and reweigh my father's heart anew, find a new balance. But as I considered this forgiveness, my father murmured, "Wake up! Your mother is trying to smooth you over. If you stay down here you'll die with the dick of a little boy. And the girl with the tits will see this. Be the Chinese brother—swallow the ocean. Swallow the ocean!"

It had been two years since he gave me an order ("Go to bed"/ "Clean your plate") but I instinctively obeyed and opened my mouth to begin swallowing water, gulping deep. Now, were Dad's instructions meant to drown me or save me? Intentionally or unintentionally, the mechanics of swallowing moved my jaw into my mother and made her wake from her trance into righteousness. She yanked my head to the surface and I coughed up chlorine.

As I gulped air, the girl climbed from the pool. Plates of bone slid beneath her shoulders, her haunches splayed from the rear, her white bikini transparent. She faced me—at that moment I knew that there is a skein that can turn transparent—was this girl's dark wedge a gift from Dad, or my separate vision? Then the girl turned to run from the pool, yelling, "Help! Mom! Mama Cass is drowning a boy in the pool!"

•

Five years later, in Texas, Sylvia and I walked through the row of tiki lights and returned to our motel room in the Wilderado. We said nothing of consequence. We watched TV from our separate beds, but I lay trying to erase the memory of my father's voice with the earlier memory of Sylvia's body. I didn't do too good.

Instead I lay remembering that after my baptism in the Mohave, my mother dressed and wedged herself inside our motel
room's closet. She planned to give thanks for our successful
immersion, her following Christ's tenet: *Don't parade your devotion in public. Hide in your closet to pray.* (My mother was
only flamboyant when necessary.) I had left our room and walked
along the slight incline behind the motel. It was a cloudy night
without moon or starlight. A shaft of light spilled out of an open
window. Inside, I saw a young woman in a slip pinning her
peach-colored hair into a bun. While I watched I became aware
of a shape beside me. It was the girl from the pool who had
witnessed my baptism.

"Last night," she whispered, "she was sitting on a man like
on a plastic pony at Piggly Wiggly."

The young woman in the room turned on the TV and then
switched off the light. The word "Bonanza" flamed on the
screen. Then, in the blue TV light, the woman crisscrossed her
arms and slipped off her slip. She leaned forward and slid naked
to her belly on the bed.

I heard my companion's intake of breath. We both watched
the woman watching *Bonanza*. We stared at the electric blue
slopes of her buttocks. Then my companion leaned her face to
mine and intuitively I kissed her. She was the first girl I had
kissed. I was intoxicated by her lips, her tongue. Her mouth was
something impossible, like hot ice cream. Our kisses lasted the
duration of two commercials until there was nothing else either
of us could think of to do. We went to her room, where the girl's
parents were slouched on the bed, drinking Millers and watching
Bonanza. Her father had eagle tattoos and a gut. An Air Force
uniform hung on a hook in the closet. Her mother was young
and pretty from the nose up, but there was something caved-in

about her chin and mouth, as if she were swallowing her face. They looked up at us and grunted and went back to the TV. No one said a word. The girl and I sat Indian-style on the floor radiated by *Bonanza*, but the concerns of the Cartwrights were insignificant to me. Imagine how exciting it was that in another room, a naked woman was taking in the same TV show as us. . .

Five years after that Cartwrighted moment, I tried recalling the woman's body. I failed. I couldn't visualize her figure. Nothing. Then I realized I couldn't recall Sylvia's body either—even though I'd seen it just that afternoon.

•

Sylvia never fleshed out. She turned brittle and broke. We made an early-morning escape from the Wilderado and out of the blue she snapped, "Stop driving and reading at the same time! I don't intend to be scraped off Texas asphalt like armadillo meat!"

And the further we penetrated the panhandle, the worse she got. The more she transformed into a reasonable woman. Into a housewife. A literate housewife, but a housewife just the same.

She ordered poached eggs for breakfast and then complained when they were inevitably poorly prepared. She skipped lunch and ate tuna salad for supper. We no longer stopped at Service Stations of the Living Dead. We were on a Pegasus trip, filling up only at Mobil stations where cornfed farmboys wore forest-

green jumpsuits with their names stitched over their hearts—
Billy, Bobby, Bo. Sylvia never spent less than ten minutes in the
ladies' room and always emerged with fresh pale pink lipstick.
She wore a bra. Her voice changed. She no longer yelled, she
whispered—a tense non-Monroe whisper with no hints of seduction. Sylvia also began talking—no, scolding—in her sleep:
"Get those boots out of here!" Another night: "Pipe down! You're
disturbing your father!" Finally: "Bad dog. Bad bad dog."

We played the radio nonstop to eliminate conversation. After an
entire day of pork-belly reports, I could forget who I was. Finally, I decided to abandon Sylvia—she was a rocket dropping
its stages from higher atmospheres of womanhood than I understood. With each gas stop I braced myself, trying to gather the
nerve to stride away from her Volkswagen. To thumb a different
ride. Then, at a gas stop in Dorothy's Kansas, she came out of
the restroom and the sun glittered off her earlobes. She had put
on earrings. When she slid behind the wheel, I saw small and
flat ear-shaped ornaments were hanging from her real ears. Rather
than playful, this seemed semiotically disturbing—as if Sylvia
now needed signs to remind herself of her body. She suddenly
reached out and grabbed my forearm, pleading, "Please, please,
please promise you won't leave me until we get to Toledo."

•

She stopped letting me drive. At an Illinois toll booth, she
threw two dollars' worth of change without making the
basket. The car behind us pounded the horn and I flipped
a quarter in from the passenger side. From then on, at each toll,

I leaned across her to drop the coins. I felt her breath on my neck. "I hope I have you around when I meet Charon," she remarked.

We had cruised the acres of steam pillars and Frankenstein electrode towers that stretched eastward from Chicago when Sylvia stopped at a lone little basket-bunker and casually tossed a handful of change overhand. Technically it was a hook shot, but she made the Arm Language her own. Each coin arced into the basket and the thing jingled like a xylophone, then Sylvia whacked the gear stick, streaking up the merging ramp at 60 mph yelling, "No coins under the tongue for me."

•

On the outskirts of Toledo, she pulled to the shoulder. Heavy traffic whizzed by as she apologized for being so difficult. "Your presence has been a comfort."

I sat paralyzed. I couldn't step out of her Volkswagen. Sylvia reached behind her seat, her earring glittering in the sun. She slapped the *Emily Dickinson* into my lap.

"This is a library book," I protested.

"Take it. I can bear the wrath of the University of Michigan."

She leaned her face toward mine. A Tim Fontanel line flashed: "The big kiss-off!" My first impulse was to offer her my cheek, but I lifted my chin, offering my lips. And she met them. Our kiss lasted longer than a moment. But just as I parted my lips to extend my clipped tongue, Sylvia lowered her head to my chest. I tasted her hair. Her shoulders shook. I sat stiffly, holding her upper arms, resting my nose in her hair. Her hair smelled of sweat but it was a good smell. Her head was a planet. I looked over its surface to the traffic. Then Sylvia pulled away and jerked back up. Her eyes were red but dry, and she was smiling. Had she been leaning into me laughing?

I was angry and opened my door. I deliberately didn't roll up my window—let the wind blow in her face. I stepped out. My foot was asleep and I almost stumbled to my knees. I slammed the door, trying to maintain my balance. Sylvia's car was already rolling as she yelled, "Be careful, Orange Boy!" then sped into traffic. It was only by a miracle of the great pagan god of I-75 that she was not bagged by a semi.

I stood beside the highway shaking the cramps out of my leg. Then I walked the shoulder in circles, cradling the *Dickinson*. Finally I turned toward the traffic and jerked out my thumb.

I would keep heading east. I would travel to Amherst. I would go to Emily—to her house—where her driveway was surely jammed with Volkswagen upon Volkswagen.

PART TWO

THE FALL OF THE HOUSE OF CUSHMAN

Her house had been built by a Puritan grandfather. It had always been called The Homestead. I was leaning on an iron gate where steep steps led to a small front porch flanked by twin Ionic columns. Although these steps were not as steep as, say, the steps from motel to mansion in *Psycho*, they were that dramatic to me. I stared up past branches—leaves New England orange—to observe Emily's window. The curtains were drawn, vanilla-colored cloth covered with plastic. A white wet look. Emily Dickinson's bedroom overflowed with ice cream.

I rattled the door, but no one answered. I left and trudged through town lugging my knapsack, past bookstores and prim houses, to Miles Standish College—a cluster of geodesic domes connected by wide concrete walkways. I squished diagonally across a wet lawn; pale kids flung Frisbees; dogs leaped and laughed. A plump bearded man tugged on a line connected to a small turquoise pyramid floating across the sky. This campus would later be described to me as the Acid Academy, the burnt-out end to which our radical elders fled after destroying the Summer of Love in order to save it. Here, the faculty with tenure tended to be ex-Weathermen hiding out from the FBI. The students were TV-literate Jackson Browne freaks, struggling to achieve their ten credits in classes such as "The History of Tibet" or "The Aerodynamics of Kite Flying"—the latter subject's prof now reeling his pyramid down from the clouds.

I asked directions to the freshman dorm, and in a bland brick building, the cinderblock hall resonating with two hundred unsynced stereos all playing *Hotel California*, I stood in a doorway and found him sitting on the edge of an unmade bed, oiling his trumpet. I found Ben Cushman. I found Sylvia's son.

•

Ben's overt genetic link to his mother was his flaming red hair. It was thick, Rapunzel length. God, I was jealous. And as he screwed a valve back on his trumpet, I saw his profile: sharp beak with sharper jaw. Sylvia had the grace of a Gibson Girl, but her son was Dick Tracy. He noticed me and looked up expectantly. For a moment he had the same open expression of Sylvia saying, "God, I feel like such a freak." But the moment he placed me—"kid lugging backpack"—his vulnerability vanished. His face became severe. Cold. After I got to know him, I'd joke that he had the face of a Salem witch burner. As I got older, I decided his facial expression was just the obvious response to this world, but then I'd watch the local New York news and see Rudolph Giuliani, D.A., announcing another indictment. I'd grin: oh, that gaunt jawline! Those rigid cheeks! That humorless upholder of justice—Yes! Yes!—Ben's twin!

These were not my observations during our first exchange. There's no reason to report the awkward dialogue of two teens except to say that extended conversation with Ben made me uncomfortable. I had treated Sylvia as a peer in the context of our journey, and it seemed I should treat her son as a peer because of our congruent ages. But I couldn't tell him I vomited Apaches with his mother. I couldn't remark on the sparsity of her red pubic hair. Ben listened to what I could reveal while diddling the valves of his trumpet. When I finished by saying I was here because of Emily Dickinson, he rolled his eyes, making me fear that I wasn't unique—I wasn't the first waif his mother had sent to Amherst. But after knowing Ben a week, I knew he had rolled his eyes because his disdain for the Acid Academy was so acute that it spread to the city limits of Amherst itself. In short— Amherst sucked. The entire Eastern Seaboard sucked. Ben originally wanted to go to the University of Anchorage, but his mother talked him east. Her motives were selfish, although Emily wasn't a factor—as frontiers went, Alaska was a wildcard, and Sylvia wanted to be the first Cushman to drive its frosty freeways or let it remain Cushmanless forever.

Ben let me crash in his room, and we spent the night spinning cool-period Miles Davis. I was unfamiliar with these albums, but managed to sway my head in a correct free-floating meter. Ben warmed up. He'd pound his mattress enthusiastically during certain riffs: "Listen! Listen! That phrase says, 'Eat shit, whitey. I own a sports car and I'm going to fuck your woman.' "

In the middle of the night, the phone rang. I looked up from my sleeping bag to see Ben's outline sitting up on his bed, cradling the receiver in his neck. The tinny voice coming from the phone was female. She was loud. Ben finally spoke: "Oh no." Then more talk from the other end. Now I recognized the voice's timbre—Sylvia! I was both nervous and excited. Did I want Ben to tell her I was here? Before I decided, Ben slammed the phone down and leapt out of bed. He paced the dark room in agitated circles. He'd just been told that his little brother Lester was in the hospital again. Another allergy attack: "Mom bought him a rain slicker and he was bombed by a reaction to the rubber. His face ballooned. He can't even open his eyes. And his heart stopped beating. For one fucking moment, it stopped beating!"

I turned on the light while Ben slid out a shoe box and began seeding dope on the lid. His hands were so shaky he spilled most of it on the floor, so I took over. After we smoked, he rounded up scissors and tape. We spent the rest of the night constructing an elaborate get-well card out of a large sheet of cardboard. We cut dozens of tiny fold-out windows in it and taped magazine illustrations inside. It was unlikely Ben's five-year-old brother would appreciate the significance of a grinning Dick Nixon with the caption: "Pardon my appearance. Get well soon!"—but at dawn, when Ben and I finished, the act of making the card together had bonded us with antiNixon Friendship.

•

Within a week, I developed my routine. I'd spend the morning at Ben's desk devouring Emily, listening to her whisper: "You invest your alabaster zest into the delights of dust." By noon, I'd bounce to the Meal Hall to down Sugar Pops for lunch with my counterfeit meal card. I tried to read Ellery Queen while I ate, but couldn't concentrate. I was too burnt on Emily's personal infinity.

Ben, himself, was an Antisocial Freak, or, as he said, "I'm into ascetic solitude." On Saturday nights, while the other students drove to the Holiday Inn to watch *Saturday Night Live* on the giant lounge TV, Ben and I trudged through a field to a railroad track where freight trains lumbered between Canada and Boston. We'd wait in the dark and exhale clouds of breath, straining to hear the first whistle of the train, but always ended up feeling the ground vibrating first. Then we'd hear the distant horn, a foghorn joining us to the curve of the earth. As the train pulled closer, the glare of the locomotive's light plowed the fields, then strobed through the bare trees. Ben and I stood just feet from the track as the diesel avalanched above us, the pounding wheels of the boxcars vibrating up our leg bones. Cleansing us. Giving us hardons.

For two months I dubbed our ritual The Amherst Wait. But then Ben revealed its true origins, its true name: The Sylvia Wait. "Mom and I would slip out of the house when *The Green Hornet* was over. We'd sneak away from Dad. I wore an eye mask and one of his old hats. I was the Green Hornet. Mom would wear an eye mask and some bent-up tennis cap she'd spray-painted black. She was Kato, the chauffeur. We'd walk out to the field behind the house and wait by the railroad track. I never knew what kind of Oriental Kato was, but Dad said Kato was South Korean. Dad stressed the 'South' part. And Dad had fought in Korea, so I figured he knew. And while Mom and I waited, she'd tell stories about where the train was coming from. It always came from North Korea. It was loaded with a thousand chauffeurs who were coming to kick ass at Chrysler-Plymouth. 'How could the train cross the ocean?' I'd ask. And Mom would say, 'Through the secret tunnel that cuts under the Pacific into California.' "—Ben paused to frown—"It would have made more sense if the trains came from Japan and were loaded with Toyotas, but it was important to Mom that the train was always filled with North Koreans—the guys who once shot at Dad during the war. And when the train finally came, the two of us would stand next to the track like you and I do. Except, man," —Ben shook his head and chuckled—"you think we stand close? We don't stand close. Mom stood close. Mom made me stand back, and then she inched closer and closer until her face was just a hair from the train. And she'd start screaming— screaming fake Oriental gibberish. I could hear her even above the roar of the engine. And when the train finally passed, she'd shut up and just stand frozen. I'd start to worry something happened. Like the train scraped off her face. Then she'd slowly turn. And she'd be wearing that dumb black cap and that spooky eye mask. And her mouth would be just a straight line. And then I'd worry that the train hurt her head, gave her amnesia. Then she'd grin and open her arms and I'd yell, 'Good work, Kato!' "

After I heard Ben's story, I became hungry in the chest. I wanted to do The Sylvia Wait and see her face kissing a whipping wall of North Korean metal. And when that train passed, I wanted to see her turn, see her smile as she started to undress . . . beginning with a flicking away of the mask.

·

The day Ben and I bussed to Detroit for Christmas Break, my radar finally zeroed in on the true vibe of his story. Because my father was dead, I assumed all children were fatherless, everyone ruled by their mother. But Ben had said: ". . . we'd sneak out of the house from Dad . . ."

From Dad?

For the first time since the Wilderado Motel, I considered this freak of nature: Sylvia had a husband. For the first time since I came to Amherst, I considered that Ben had a father. I had figured that his genetic makeup was coded from Sylvia, forgetting that half had rolled down from Dad—a man named Joshua. And what was it about this Joshua that made Sylvia and Ben, his wife and son, creep into the snow to embrace North Korean locomotive light? Was it the same thing that made Sylvia drive the desert?

When my grandfather, Rex Ringer, finished the first draft of the manuscript you are reading, he snorted and burst into laughter. Him: "You don't see it even now, do you?" Me: See what? Him: "You keep insisting you're writing a book about Sylvia Cushman." Me: Yeah? So what? Him: "This book isn't about Sylvia Cushman. That bastard tricked you good." Me: Huh? Him: "Sylvia's husband. You spent a couple years writing about her husband. You wrote a book about Joshua Cushman."

•

The House of Cushman stood in suburban Detroit, but that label "suburban" or the twinkling Christmas lights looped along the porch didn't negate the Gothic extremity lurking inside. I first entered the house with Ben, both of us carrying grocery bags of frozen broccoli, frozen beets, frozen chicken— food as weapons—while Sylvia followed with the Sunkist oranges. She was dressed in a lime-green '40s nightclub dress— the cleavage covered with various folds like a Roman toga while the dorsal zone was pulled tremendously tight making one want to burn incense at the glory of her hips. She was an extravagant thing to be greeted by in the Detroit bus station, let alone follow down a grocery aisle lined with frozen food. And Sylvia had secretly indicated that she wore this dress for me.

After I learned this, my brain floated around the bus station and then the supermarket. Although Sylvia and I had traveled, in our own fashion, chastely from Yuma to Toledo, had my absence kindled desire in her? Did Sylvia plan to seduce me in her very home, under the nose of her husband?

Seduction made me think of Raymond Chandler. Chandler's wife, Cissy, had been twenty years older than him. She was reportedly "delightfully crazy" like a character in a novel. And she had divorced another to be Chandler's wife. Then I entered the Cushman kitchen. My mouth hung open. Maybe Sylvia was no Cissy. Maybe Sylvia was dangerously bonkers. The kitchen was as padded as the asylum cells in *Shock Corridor*.

Not only were the walls padded, but the ceiling too. There were no sharp corners anywhere. Kitchen utensils had leather handles and were connected to the wall with curlicue telephone cords. The drawers in all the cabinets were lined with felt. Unpacking a bag, I dropped an orange, and it silently bounced on the spongy wrestling mat floor. The room oppressively absorbed all peripheral sounds. I heard the blood cascading through my ears. The rumpling of a grocery bag was World War II.

Sylvia was chattering neighborhood gossip to Ben. Was he so used to the kitchen, he forgot to warn me? Or was this a test? He was acting as if his mother wore green torch singer dresses all the time. When she had greeted us at the bus station, she smiled, opened her mouth as if she were going to purr "I Get a Kick Out of You," but then pecked her son's cheek. She turned to me and paused curiously as if she didn't know me. Back at Standish, Ben instructed me that his father detested his mother's driving trips, so we would tell him I was just a college roommate. Here in the bus station, Sylvia stared as if this fiction were true. Had she forgotten who I was? Ben ducked in the men's room for a post-trip visit. I waited with Sylvia, lamely holding my two knapsacks —one filled with books and the other dirty clothes. After a long silent pause, Sylvia suddenly swirled her skirt, saying, "Don't you recognize it, Orange Boy?"

I was too glazed to even shake my head. She slipped her hand in her bag and pulled out a paperback. The pages were yellowed. It was from the thirties or forties. Sylvia faced the cover to me. On it, a blonde sang into a microphone oblivious to the thug that was gunning down the band-leader. Sylvia was wearing the same dress as the singer. The book was called, *Too Late for Tootsies*. By Rex Ringer.

"Close your mouth, Orange Boy," Sylvia said, sliding the book back in her bag. "I couldn't believe it when I found your grandfather, and then this dress."

Ben bopped up from the bathroom, and she silenced me with her eyes. She avoided my stare both in the supermarket and on the drive home. After we unpacked the groceries, she ushered Ben and me to a table and then stood at the stove boiling milk for hot chocolate, needlessly slapping the spoon every few seconds on the pan—whap! whap!

Edsel, the family dog, suddenly wheezed into the room. Edsel was a basenji, an Africa breed of barkless dog, and resembled a waddling loaf of bread. He sat staring up at the back door as if he were reading a newspaper. Ben opened the foam-rubber-lined door and let the dog out. The corner of the door was taped with a dozen slips of paper that fluttered in the cold outside air. While Edsel explored the crust of gray snow that stretched from the Cushmans' half-submerged black barbecue grill to the backyard of a neighboring auto-executive, I stood and checked out these slips. Traffic tickets. All made out to Sylvia Cushman from two Michigan towns with the names of Muttonville and Lamb. On each, Sylvia was charged with reckless driving.

"Hey, you're responsible for my sinking driving record, Orange Boy," Sylvia yelled. "Those are all tickets for pitching oranges while driving a motor vehicle. Between Halloween and Thanksgiving, I used to drive to Canada where the foliage was spectacular. I kept remembering your speech about how angels are plants and man is meat, so I figured by pitching a little Sunkist in Lamb I'd be doing the Lord's work."

The familiarity of Sylvia sailing citrus eased my unease. Perhaps this kitchen was only an extraordinary indulgence. Perhaps swiftly swirling milk or soup made Sylvia reflexively pitch whatever was handiest—a pan or a dish—into the wall. So they padded the kitchen. But both this theory, as well as my earlier flash concerning padded cells were wrong. This kitchen wasn't designed for Sylvia. It was for her husband—the man my grandfather claims I've written this book about.

•

M r. Cushman entered the kitchen a little after Sylvia finished pouring hot chocolate into our rubber mugs, and asked: "So Orange Boy, where do you sleep when my son invites coeds to his room?"

Without thinking I had said, "There are no girls." I then immediately flushed. I should never reveal such a truth.

But surprisingly, Sylvia responded with: "Good. Good."

That surprised me. I took it for granted that Sylvia would want a heartbreaker son.

"What's good?" a hoarse voice asked. A barely audible voice that rasped rather than spoke. We all jumped because we hadn't heard him enter. Joshua Cushman walked into the kitchen. His kitchen. Ben let Edsel in from the backyard, but the dog immediately snuck back out.

On first impression, Mr. Cushman looked as if he could be typecast as a Russian premier. He was a hulking short and burly man in a trench coat and wore an out-of-date fedora. He reminded me of the Khrushchev drivers who had tailgated Sylvia and me in New Mexico. He seemed to lack good nature, and radiated the menacing essence of a petty bureaucrat. He lowered his bulk into a chair and removed his hat. He was bald. I noticed his upper lip was scarred. His grievance wasn't as long as mine, but it was deeper. I felt simpatico and began unconsciously running my tongue along my own scar. Mr. Cushman glared with frank disgust. I must have looked like a slobbering joyboy.

Sylvia gave a lingering touch to his shoulder, then left the kitchen. Mr. Cushman acknowledged his son with a handshake. I extended my hand, trying to think of something to say, but he ignored me. On the bus, Ben warned that his father was rude, an affliction that couldn't be helped, and said I should treat his father like a hunchback or a man who pissed in public.

Sylvia returned to the room—head lowered and silently shuffling geisha-style. She poured her husband's hot chocolate so gingerly we heard the steam rising from the delicate laps of milk.

She had held her head down as she walked, but raised it to follow the stream of milk so I saw she had just put on lipstick. Extravagantly rubescent lipstick. I'd never seen Sylvia wear anything other then a faded puce when she started doctoring her face in Missouri. Also, her ears now glittered. She'd put on her little ear-shaped earrings.

Mr. Cushman never raised his eyes. He was gripping the table, then abruptly pointed at his son asking: "How did you deal with lime ridge?"

After living with Ben, I'd absorbed some history of swing and bop, and knew *lime ridge* was Lime Ridge, Pennsylvania. The spot where Clifford Brown died. Ben closed his eyes and said, "As our Greyhound passed, I started crying."

His father nodded. They began a revelry—Ben talking, his father grunting affirmatively—about Clifford Brown—promised prince of bebop, a trumpet-boy who might have deposed Miles Davis but for an icy road in 1956 when the 25-year-old Brown lost control of his wheel and James Dean escorted him up to heaven. While Ben focused on the subject of his own weeping —describing his tears as if it were a wonder to express grief with water, not merely clenched jaw—I stared at Sylvia and took her in. Her lower lip was raspberry. It seemed her slightest and strongest muscle of sensuality. I figured Sylvia was wearing this lipstick for her husband, but would Mr. Cushman suspect she wore the dress for me? And in the hard kitchen light her earrings seemed made of a metal less substantial than silver. They looked tin. And if that was true—Sylvia had "tin ears." Were her ears an ironic comment about her son's or husband's musical tastes? As a signaler—passion/infidelity/disrespect—Sylvia was confusing.

I looked away. Both Ben and Mr. Cushman had been watching me watch Sylvia's lower lip. They were both staring at me in passive attention—as if I were a professor paused in the middle of a lecture. This was unnerving. Sylvia rescued me from their scrutiny by saying: "I don't know about you, boys, but from now on, I'm going to wear my seat belt. Indians and ancient Hawaiians both believe one should never speak the names of the dead. Their spirit ears hear and they are drawn to you like plague. If Cliff hears his name, he may try to tug one of us to car-crash heaven."

•

Now is the time when I must describe the calamities that befell Mr. Cushman's head, but first, I want to stress that my grandfather was wrong when he said I wrote this novel about Joshua Cushman. I'm going to describe the grievances done to Cushman's head and ears not for his character development, but for Sylvia's. She married the man for this pain, believing she could heal him. After two decades of failure, her bad Florence Nightingale trip left her with nowhere to turn but to God. And He was the Catholic god of the Southwest high desert. Sylvia's ornamental ears were made of tin—tin ears from a New Mexican church famous for healing the crippled. Tiny tin body parts (arms, hearts, legs), representing the injured part of the anatomy, were placed at the church's altar. The applicant then prayed for healing. The church was circled with crutches, left by the lame who could now walk and drive cars.

Sylvia wore the tin ears beside her skull—the closest point to her brain, the next best place to New Mexico—because of her husband's calamity, his "Silence Trip"—which began in the late '40s when his ears were fine. During this time, Cushman played trumpet and even gigged around the country with the Stan Kenton Orchestra until he was drafted to '51 Korea. He signed up for the Army band to blow his way out of combat. Then one night after five bourbons at the Five Spot in New York, he wrapped his Buick around the street sign on the corner of Bowery and Houston. His head bombed the windshield and he shredded his lips on the glass. The Devil kissed his embou-chure goodbye.

Because Cushman could no longer blow, he spent a sorry year in someplace called Yangyang, freezing his ass voluntarily pulling midnight sentry. Since Cushman had been forever de-nied the gratification of playing music, he now funnelled his life into listening to it. It was in the midnight hour that the U.S.O. radio station broke its stream of white Big Band with heavenly bits of Duke Ellington and Armstrong. The Army was experi-menting with a prototype of the transistor radio (having a vision of each soldier in the midst of combat simultaneously connected to General Ridgeway's voice), and Cushman would stand at his post swaying in the night snow with his "cigarette-pack" radio pressed into his ear.

It was just after dawn one morning when Cushman had his second visit from the Devil. The snow was falling in pellets like rice. It was Cushman's turn to clean the latrine and as he lugged a bucket of frozen shit across the yard, a fellow bebop lover stepped out of the barracks to blow reveille, saw Cushman, and instead blew three bars of Ellington's "What Am I Here For." The music appeared to literally hit Cushman in the head. He fell to the ground and bucked up and down holding his ears, screaming in the blizzard like a baby. Three privates hauled his twisting body back into the barracks and tied him to a bunk. Cushman couldn't stop screaming long enough to tell them what was wrong. The base doc said Cushman was faking, but after three days of nonstop screaming, they shot him full of morphine and shipped him east to a psycho-ward in Japan.

He spent the next two years stateside in the Vets' Hospital in San Francisco until a doc figured out that the combination of car crash and Korean winter had irreparably damaged Mr. Cushman's "oval window," the small gateway that connects the outer to the inner ear. As a result, sound caused pain. While the gently stirred molecules of "I Cover the Waterfront" do a blissful tiptoe across the trilogy of our delicate ear bones, those same molecules were a hurricane to Cushman. A lover's whisper or the flap of a sparrow's wing was amplified, jackhammering the pulp of his brain.

Although Cushman's affliction was incurable it was not constant or consistent. Cushman had good and bad days, even good and bad years. When he was diagnosed, he left the hospital to get on with his life, having visions of manning a weather station in Antarctica, presumably the most silent place on earth. Instead he went to Wisconsin—to the university at Madison—where he apathetically embraced the Eisenhower-era fad of engineering, choosing "automotive design." Because his fellow students all craved jobs fashioning shark-finned sports cars, Cushman became a specialist in an unpopulated field—auto safety; so that now, as Ben described it: "Dad crashes cars for a living"—

earning a salary that allowed him to construct a home for his ears—his Quiet House: the House of Cushman—where the residents tiptoed, carefully clicked light switches, and whispered when they spoke. The only member of his household exempt from its laws was Lester—now a five-year-old with the serious brow of an old man.

As Ben and his father finished discussing Clifford Brown, Lester himself padded into the kitchen. He'd been over his allergy attack for a month and demanded his daily Bosco in a loud frog-child voice. Mr. Cushman winced, but said nothing.

•

When Ben had been born his father moved out of the house for a year because the baby's crying was unbearable. Yet Lester was born during one of Cushman's "good years." The man was able to walk his child at night. But then Lester was mute as Edsel. At first Cushman was grateful to be spared the needless din of babytalk. But when Lester was four and still hadn't spoken, the child's silence implied autism, a condition reflecting badly on Cushman's genes. He became obsessed that his child talk. He bought flashcards of insects and animals, and sat in front of the child mouthing, "Beetle. Bunny." "Adam naming the animals," Sylvia mocked. And then one day, Sylvia returned from shopping and found a terrified Lester with rolling eyes, pointing all over the room jabbering: "Father. Window. Dog. Me. Chair . . ." It took a week before the child calmed and began to speak more or less coherent sentences. Sylvia couldn't figure out how her husband made Lester speak

—had he threatened the child? In any case, Lester had become the family orator. And while we all sat drinking hot chocolate Lester croaked about his latest finger-paintings. Could Jackson Pollock have described his work with words any more elegant? "I like where it looks like I swallowed a whole pot of purple paint and green paint and then spit it all out at a hundred miles an hour."

Sylvia said that once when Lester was describing a finger-painted self-portrait that was all teeth and mouth, she just blurted, "How did Daddy teach you to talk?" The child paused, then abruptly screwed up his face and screamed, "Daddy showed me the dogs! Daddy showed me the dogs!" before pitching his milk across the room.

•

After a dinner of frozen fried chicken—I spent the meal holding my chicken and knuckles over my face so I could surreptitiously dart glances at Sylvia's red lips—she told Ben and me that we were going to pick out a Christmas tree, then she went to change her clothes. Now because of Scripture, my mother forbade Christmas trees, so I saw this ritual as something other families did. It didn't dawn on me this was a strange mission for a Jewish household.

Sylvia reappeared wearing jeans and a gray sweater. She'd taken off her tin ears. Down in the sunken garage, she threw Ben the keys to the station wagon, and the three of us crowded together in the front seat. As I started to buckle my seat belt, Sylvia laughed, "Ben, dig this! Orange Boy is worried about your driving." Ben peered over: "What are you—a pussy?" I released the belt.

Ben started the car and Sylvia wiped off her lipstick with a Kleenex, carelessly tossing it behind the seat. As Ben backed up out of the driveway, he twisted in his seat and touched his mother's shoulder with his right hand. We reached the street and swung around Sylvia's VW—cold metal parked and gleaming under a streetlight.

"Note this technicality, Orange Boy," Sylvia said, pointing to the Volkswagen. "You can only pitch oranges from a convertible when it's warm enough to drive with the top down. When the top is up, it screws up the arc of your pitch. I'm out of commission until spring training."

●

It was unsettling sitting beside Sylvia inside a car that neither of us was driving. The station wagon was wide enough that we could sit without touching. I wanted her to move closer, but when Ben swung a sharp turn and she slid into me, I flinched away toward the door.

I figured we were going to buy a tree at some supermarket parking lot, but Ben passed several shopping centers and headed down a dark road that wound around hills where houses sat roped in elaborate strings of Christmas lights.

"Ritzy digs," I remarked.

"Ha!" Sylvia snorted, her breath staining the windshield. "Bloomfield Hills is just nouveau riche. You want class, go see Grosse Pointe."

We drove further, and I considered the genetic shakedown of Cushman driving techniques. Sylvia drove in abstracted sheets of motion while her son drove in sparse, violently efficient motions. He was a terse Dashiel Hammett sentence on wheels.

Sylvia sliced the air with her hand and Ben crunched the station wagon onto the gravel shoulder, then cut the engine. Both sides of the road were walled by dark trees, the only illumination a cone of light beneath a lone streetlight in the distance. I leapt out of the car, my breath glowing in the dark. Sylvia leaned over the seat and then crawled out of the car hugging an axe. We followed her into the trees. Ben walked parallel to his mother and suddenly had his arm around her shoulder. It was a touching tableau in a Cushmanian way: Mother. Son. Axe.

We stepped out of the woods onto the edge of a clearing where a rotund plastic Santa glowed—the pagan object the size of a child and lit from within.

"Now, follow in single file," Sylvia said. I was puzzled but followed behind her and Ben, all of us now traveling like ducklings up to the house. Near the shoveled front walk was a row of cupcake hedges iced with snow that curved around a fair-sized evergreen.

"Thar she is," Sylvia whispered. Ben walked over and shook the tree. Inexplicably it gave a high-pitched shriek and we all jumped as something flapped away. Sylvia laughed, "Big Bird," and picked up her axe.

"I'll go get the car ready." Ben turned and darted back down the lawn.

I was alone with Sylvia again. Our motel history came back to me, but I wasn't sure what to do with it. She was kneeling and breaking off the smaller branches at the base of the tree. Then she rose and raised the axe over her shoulder. I moved back out of her arc. "Paul Bunyan was my dad," she grunted, and gave the tree a smart whack. At that moment, the head of an Afghan appeared in an unlit window, barking hysterically. With its flopping hair and long snout, it was Pete Townsend. Then a car began pulling up the long driveway running parallel to the front yard. I stood paralyzed watching the headlights race towards us across the blue snow until Sylvia grabbed my waist yelling, "Hit the dirt!" and threw me down to the snow.

The headlights rolled across our embrace as Sylvia's lips pressed in my ear panting, *"Come on you patriot. Make it one. Make it one."*

There, lying in the snow, I instantly knew what she meant— Emily Dickinson's 'Patriot Sleep' letter, the smoking gun signifying she had lain with Judge Ottis Lord in love (theoretically on a bed, not a snowy lawn). After Emily's death, her brother discovered drafts of her letters, and he cut out the racy parts. But her brother missed the Patriot Sleep letter. Emily had disguised her passion in coded metaphor.

Sylvia's face was now about two nose-lengths away and I recited Emily's letter from memory, " *'We went to sleep as if it were a country, — let us make it one. We will make it one, my native Land, my Darling. Come, oh, be a patriot now.'* "

Sylvia looked over with pure admiration. This was the first time she'd given me such a visual blanket. Then we heard four car doors slam. Voices. Footsteps. I heard something hit the window and peered over her shoulder. The dog was hurling itself at the glass, then disappearing for a moment, before returning to bang-and-bark again. We heard the front door open and shut.

Sylvia helped me up. As I brushed the snow off my legs, Sylvia rushed over and felled the evergreen in two swift strokes. I tried to catch it, to brace its fall, but the tree was heavier than it looked. It landed in the snow.

"We'll drag it over our tracks," Sylvia instructed. We stooped and grabbed the bottom branches and began shuffling backward, lugging the evergreen down the lawn toward the tree line. When we reached the woods, Sylvia stopped and handed me two oranges.

"Take your gloves off," Sylvia commanded. "You have to feel the orange skin as you pitch."

I followed her order and whipped fruit at Santa. As Sylvia did her windup and pitch, each fold of her vinyl jacket gave a different texture of sound. We both missed. Santa just grinned.

•

I helped Ben drag the tree into the living room where his father was talking on the phone wearing earmuffs. Mr. Cushman hung up, took off his earmuffs, then walked over to pinch the branches. Checking for bugs? Lester was circling us all, jumping up and down, psyched out on yuletide adrenalin.

"All this noise over a tree," Mr. Cushman finally rasped, shaking his head. He retreated down into the soundproof bunker he'd built in the basement. There (according to Ben) Mr. Cushman would sit and dream over a stack of brittle, antique Clifford Brown albums from the '50s. But Ben's dad wouldn't play them. He had taken a vow that music would never again turn on him as a sudden sonic whip. And he masochistically followed this vow as if it were some *Manchurian Candidate* brain programming. For example, see Cushman in the basement watching Dizzy Gillespie on TV. The sound is off—the set gives off nothing but an electric hum. Cushman hunches religiously in front of the silent blue screen, conceptualizing Gillespie's notes by the position of the man's fingers on his trumpet valves and reading the topography of the man's frog cheeks as he blows.

On this particular night, Cushman spun records on his imaginary stereo, while his wife returned wearing her green Rex Ringer film noir dress, and holding a box of glass ornaments the same color—her pucker again smeared with lipstick, the red of Bible ribbons.

She and Lester began hooking the bulbs to the tree-sprigs, while Ben slouched sideways on an armchair scanning one of his father's old big-band charts. The living room filled with the smell of evergreen. Lester ran up clutching a fistful of tinsel, laughing, "Look, mom! Silver spaghetti!" "No, it's linguine, dear," Sylvia said and looked back over her shoulder at me. "Isn't this Christian business intensely nostalgic for you, Orange Boy?"

I looked down at the thick carpet. My mother said Christmas was a pagan holiday with roots in Druid England. In the ring of Stonehenge, white-robed priests had impaled squirming naked virgins on evergreens—angels on the tops of Christmas trees. Even worse, according to the position of biblical-era stars, Jesus was actually born on February 2—Groundhog Day. My mother's homily: "Jesus was mankind's groundhog and the *Book of Revelations*' prediction for the length of Satan's winter."

I declined to share this information and bomb the yuletide vibe. But then I asked, "Why do you guys do such an elaborate Christmas tree trip if you're Jewish?"

"We're not," Ben snorted. "We're Ethical Culturists." I looked blank. "We're the Semitic version of Unitarians," Sylvia explained. "We started stringing a tree when Ben was a baby because we didn't want our little boy to feel like a freak among the Deerbourne goys." She smiled. "Then we just got into it."

Mother and son hooked the final brittle green bulb, and the tree, rather than looking festively flashy, became a cold geometric object of green needles and bubbles. Lester slipped out of the room and ran wildly back waving one of his G.I. Joes decked out in camouflage and combat gear. Sylvia lifted the boy over her head, and he stuck the mercenary on the top of the tree.

"Death from above," Sylvia said. "Kill them all and let Santa sort them out."

•

Santa broke my heart and sent catastrophe from above. I was sleeping on a rollaway bed upstairs in a small padded cell used as the Cushmans' guest room and office. I awoke to muffled screaming and jerked open the door. Feet were pounding down the dark hallway. A light suddenly shot on. I was blinded by the glare. Brief flashes: Sylvia Cushman. Rear view. Aqua underpants. The bones of her back. Now whipping a nightgown over her head. Sylvia disappearing, then running back clutching a small body. Lester. Now Sylvia kicking Ben's door—savage kicks—screaming, "Quick, Ben! Goddammit, wake up! Get the car started!"

Sylvia ran down the stairs with Lester. I pulled on my pants and followed. Downstairs, Sylvia knelt in front of the couch wrapping Lester in a blanket. When I got closer, I saw that her son was no longer her son. He was Bug Baby, a lump of dough with puffed-out head, eyes wet and swollen—his fat lids the color of peeled hardboiled eggs. Lester was mindlessly waving his swollen hands at his face as if he were swatting at flies.

Mr. Cushman ran up from his bunker wrapped in a ratty bath-robe, rasping, "What's all this noise?"

"Oh god, oh god, Lester's got another attack," Sylvia said, her voice cracking.

"Well, let's have a little control if we can," Mr. Cushman whispered, running his hand across his bald head.

Ben dashed down the stairs two at a time, took a look at his brother, and said, "Oh Christ shit okay let's split. Where's the keys?"

Sylvia threw him the keys and lifted Lester. Mr. Cushman shot out his hand, rasping, "Hey, just wait. He looks pretty swollen, but I'm sure he'll be all right 'till morning. Then we can drive him to my father's."

"We'll do no such thing!" Sylvia screamed—a strange sound bouncing off the cork ceiling. She paused and stared at him, her face pale and drained. "He's going to the hospital!"

Mr. Cushman winced at her voice. He stood blocking the hall-way and didn't move as Sylvia rushed up cradling Lester. She paused and said, "You go with your dogs and silence, but you go too far here." Then she swung her hips and butted Cushman out of the way. She hauled Lester out the door. Even though the doorframe was padded with a leather lining, it made a thudding slam. Mr. Cushman whimpered.

I just stood rubbing my bare feet on the carpet. "Dogs and silence"? Huh? As I contemplated this term, I noticed tiny green lights strung on the Christmas tree blinking in lazy Morse code. Mr. Cushman rushed over and choked, "I'll be damned if we'll be bled by Detroit Edison!" He ripped the plug out of the wall. The tree shook. The G.I. Joe toppled and fell.

Mr. Cushman spun and stomped upstairs. I heard him enter the guest room. The wall of that room was lined with framed album covers. Jazz records from the '50s.

When I'd first entered the guest room, I hadn't paid them any attention, but leaned on the shut door and slid out the Kleenex Sylvia had wiped off her lipstick with—I'd snatched it from the floor of the station wagon when I helped Ben position the ever-green in the payload. The lower third of this Kleenex was marked with a single successful impression of Sylvia's complete lips. The Kleenex was confusingly erotic—the Shroud of Turin of Sylvia's mouth. I had carefully placed it on the desktop, then checked out the albums covers—the bright blue, orange, and green that art directors of the 1950s were so fond of—colors now beautiful in their antique garishness. There was a Duke Ellington record. A Clifford Brown. Of all things—a Steve Allen. And a Chet Baker: *Things That Aren't There*. In an obvious staged set, Baker sat at a nightclub table before both his trumpet and a smoking ashtray. A standing blonde leaned beside him, breasts heavy, whispering in his ear. Her lips were a bright red "O." She wore a lime-green dress. She wore Sylvia's dress. Whatever it meant that Sylvia wore it to the bus station, I now knew the dress was first and foremost a reference to this album. And Sylvia wore it to honor both her husband's love of jazz and his loss. And just as her garb was for her husband, so was this flag from her lips.

•

I was still standing in the living room beside the unlit tree when Cushman clumped down, holding that Kleenex, pinching it more delicately than I did. He gave me a quick look, then retreated down to his bunker. Edsel trotted into the room. I considered if Sylvia's "dogs and silence" was a simple reference to the mute family canine. Edsel paced up to the now-dark Christmas tree. He snuck me a look, then lifted his leg and pissed on it.

•

The next morning Ben said we should promenade the subdivision and he'd explain. As we walked out into the garage and up the driveway, I saw Sylvia framed in the living room window. She sat on the couch cradling Lester, a Madonna with child growing worse—his face fatter, straining to burst. Behind them stood the blaze of the Christmas tree.

As Ben and I slid down the front walk, he told me how the doctors hadn't a clue what Lester was allergic to—"No one with blue dye. The next year—no more ice cream and stay away from cats. Soon, they'll find out TV-rays make him blow up."

Last night, the doctors had shot the boy up with adrenalin hoping that would make the swelling subside.

"If Lester's allergies don't bottom out, Mom's going to lose it," Ben said kicking a lump of snow. "She's climbing the walls trying to figure this attack."

I asked Ben to explain Mr. Cushman's suggestion: "We'll drive Lester over to my father's."

"Grandpa Cushman—ha! He's an M.D., a jerk-off quack who doesn't know where shit drops from."

Ben proceeded to give me the tour of the neighborhood, a subdivision just hilly enough to give one a sense of its depressing flatness. The neighbors lived in clunky ranch houses, childlike versions of the Frank Lloyd Wright mansion in *North by Northwest*. Their lawns were covered with gray snow, and in daylight their Christmas decorations seemed gaudy. While we walked, several big Buicks and Cadillacs—all chrome and plum-black paint jobs—pulled over and stopped us. The electric windows slid down and the drivers curtly asked where we lived. Ben answered quietly, politely, leaning forward to better understand each pudgy businessman, each matron smeared with lipstick. Once he even held his knit ski hat in his hands like some peasant as the overlord trots by.

"If a longhair gives them any lip, they call the cops," Ben explained. We walked several paces, and then stopped. He looked up at the sky. "I hope the Russians drop a bomb on this fucking town."

•

Ben and I were stomping the snow off our feet when we heard Sylvia's muffled raving—the angry housewife. Growing up, I heard similar raging from the neighbors' homes. What was lacking here were husbandly responses. Because of the cork ceilings, it took a while to find her, to find Sylvia in the living room, standing beside the Christmas tree, clutching a brown box marked with canceled stamps. The positioning of her fingers made it look like a weapon. When I rushed in she went silent. Mr. Cushman, hunched, began whispering with clenched jaw: "You treat that boy like a sedan with faulty filters. Boys can heal themselves."—pause—"You don't worry about our son when you're off on your little lone feminine driving jaunts across the desert."

Silence. Then, Sylvia shrieked: " 'Feminine driving jaunts'?" I jumped. Cushman winced. Sylvia yelled as if she were an inexperienced actress testing her ability to project her voice.

"You loud woman!" Mr. Cushman rasped, slapping the cushioned table. At the sound of his slap, he exhaled an "Ugh!" He stood up, croaking, "I can't whisper to you when you're unreasonable like this."

Sylvia stood quietly for a moment. (Had Cushman actually said "whisper"?) Sylvia narrowed her eyes, letting his comment twist in the air—while Mr. Cushman appraised me as if I were responsible for this disorder in his household. He didn't catch Sylvia flapping up her arms while simultaneously taking a deep breath. When she dropped them she let loose with a single high-pitched "Ha!"—an operatic tremolo so shrill even I winced. Mr. Cushman stumbled up, eyes bugged-out, clamping his forearms to his ears and blundering into the table. He knocked it over, and we jumped out of the way. The little premier tripped down his hallway, while his wife danced after him, singing louder and louder. Who knows how Mr. Cushman's damaged "oval window" took this sound? Sylvia might just as well have been poking his eardrums with an ice pick. Mr. Cushman clawed at his bunker door trying to yank it open. When he succeeded, he jumped down the steps, pulling the door shut. Sylvia wiggled the doorknob. Locked. She kicked the door with the side of her shoe and said: *"An ear can break a human heart/as quickly as a spear!"*

Then she turned, blew a curl from her forehead, and began both weeping and laughing. "Well, Orange Boy—was it live or was it Memorex?" She then ripped open her box and rustled through shredded newspaper. Something silver glittered. She lowered her hands, and I saw she was wearing a single earring, pirate style: a tin baby. She wore a tin Lester near the bottom of her New Mexican skull.

•

A year later, Ben and I stand in a New Orleans cemetery under the shadow of a vandalized French mausoleum. Ben raises his cornet and begins blowing a dirge for his dead mother before an audience of rain-beat cherubim. A century of storms had smeared each stone face featureless—a remnant of swelled-Lester. When that little cherub's allergy had peaked at its worst, Mr. Cushman sulked in the basement, while Sylvia, Ben, and I sat up with the child to make sure he didn't suffocate on his own swollen cheeks. Sylvia found a box of old baby bottles, and popped the nipple off one. With a paring knife, she sliced off the nipple-top, then stuck the plug in Lester's mouth. "At least now he can breathe," she said, then whispered, "poor little Pillsbury Doughboy . . ." She looked up at Ben and me, tin baby glittering from her ear, letting us know it was all right to laugh.

On our first night of guarding Lester, Ben lasted until 3:00 a.m., then crashed. By 3:30, Sylvia's head began wobbling at the Japanese monster movie we were watching on TV. In the garish TV light she was looking fifty years old, the skin that circled her eyes gray as a bruise. Lester started to moan. I reached out to turn off the volume, telling Sylvia to go to bed—"I'll stay up and make sure he keeps breathing."

She left the room and returned to thump a box of typewriter paper on the TV table, singing, "Ta-da! The great thesis." I looked at the cover page: *An Analysis of Spherical Symbolist in the Verse of Emily Dickinson, by Sylvia A. Cushman.* "It's still a work-in-progress," she said. "Give it a read and tell me how wonderful it is."

It took two hours of wading. The text was dense lit-crit, but as much as I could make out, Sylvia had cataloged every circle, sphere, and dot that spun in Dickinson's poetry ("Soundless as dots—on a Disc of Snow," etc.). Her thesis climaxed in a philosophical discussion of the genesis of sphericity—how the fertilized egg is a perfect circle at fertilization, and only later warps into ovality—and Sylvia coupled this with the irony that Emily never bore children. While I read, Sylvia didn't go immediately to bed. She said she was too wired. She slipped on a parka and took a full grocery bag and went outside to pitch oranges against the back bricks of the house—soundless as citrus on a disc of . . . etc.

Her oranges gone, she came in and went up to bed. I had just reached a point where Sylvia makes a leap from conventional college repertoire into pure Sylvianese: ". . . Emily Dickinson's relentless obsession with the particle—with the atomic scale, if you will—makes Dickinson, the American, the founder of particle physics. It's not a stretch to state that Emily Dickinson is the mother of Los Alamos."

•

finished Sylvia's thesis and looked up at the television. The screen was swarming with blue static. Little blue atoms. Busy blue bees. Have you ever seen your TV actually filled with swarming bees? The camera pulls back and shows you the hive. The hive shaped like a cross. Don't switch channels! See the figure lumber up to the cross. A deep-sea diver? No. My mother. In a bee bonnet. She has come to gather the Lord's honey.

You must admire the novelty of beginning a religious broadcast this way. Its bizarreness factor is minimized if you are familiar with Proverbs 12:13: *"Eat Thou the honeycomb, which is sweet to Thy taste. So shall wisdom be unto Thy soul. When Thou has found it, Thy expectation shall not be cut off."* And when the credits roll, the shot changes to a live broadcast from the Tabernacle of the Speckled Bird. My mother appears, dressed in a frilly white dress, hair cascading in ringlets to the slump of her shoulders. She waddles across the stage swinging a pail—a simple tin milk pail glaring in the floodlights. When it tips towards the camera, something golden glistens inside. My mother then turns her head away from the current camera a millisecond before the second camera picks her up. At first you think this is clumsy camera work. Then you realize that my mother is willing the cameras to change angles.

Once the second camera is in place, it tracks her as she walks over to the wretches—several drooling Mongoloids in rompers or a skeletal waif twisted in his wheelchair. And my mother pulls a ladle from her pail. And my mother prays: "Dear Lord, see these humble lambs. Their expectations have been cut off. Their expectations have been cut. I offer them Thy honeycomb to eat. I offer them Thy honeycomb." And what happens next is this: exactly nothing. The lame do not walk. The idiot does not recite the alphabet. But in the immediate viewing present, healing is not expected. This is no holy-roller tent revival. As Sylvia put it, my mother's honey ritual signifies a larger gestalt—the viewer at home realizing that deep within himself is a huddled crippled child, baby lips hungering for holy honey.

I knew that twisted boy in the wheelchair. He was the nephew of my mother's media-adviser. I never knew the specifics, but he was obviously brain-damaged—mouth hung slack, his eye nullified with vacant gaze. His hands dangled at the wrist. I remember studying those wrists for inspiration when I had to play a dog in a grade-school play. Occasionally, in a gesture that might seem cynical to an outsider, this particular child was wheeled in front of my mother's cameras when there was a shortage of other deformed children to be fed their smear of honey. From a tactical viewpoint, he was so touching in his pathos that my mother knew hundreds of sinners embraced Christ whenever this crippled child appeared. On his last TV appearance, my mother paused longer than usual with her ladle in front of his body, lapsing into a ferocious rap: "O' Lord, the bees that secreted Thy food were holy. And O' Lord, the workers were righteous, the drones were blessed. And O' Lord, the queen was a blessed and righteous queen. And the bees danced in the joy of Thy name, Amen. And the bees flicked flowers in Your blessed fields, Amen. And the hive swarmed in Thy name, Amen. All so this honey could be secreted in Thy sweet holy name. And I am praying to You, Dear Jesus, to make this honey taste as sweet to this poor lamb's lips as the sound of Thy sweet holy name is to his little ears. Oh blessed Jesus, thank You thank You thank You."

I had been waiting on a hallway bench outside the studio, swinging my feet. This child was wheeled beside me. "Watch him for a moment," the media-adviser asked, and clicked away on her heels. My mother's honey drooled from the boy's salamander lips. As I heard the muffled sound of my mother's preaching from inside the studio, the child continued his dull gaze. I found the honey dripping down his face unbearably disturbing. Hadn't I just learned to manufacture a similar substance? I had to wipe it away. I bunched up my sleeve and carefully reached over to rub his mouth. At my touch, the boy quivered. I froze. Oh shit! Was it wrong to touch him? But then the child's hunched body began unfolding—the wet insect exits its egg case. His arms uncurled. His fingers wiggled. His legs extended and stretched out. He shifted on the ladder of his spine and sat erect.

And I thought: My god! This boy is as tall as I am! Were we even the same age—his deformities only making him look like a child? Then the boy looked down at me. His eyes were wide and the irises turned from milky-gray to a spectacular blue—somewhere Paul Newman was slipping on a pair of shades in shame! And while this boy pierced me with those eyes, he lowered his jaw. And he spoke. This once-idiot who lacked even the rudiments of babytalk now spoke in a soft, melodious voice. The boy clearly said: "Christ sees you like an X ray."

I scrambled quickly for his aunt. But when we returned, the boy lay on the floor. He was still. He was dead.

I could have informed my mother that she had healed the child. That even though he died, he had that moment of healed clarity—certainly a miracle. But I didn't. My mother and her adviser were leaning over his body, completely ignorant of his transformation, too taken up by concerns over adverse publicity. "This is bad. So soon after the honey sacrament," the media-adviser grimly mused.

"No. no. no. Jesus heard my call and decided to take him now," my mother said, patting the woman's shoulder. "He's up playing Little League in heaven."

"Yes, yes, that's right," the other woman agreed. "Jesus needed him." Both women then said: "It was a good thing."

I stayed clammed. If my mother knew the extent of her prayer power she might use her words to smooth me over. But now eight years later in the House of Cushman, I turned from the bees on the television to consider Lester. Didn't Sylvia's child, this stricken lump with suet cheeks, deserve to be healed like that boy? What if healing prayer power was genetic? Even though I had never been on television, could I heal Lester?

I knelt on the Cushmans' carpet. I folded my hands and I began to pray. I pushed my petition for Lester's healing out of a spout in my crown, and my words shot through the ceiling. My words rose above the sleeping homes of Bloomfield Hills. If you had been flying above, you would have seen these words—my words —as luminous balls flaring past the windows of your jet.

But two hours of prayer did not heal Lester. At 8:00 a.m., Sylvia bundled Lester in a blanket to take him back to the hospital for more shots of adrenalin. As the Volkswagen pulled away, Mr. Cushman crept into the room. I caught his shape out of the corner of my eye and jumped. We stood considering each other for a full minute before he whispered: "What were you doing to the boy last night?"

I shivered. I felt like I had been caught jerking off. Cushman must have spied me kneeling in his living room praying over the body of his son. But then I thought: Wait a minute, wait a minute. This man is a Jew. I can get away with this . . . And so I said, "I was praying," saying it matter-of-factly, as if this was something all Christians did.

Mr. Cushman rubbed the stubble on his jaw and gave the slightest of smiles. "Get on your coat. I want to show you something."

I got dressed and Mr. Cushman showed me the dogs.

•

He waved me into the Cushman station wagon and insisted that I strap on the seat belt-harness, which hugged tighter than I was used to. "Euro-design," he whispered. "No leeway. Detroit standards are for shit. Two inches of slack at even 30 miles per hour and your brains are yolk on the dash."

Those were his only words for the next hour. We drove out of their subdivision between storm clouds and aluminum fields, the monotony of which was only broken by bands of lemon-colored factory smoke pouring into the sky. We passed dismal towns with the names of automobiles. At one point I reached over and turned the radio on. Cushman reached over and turned the radio off. I fidgeted in my harness, waiting for him to speak. He knew nothing of Sylvia and me other than that I coveted her lipstick banner. But did he sense that I once had seen his wife naked? I blinked into my sideview mirror. Did he now have the right to poke out my eyes with a stick?

Mr. Cushman suddenly swooped us into a gas station, the abruptness of his gesture startlingly familiar. Cushman started out our trip driving like a surgeon, but he now drove abrupt and jerky like his wife. He made a sharp Sylvian turn and al-

most sideswiped the pumps. He braked by the open wash-
rooms.

The station didn't appear to be open. Cushman got out of the
car to shake hands with a guy not much older than me. He had
a cowlick and a parka of hunter's orange. They talked. Then this
orange boy disappeared into the garage and returned with the
dogs.

The dogs were an incongruous Disney-vision of four Dalmatians. They were dragged to the back of our wagon and herded
in, the car instantly smelling of dog—not of unwashed dog, but
old dog. At least three of them were male, their plump, pink
scrotums bouncing. Two immediately lay belly-down to start a
session of serious panting. Another jabbed his snoot into my
face. The fourth crouched at the back door, whining.

I dug my fingers into the soft flap of skin on the back of my
Dalmatian's skull and began scratching. Cushman opened the
driver's door. He was carrying a cardboard case of highball
glasses. Each one had a goose printed on its side with the
expression: "I'm a Michi-gander."

Cushman jerked the ignition on and bumped us out of the
station, heading up the highway. I continued scratching my dog
and considering his brethren. An untrained observer might see
the four as duplicates. When I was a boy, my father once
brought one of Lassie's TV trainers home for beers. Dad wanted
information about a client's cheating wife, but all the trainer
would do was talk about dogs. Near the end of the evening, the

trainer was ranting, "Half a dozen bitches play Lassie in any given show. I can't believe the idiot viewing public thinks it's the same dog."

As for Cushman's Dalmatians, I had already named them mentally—Friendly, Sleepy, Rascal, and Nixon. The one I was scratching was clearly Friendly. Sleepy lay extended with snoot in paws, asleep. Rascal lay on his side and occasionally gnawed Sleepy's hind paw. And Nixon was the dog whining at the tailgate wanting to escape.

My spine was getting twisted, so I turned back around and faced the front. Our car took a two-lane through dense pines. A high chain-link fence topped with barbed wire ran parallel to the road; below—a moat of frozen water. Cushman swerved us into an unmarked gate where a guard was huddled in his pillbox watching TV cartoons. Mr. Cushman flashed some sort of I.D. at him, and we drove through, following a gravel road through naked trees. Then as we bumped along, Mr. Cushman's eyes still fixed on the road, he began whispering. I strained against my harness, leaning closer to hear him, feeling the steam of his breath. "It kills me you kids think you know it all," he said, then paused. "You know it all about ecology. You know it all about Red China. You know it all about pot and granola. You know it all about having some fairy dick you in the back seat of a Jap sedan and then drive you home so you can tell poor stupid old Dad why he can't vote for Gerry Ford anymore. You know it all, don't you? You know everything about everything. You know so much you can even pray and tell God why he can't vote for Gerry Ford, either." Then he abruptly braked. The seat belts were good. My skull whipped forward, but my upper torso stayed put. Cushman then dug his fingers into my collarbone, a curious gesture halfway between a teacher grabbing a disobedient child and Casanova unbuttoning a beloved's blouse. Cushman silently stared at me. I studied his whisker pits. Then he spat, and made his voice not only audible, but almost a proper volume for anger: "Well, let me tell you something, little boy. You let me tell you something. You don't know squat about anything. Anything! You don't know squat about God, and you don't know squat about Gerry Ford, and you certainly don't know jackshit about the automobile industry."

•

Our car entered a vast flat field bordered by pines. A wide runway ran the longest length of the plain, ending at a wall—a monstrous concrete slab marked by black scorches. There were no airplanes to be seen.

The road led to the rear of a tin-roofed hangar. Cushman parked next to a fire truck. Curiously, that vehicle was unmarked and painted gray. As soon as we had slowed, all four dogs sprang up attentively and began panting. Cushman slammed his door, and I joined him outside. For some reason, I asked if I should lock my door. He didn't answer. I waited for him to let the dogs out, but instead we entered the hangar. A dozen men in white lab coats snapped to attention when they saw Cushman. Someone continued whistling, "How Much Is that Doggie in the Window?" then gave me (I assume) a wolf whistle. I didn't want any anti-longhair hard times, so I turned away.

The wall behind me was covered with mannequins. Whole families hung from hooks—Mom, Pop, brother, little sis. The bodies weren't rigid like department store dummies, but had flexible limbs. And they were naked. I found myself feeling lust towards the women, and this seemed childish, like when I was a boy and peeked under mannequins' dresses at Sears. The women lacked nipples, but unlike their department-store sisters, their breasts had realistic weight and slight sag. I walked closer and examined their slack jaws. What incredibly detailed mouths— lips, teeth, tongues! I then noticed why my general lust had been ignited: each female mannequin had red hair—Sylvia's exact shade. My lust was chilled when I noticed the twisted red-haired bodies piled over in the corner. They were half melted or gashed, revealing puckers of torn plastic. Their interiors were filled with rubber organs and offal. Hospital bracelets were wrapped around their wrists, or, if necessary, their ankles. Mathematical equations were written in black Magic Marker around the wounds. Despite their conditions, the redheads' rose-lipped expressions still looked regal, the way cracked busts of Egyptian queens look in museums.

I was then aware of a continual high-pitched yelp. Animals or babies? I headed towards the sound. Mr. Cushman had a white lab coat draped over his shoulders and was wearing huge earphones—the kind flight crews wear when they guide jets down runways.

I walked outside; a group of labcoats were gathered around a midsize sedan—black with a long antenna arcing out of the hood. White numbers and arrows were painted over the car's body like star charts. I peered inside the car and saw my four

Dalmatians strapped to the seats in harnesses. Friendly and Rascal were in the front panting over the dashboard, Sleepy and Nixon in back. Sleepy was pulled too tight in his harness to actually sleep, and just sat looking drowsy. Nixon strained against his restraint, giving the high-pitched yelp.

There was a rattling sound behind me, and a black guy shuffled up shaking a Milk Bone box, singing: "As I was motorvating over a hill, I saw Rin Tin Tin in a Coupe deVille . . ."

He offered the biscuits through the open windows to the dogs, who spit them out. A voice yelled, "Stand back. Start the engines." Then everyone scattered.

The windows automatically slid up. The dog car's engine kicked. A few stragglers jumped away, labcoats flapping, just as the vehicle gave a short peal of rubber and then shrieked down the runway. They taught the Dalmatians to drive? Dogs driving cars! Dogs smoking cigars! But it wasn't a Dalmatian pawing the pedal. It was Mr. Cushman standing and calmly working a joy stick connected to a thick black cable.

Without knowing why, I ran after the Dog Car, chasing its dwindling back bumper. As the Dog Car reached freeway velocity, I wondered if the Dalmatians were enjoying the speed. Then I understood that the dogcar was driving straight towards the wall.

Because the sky is gray, there are no shadows on the runway. I have no depth perception. Visually speaking, the dogcar I'm chasing could be an image on a drive-in screen at twilight . . .

And tonight we're screening those particular movies where cars are the chariots of death; like Robert Mitchum deliberately driving himself and his lover off into the dark to be gunned down at a roadblock (*Out of the Past*, 1947); followed by Ralph Meeker (the now-obscure actor) speeding his sports car through the night just as a woman in a trenchcoat darts into his lights (*Kiss Me Deadly*, 1956). He swerves. Screeches to a stop. She jumps in. She's naked beneath the coat. Midway, a character clarifies the story's direction by saying: "Listen, these are just a bunch of letters scrambled together, but their meaning is very important: Manhattan Project . . . Los Alamos . . . Emily Dickinson." The movie ends when a lead box is opened, and we last see Ralph running down a black beach as the ocean transforms into atomic fire.

It's anticlimactic and redundant to write a variation of the Death Car motif. A writer must move dramatically sideways across the food chain. For my novel, just see my Dog Car several car lengths from impact. Inside, the Dalmatians sense disaster, but don't cover their eyes. They sit in the speeding car with snouts attentively forward, numb with confused apprehension.

The Dog Car crashes. The hood hits, then the top of the car flips and slaps the wall, revealing the axles and Panhard rods. Two hoops fly east and west: tires. Then the car bounces back down and there's a whizzing behind me. Two golf carts driven by labcoats zip by. I continue running. The carts stop simultaneously beside the wreckage. One man hops out lugging a fire extinguisher and assumes an exaggerated samurai pose. The other looks like a 1930s newshound. He lackadaisically picks up an old flash camera and begins photographing the wreck.

I'm now close enough to realize the crash is far worse than I imagined. This was no test of safety belts. This was a complete wreck-up. And now I hear the new song—a high-pitched fluctuating wail. Jimi Hendrix. A song released by dogbone. Up close, I see the black scorches along the concrete wall have delicate gradations between black and gray. I lean on the car, but can't see in through the windows spiderwebbed with cracks. The photographer begins struggling with the crumbled driver's door. It won't open. Creased frame. Finally, he really tugs and the driver's door is torn open: the sharp snout of a Dalmatian appears. Front paws. The dog leans over the driver's seat. I recognize him. He still has a sparkle in his eye. It's Friendly. He's free of his torn harness and looks up at me. My dog sees me. He dips his head—dipping his head the way a dog dips in playful joy at the master. And I am electrified. My eyes start tearing. The dog is mightier than runaway metal and gasoline. The Dalmatian dips his head again and slides out of the car. And then what I see can't be right—because the dog that slides out of the driver's seat is only the front of the dog—the front of the dog still alive, the front of the dog using its two front paws to paddle across the concrete, trailing tissue and filaments. This front of the Dalmatian paws over to me and rests his muzzle on my tennis shoes.

He frowns up as if it's time to throw him the ball, to play fetch.

I'm missing my cue; I have no ball.

S ylvia Cushman had shown me oranges. Her breasts. Emily
Dickinson. Joshua Cushman showed me the dogs.

•

A s we returned to Bloomfield Hills, Mr. Cushman talked to
me with the concern of a guidance counselor: "Those
bleeding-heart Humane Society jerks think my work is
inhuman. And it is. But there is certain safety status we can't get
from prosthetics . . ." His whispering monotony merged with
the swish of the windshield wipers. Cushman rolled us down his
narrow driveway to the underground garage. He braked and
whispered, "Open the garage."

I faced him. "No."

Mr. Cushman ground his teeth, but climbed out of the car.
There was maybe two feet of space on either side of the car. It
was almost too narrow for Cushman. He had to slide sideways,
his back bumping bricks while the hood pressed his ample gut.
At the front of the car, he stooped for the handle of the garage
door. That was the moment I unsnapped my harness, slid behind the wheel, and shifted into drive. The station wagon rolled
forward. Mr. Cushman jumped up, flashing irritation because I
wasn't wearing the Euro-design driver's harness. Then his eyes
widened in panic. He believed I was going to run him over and
whipped his arms up to stop the car. I braked, boxing the man
in between the grille of the station wagon and the garage. For

his benefit, I raised my hands, posing them above the steering wheel. I wanted to look like Glenn Gould about to bang Bach . . . Mr. Cushman could show me the dogs, but I could show him my hands. And I would even play him a song—this song: I slammed the heels of both palms against the horn, and the car sounded its electric note, a bellow somewhere between French horn and elephant. The sound ripped through Mr. Cushman's damaged ears up to his brain Jell-O. He tried scrambling over the hood, tipping the car forward with his weight, but he fell back and rolled out of sight. I kept pressing the horn and the car kept singing. The garage door raised slightly, then fell. I pressed the horn a little longer, then reversed the car. I got out and saw Mr. Cushman was gone—he had bellied into the garage. I heard deep-chested weeping and went to the front of the car to lug open the door. Mr. Cushman was inside. On his stomach. His hands pressed to his ears. Squirming.

•

I walked to the front door and pounded the heavy American-eagle door knocker. With each pound something became clearer to me: I saw the specific evil that had entered the House of Cushman.

Ben whipped open the door and yelled, "What? What?"

I tried to speak, but just pushed him aside and marched into the living room. Lester was rolled in a ball on the couch with Sylvia rubbing his head.

"I've solved it!" I shouted. "I know what he is allergic to!"

I paused. Sylvia scrunched her forehead, then screamed: "What? What? Tell me what!"

"He was fine until we brought the tree home. Lester is allergic to the Christmas tree!"

Sylvia sat with her mouth open as we all were enveloped by the evergreen smell, the tree quietly blinking its firefly lights in the corner.

Sylvia sprang screaming from the couch and tackled the evil tree, green bulbs flying. Then mother and son grabbed the tree while I ran around the room struggling to open the storm windows. Cold air rushed in, blowing a row of open Christmas cards off the mantel. Sylvia gripped the tree's upper branches while Ben held the trunk. They carried the thing down the hall, shattering ornaments against the wall. Covered with tinsel, Edsel was wheezing from room to room. Sylvia and Ben had the tree in the kitchen and were trying to stuff it out the back door.

"It's too big," Ben said, turning toward the door that lead to the garage.

I panicked. Cushman the monster was sprawled out there. Then Sylvia yelled, "Fuck it!" She picked up a chair and holding it up like a lion tamer, she lifted it above the kitchen table, scattering grocery bags full of fruit, and then smashed it into the wide window. Unlike the movies, the glass wouldn't shatter. With the next smash, a chair leg broke off and rattled into the sink. Ben reached and pushed a lever. The window slid open. Mother and son then swooped the tree out. As the thing flew through the air, I saw it wriggling and giving off frozen breath. Ben and Sylvia had turned to hug each other, making me the only witness to see the Christmas tree thumping up and down in the snow and oranges before finally dying.

PART THREE

SLEEPERS EAST

In March, three months after we killed the evil Christmas Tree, Sylvia called Amherst from the Ann Arbor. She called from the rooming house where she was now living (with Lester) after leaving her husband—

No more Mr. Cushman . . .

"How come my eldest alleged son is never around when I call?" she demanded.

I paused, strung between discretion and confession. I chose both. First, I told her Ben was with his new girlfriend every night. Sylvia sighed—a sad sigh—and wanted the lowdown: "Is she cute? Is her daddy rich? What does she read?"

I started by saying, "The girl has Rita Hayworth's hips and Iggy Pop's chest. She has olive skin. Coal-black hair. Coal-black eyebrows . . . Najaf does have eyebrows! Imagine a cross between Twiggy and Groucho Marx . . ."

I paused, wanting to describe Najaf with more allure. Ben and I had met her on a night when Ben was lying on the floor blowing his 3 a.m. rendition of "Sketches of Spain" at the ceiling. The door flung open and his new neighbor stood there, wrapped in a purple silk bathrobe, raven hair piled above her head with a scarlet snood. She whipped up her left arm—flagging her gown open—and pointed at Ben: "Stop stop stop. I'm trying to study. Go to sleep. Be silent."

Telling this to Sylvia made me replay that scene: As the girl with the slight, sharp breasts stood, wagging her arm in wrath, I was slouched on Ben's bed. I saw she gripped a hardcover in her cocked right hand—its spine perpendicular to her dark pelvis, her pointer marking her place. I wanted to know the title. I tilted my head and read: *Football and a Woman's Anger During Childbirth*.

I knew she wasn't a pregnant reader—she was holding a title from a feminist professor's syllabus, a book with the thesis that men displaced their shame at lacking a womb by stomping each other on autumn grass. And in his own way, Ben lay on the floor synchronizing himself with that title. His body was sprawled in the birthing position, and he clenched his teeth so hard that his chin was shaped like a football. But as Ben took this female intruder in, his face softened. Anger washed into confusion. He brushed the hair out of his eyes. And he smiled. He couldn't help himself—he just smiled . . . He was discovering his heart's number: he was into enraged womanhood.

•

Although I spilled the existence of Najaf to Sylvia, I was technically lying. Ben split each night at 11:00, but he never went directly to his girl. The month before, I had spied him slipping into a Student Union phone booth. This confused me. There was a dirty yellow institutional phone up in the room. On the next night, I tried getting close enough to eavesdrop, but failed. The third night, I hid behind a cigarette machine with binoculars and studied Ben's fingers as they dialed (a Tim Fontanel technique—*The Corpse Called Long-Distance*). I had caught the area code—313/Lower Michigan— when a coed began beating my machine to make her Marlboros pop out. It took me three nights to view the entire number— 313 432–7696.

Every night Ben was phoning Mr. Cushman.

What did they talk about—Sylvia? Lester? Historical Bebop? One night Ben crowded into the booth with his trumpet and played a phrase from " 'Round Midnight" over and over, pausing every few bars to listen to his father.

etting back to Sylvia—to answer her question: "Yes. This girl's daddy is rich." But this statement needs elaboration. Najaf was a Middle Eastern deb from an immeasurably wealthy family. She was born with six midwives assisting her mother. She spoke her first words on the family jet and learned to read on the Riviera. When she was 12, she was given her own Mercedes with driving lessons from a retired Grand Prix winner. Najaf was born in Iran. The Shah's Iran.

When Ben and I returned to Standish at Christmas, we found every empty dorm room filled with children of the teetering Shah's government. Their parents had paid international brokers to get them into America on student visas, and then paid full tuition for just half a semester—an arrangement which saved many small colleges from Armageddon.

The man who paid Najaf's tuition, Najaf's father, deserves congruent mention with Joshua Cushman. One man crashed dogs and the other, the interiors of men. Najaf's father was a high-ranking Savak official, a man renowned in interrogation circles as the inventor of "Apollo"—a chair with a tin bucket attached to the headrest. Apollo's operating instructions were simple: you strapped the interrogatee in the seat, put the bucket over his head, then questioned him in the usual manner (electricity, pliers, etc.). In addition to afflictions of the flesh, the prisoners were tortured by their own screams.

As for the furniture-maker's child, she possessed the kind of arrogance we'd all have if Dad ran the dungeon.

•

Although these two fathers never met, the daughter of one and the wife of the other did. It was in the beginning of the New England spring—a season that begins in theory only. The landscape was still crusted with snow. An afternoon ice storm had sheeted the oaks. And beneath those gleaming branches, Sylvia and Najaf approached each other generating some feminine magnetic energy—not of attraction, but of polar opposites. Or perhaps feline energy. Imagine two cats becoming magnets.

Najaf and I had been heading off campus, gingerly slipping our way down the dark iced sidewalk when we came upon Sylvia Cushman standing beneath a street lamp. How could this be? She was in Michigan. An electric glow illuminated the corners of her hair. Sylvia's head was on fire.

"Where the hell is Duck Street?" she shouted.

"The street flows before you," I yelled back.

"Then where's the renowned Miles Standish campus?" Sylvia shouted again.

I waved my hands, saying, "You are surrounded by it."

Sylvia looked up at the lit geodesic dome hovering above the bare trees and laughed, "Oh! How could I not recognize the Athens of the East?"

Sylvia asked where we were going. I told her. To the railroad. Ben was back in his room cramming for a test on the assassination of McKinley, and I had asked Najaf to come outside. I intended to initiate her into the Amherst Wait.

"Let me lock my Avis and I'll join you."

Najaf said nothing, breathing heavily through her nose.

Sylvia reappeared, and the three of us tramped into the woods through the snow. I asked Sylvia where Lester was and she said with her sister in Lavonia. Sylvia then gave Najaf a long peer, and began ranting that Emily Dickinson's works had been translated into Farsi. Apparently Emily has already been translated into half a dozen Moslem tongues with her name disguised as *Emile* Dickinson. "The gender problem here is not that they don't like women—they just don't like intact women."

The woods were filled with drifts and Sylvia waded into one as I scrunched up my face. "Intact? What are you talking about?"

Najaf spoke up dryly: "When Arab girls turn eleven, it is customary for them to be held down in the bathroom by the village crone. Her bare flesh presses the cold tiles. The crone yanks the girl's legs apart for Father. And Father leans forward. There is a straight razor in his hand. Father only has to slash once or twice."

Najaf continued: "The girl is too young to understand the purpose of this disfigurement—when she grows older and marries, she will be incapable of having an orgasm. Thus she'll never commit adultery." Najaf paused and exhaled a tiny cirrus cloud.

The two females faced each other. Najaf was taller than Sylvia, and continued speaking to the shorter woman, "But to the little girl, the real horror, even worse than the pain, is the image of her mother coolly watching from the bathroom door. This act had once been performed on her. And in one split second, the child understands that Mother wants Daughter to be as diminished as her."

Sylvia peered up at Najaf with drowsy Robert Mitchum eyes. Someone was going to get decked. But then she just turned away, raising her mittens to her face, muttering, "Oh god, forget what I said. I'm acting like a jealous mother from Cranbrook Bridge Club."

Sylvia trudged ahead through the woods. I couldn't hear her crying, but she kept rubbing her face with the mittens. The trees ended at the edge of the tracks. We all paused and listened: a distant dog . . . a branch snapping from the weight of the ice— a sound like breaking pottery . . . Then the tracks began ringing: an approaching train. I said, "It sounds like a Slinky."

Both females gave me quick glares. Apparently, this was not the time to mention toys. The rails began vibrating more loudly, followed by a wind roar of distant diesel. Then a sustained honk —the horn. A massive prison-break spotlight swept the snow. I turned, intending to teach the correct pose to Najaf, but there was Sylvia, the choreographer of the gesture, gripping the girl's shoulders, gliding her up to the track. Sylvia stepped back and quickly scrutinized Najaf's position. She put her palm on the girl's right shoulder and pushed her closer. Najaf stood only four feet from the track. Sylvia then took her own position—a foot closer—and stood with cocked hip, posing as if she were playing volleyball and impatiently waiting for the other team to retrieve a renegade ball.

The cold rails began banging. They were slices of frozen gasoline. Then the train pounded before us. The locomotive's frigid blast blew my hair across my face. Out of the corner of my eye, I saw Sylvia inching forward. I inched forward too. There was nothing but a black blur with occasional metallic glints. The massive wheels were hip-level and I felt their mad vibration up my pelvis, sucking me towards the train. I got a hardon. Both Najaf and Sylvia were also standing with straddled legs and pelvises trust forward. I obviously stood with two hermaphrodites that had hardons too. A string of empty boxcars roared by—both sets of doors open, visions of the white ice on the other side of the tracks strobing into our eyes. Then the black bellies of oil tankers. Then my toes hit gravel and I realized how close we'd moved. I stopped. But Najaf and Sylvia kept inching forward. Both hermaphrodites were certain to be smeared—their bodies entering that sheet of railroad light!

The train passed.

I had a sudden view of the snow on the opposite side of the track and was blinded by this light. Then inexplicably, Sylvia and

Najaf were on the other side of the track too, laughing and rolling together into the snow. It was obvious that their bodies had passed through the moving train.

•

The next morning, Sylvia nudged me through my sleeping bag with her boot, calling, "Crawl out, crawl out, Orange Boy! You have a rendezvous with destiny."

Dressing for destiny, I discovered Ben had already left, his bullet-to-McKinley's-skull trajectory diagrams still scattered on his desk. Outside, I saw Sylvia intended to drive us to destiny in an enormous red rental. The car's seats were like cushioned armchairs. Although its engine revved instantly, we just sat there. Sylvia leaned her chin on the wheel and told me how she'd just taken Ben to Howard Johnson's to give "motherly approval of Najaf." He had nodded woodenly over his breakfast hamburger, then launched into a non-sequitur tirade against the East Coast.

She ended the story by extending her blank ring finger, saying that neither Ben nor she brought up the husband/father situation. She then jerked our car out of the lot, narrowly avoiding nailing some cross-country skiers.

"What happened to your VW?" I asked, trying to figure out how to sit so when we crashed I wouldn't fly through the windshield.

"It sank," she said cheerfully.

"What do you mean it sank? Your husband? Were dogs involved?"

"No pooches were damaged," Sylvia laughed. "I was pitching Sunkist underhand, and flipped down an embankment on Telegraph Road."

"Were you hurt?"

"Nope! Just a cut on the head." She faced me and pulled up her bangs to display her forehead, the skin black and laced with Frankenstein stitches.

"But the Volkswagen sank?"

"Yeah. The V.W. landed on a frozen lake and began skidding across the ice. Oh it was wild! These ice-skaters madly sliding out of my way! I had a little blood in my eyes, so I wiped them with my mittens, and then the next thing I see is this sign proclaiming: *Danger, Thin Ice!* My car decides to stop and I sit there listening to the ice start to crack. A small crowd had gathered, but no one would come get me because they were afraid the ice would give. So I rolled down the window and yelled, 'Adrift! A little boat adrift! And night is coming down! Will no one guide a little boat unto the nearest town?' Then I turned the radio on. The station I hit was playing ice-skating music! (You know, one of those bouncy organs prancing away with roomy echoes.) Suddenly, this little boy skated up, yelling, 'Come on, lady. Get out of there.' So I climbed out. The kid took my hand and we slid toward the crowd. Then there was this monstrous cracking noise, and I turned to see my little red

Volkswagen sinking. I could still hear the radio through the water and ice."

With great concentration, Sylvia began running her finger along the steering wheel scallops and said, "Losing the car made me finally leave Josh for good. I mean if a husband in the auto-safety racket can't protect you from drowning behind the wheel —what the hell good is he?"

Sylvia cut through a filling station, scattering a cluster of kids with knapsacks. "God, not even Ann Arbor has this many pedants!" she laughed.

I twisted around looking for cops. "Where are we going?"

"The Homestead!" she said, honking the horn for emphasis. "I was going to save this pilgrimage for when I finished the thesis. But I've hit a snag." She made a left turn against the light. "I've been writing myself senseless."

She raised her hand to hit the horn again, but slapped the mirror instead. This gave her a prime view of my forehead. "Orange Boy, I know you're an idiot about mathematics, so follow me closely: before she was thirty, Emily Dickinson wrote 1,775 poems. I've spent my prime struggling with one goddamn thesis. And now I realize my thesis is invalid: Emily Dickinson didn't just write about spheres. No! She constructed an entire geometry for God. Each poem was an individual piece of a spiral, a spiral duplicating the gnomonic spiral of the brain as it evolved from amphibian to man to angel. Follow me? . . . So now I desperately need to stand in her room. And pray she'll bless me. She'll bless my work. Pray she'll square her sacred circle."

"Circle": the moment her tongue released the word, we topped the hill and saw Emily Dickinson's street blocked by elephants.

They were long-tusked African elephants, awkwardly mis-clothed with India-style pomp and circumstance—gold tassels dangling from their tusks, massive skulls covered with purple prayer-caps. Sylvia braked, and we sat open-mouthed while the elephants dragged their trunks like vacuum cleaners over the slush.

We sat stunned until Sylvia cried, "Fucking Republicans! They've blocked off her house!"

Then it hit me: "Sylvia! Those elephants are a message directly from her. Directly from Emily."

Sylvia creased her brow. "You're now receiving messages from Emily? You only learned who the hell she was six months ago, back in cowboy country."

The elephants began snorting clouds of white breath. I grabbed her shoulder and said: "Sylvia, I've taken the tour. I've been in her bedroom. The tour guide opens the door and the closet is empty except for one thing: Emily's dress. The white dress is encased in a thick plastic sleeve for protection. The tour guide lifts the dress on its wooden hanger and spreads it open."

"So?"

"Sylvia," I said, "Emily Dickinson's white dress is as wide as a tablecloth."

Sylvia creased her brow in confusion. I continued, "Her poetry was spare, but Emily Dickinson was fat."

"Oh Christ!" Sylvia shouted, cupping her face and dropping her head to the wheel. She accidentally beeped the horn with her forehead, and whipped back up: "Listen up, Orange Boy, project your Big Mother on every woman but Emily. No no no. Not on Emily. She's not anyone's Big Mom. You've seen the photo—Emily Dickinson was thinner than Catherine Deneuve. Thinner than Diana Rigg. Thinner than . . ."

I had never seen a Catherine Deneuve movie, and Diana Rigg didn't seem particularly slender . . . Sylvia was going to sit there reciting the names of moderately-sized woman for the rest of the day, so I said: "No no no! Emily Dickinson was slender for her photo at seventeen, but she thickened up. I know what I'm talking about. I've seen her dress." Then I grabbed her shoulder and said, "Why do you think Emily signed her letters to the Judge as 'Jumbo'?" I paused. "She called herself 'Jumbo' and here are a dozen elephants with the same name!"

Sylvia jerked her door open and scrambled out. I followed. We left the Buick and slid down the ice toward the elephant line. We did a Chaplinesque ice-skid around a post office and saw a semi in the intersection tipped on its side—a Coca-Cola truck leaking black soda. I thought of the man who had been ruined by Coke and knew Fatty Arbuckle was blocking these elephants.

Up the street, behind the animals, we could see a marching band, the front row of trombone players dipping their slides as they kicked snow. A tuba player began blowing "A Hard Day's Night." An elephant with a tinsel tiara perked up its ears and with a bellow, rolled its trunk into its mouth.

Sylvia stomped from the curb and a policeman shouted: "Miss! Miss! Keep back! You can't cross between the animals!" Sylvia shook her head and passed between two elephants. She paused beneath Emily's bedroom window—a cold sheet of reflected sunlight. The Homestead's front steps were crowded with college kids drinking Cokes. Sylvia jerked her arms and plowed up between them. Soda was spilled. Kids began yelling indignant *Hey!*s. Then Sylvia turned and stared down so wide-eyed homicidal that everyone scooted away.

She rattled Emily's front door. It was locked. Sylvia pounded on the glass. She jumped off the porch and circled the Homestead, casing it like a second-story man. The back door was as massive as the front and also locked. I talked her out of "just pitching a rock through a window" to climb inside.

"Jumbolaya or not—I came 500 miles and will not be denied," Sylvia shouted, thrusting her jaw until it looked like an elbow. She stomped down the block to a payphone while I watched the elephants. They began kneeling on the ice, and closing their eyes, beginning their daily prayers to Dumbo.

A cop told me the elephants were here for Amherst's 300th anniversary. The parade had been delayed because of the overturned Coke truck. Then Sylvia ran up crying, "Her house is closed every day this week!"

"The parade can't last seven days!" I said.

"No. Her bedroom stuff and her papers were just shipped to the New York Public Library!" Sylvia punched down at the air circling her hips, crying, "For an exhibit or something. Even her white dress is gone."

•

We headed for New York the next day. Ben drove Sylvia's rental. She insisted on sitting in front beside her son. Najaf and I sat in the back. The auto's remaining interior, and exterior, held a dozen Najafian suitcases. On bad bumps, the back end scraped the road.

We weren't really advancing to New York as much as we were fleeing Amherst, a flight generated by Walter Cronkite and Jimmy Carter. Literally! On the night of the elephants, the Cronkite news did a feature on the Iranian student/broker deals using Standish College as an example. The next morning, Carter's Bureau of Immigration raided the campus to round up Iranians. Najaf hid under her bed—literally!—and we later sprinted her out of the dorm. She instructed us to take her to Manhattan because she had an uncle there—"He's a diplomat. He can help."

The sun was setting as we crossed a girder bridge out by Co-op City. Sylvia said, "Look, the sky is the color of peanut butter."

•

N ajaf's uncle lived in an art deco fortress on East 73rd Street, the kind of building I didn't know existed east of Warner Brothers. Ben double parked and let us out, saying he'd wait and work on his "Blowing-away President Garfield" paper by streetlight. The rest of us entered the lobby. The doorman was leaning back in his chair snoring into his epaulets. We tiptoed across a marble floor to a marble-framed elevator. In the corner of the lobby, a Christmas tree still stood, ringed by four-month-old presents. As the elevator doors opened, Sylvia bobbed down and grabbed a box. In the elevator, she shook it and frowned. "It's empty."

The sixteenth-floor hallways had pool-table green carpet and fern-colored wallpaper. Najaf knocked at an intricate oak door that belonged in the last half-hour of *Citizen Kane*. She barely retracted her fist when it swung open and two Dobermans pinned us in an alcove. A man with dark Aladdin skin popped out, training a tiny gun on us that resembled a hair dryer. He gave a short whistle. The disappointed dogs trotted back inside. The man with the gun took Sylvia's present and began sniffing it. "It's okay, Moq," Najaf said. "It's not a bomb."

Moq motioned us into the apartment. At the end of a long hall stood a male silhouette, wearing either a barber's smock or bathrobe. Sylvia and I were instructed to wait in the massive kitchen, chaperoned by the gunman, while Najaf went to talk to the silhouette—her uncle. Moq held his tiny gun while channel-hopping on a portable b&w TV that sat by the sink. Occasionally, he'd take out a little notebook and make notes in Arabic. Although he didn't explain himself, the Iranian seemed interested, but perplexed, by the laugh-tracks.

A half hour later, Najaf returned, energized and lugging a satchel. We left. The doorman still slept. In the car, Sylvia and Ben argued about who would drive while Najaf tugged open the satchel. Sylvia won. Najaf found bundles of dead presidents— cash that was to last until the end of the month, when she was to zip to Switzerland. Then she held up her hand and jingled some keys. She'd been given a loft to mark time in. "None of us has to go back. My uncle said we can all live there." For some reason we all—even Sylvia—looked at Ben for approval. He was pensive for a moment, then grabbed his paper on Garfield and sailed it out the window to the street.

Sylvia successfully navigated us down to Crosby Street—a barren alleyway on the rim of SoHo. She told us Diane Keaton lived here. "We should look for Woody Allen's white Rolls," Sylvia said. "There's a car I want to pitch citrus from."

Our loft was a large third-story floor-through owned by a sculptor. He had been given a grant by the Shah to construct a giant obelisk in the middle of the Dasht-e Kauier, an immense desert stretching east of Teheran. ". . . where the camels are into Minimalism," Najaf told us.

This loft had the ambience of a parking garage. One wall was lined with sculptures—huge wooden cubes of various sizes—the average being that of a refrigerator. These boxes were plain. Unpainted. Devoid of chisel work. Najaf explained they were meditations on the essence of wood (—and indirectly, Ben remarked, boredom).

We shoved them like giant children's blocks and partitioned rooms for ourselves. When we finished, Sylvia insisted that "communes should have names." I was sure Dickinson's verse would figure in the title, but I was wrong. Together, Najaf and Sylvia christened our loft: Chateau de la Sam. Najaf came up with the French syntax. The remaining part was topical—Son of Sam was still shooting couples on Lovers' Lane. This black-hearted reference to Samuel was Sylvia's.

•

To adapt to the anti-New England terrain, I shelved Emily (Najaf taking these books under Sylvia's influence) and mainlined detective novels instead—but only those set in New York, such as *Cat of Many Tails* by Ellery Queen, or *Black Mask* tonics like *Red 71st Street* by Paul Cain. I decided to read them only on the street, propping myself in seedy doorways flipping pages. I was leaning into such a wedge near Port Authority when Sylvia strutted by across the street.

She was dressed in jeans and a sloppy sweater like an over-age art student. Suddenly, she was stopped by a businessman who gestured with confused Arm Language. Sylvia sliced her palm toward the sunset and kept walking. I assumed she had just been asked for directions (which was crazy because Sylvia was so geographically scrambled that she could walk west on 22nd figuring she'd eventually hit 23rd).

Sylvia hadn't seen me, so I tailed her along 42nd. We passed a barrage of theaters with slasher-flick marquees (a new genre). Dudes made sucking noises at her. She crossed Sixth Avenue into a prim little park stuck at the back of a stone building, then circled to the front of the building. These words were etched in stone near the roof line: The Public Library. She climbed some tiered steps between frowning stone lions and gave a Boy Scout salute to the southernmost one. I followed her into a large echoing lobby, up two interior flights of steps, then hung back. She clicked down a marble hallway into a door marked, "Rare Book Room." I followed her in. It was half-full of the lingering elderly, half-moon glasses balancing on their noses. A billboard-size photo of a teenage Emily Dickinson hung over long glass coffin-cases. To the side of the room sat Emily's bed. Seeing it roped off that way made me think of a crime scene. I leaned on a glass case, and studied spidery handwriting scrawled on the brown papers.

I spun when Sylvia goosed me. She displayed no surprise at my presence. Had she known all along that I was tailing her? She took my hand and we leaned over a poem that Emily had dashed in the margin of a laundry list. The list was one hundred years old and not much different from the list that the four of us had composed that morning. "Look at how different words are capitalized," Sylvia said. " 'A *Tongue—to tell Him I am true!*' " and then with abrupt tears in her eyes, Sylvia looked up at me: "Orange Boy, you know I've come so far for beauty and left so much behind. I've lost my patience and my family. It's all blown away."

Her lower lip quivered. She looked like she wanted to start smashing glass with her head. I took her by the shoulder and steered her into a large rotunda lined with murals. As Sylvia began crying in earnest, I held her, her head level with my nose. I smelled her hair and studied the murals. They were painted with the dreary colors of Classic Comics covers. On the east wall were two dismissible murals of obvious library subjects: one was of bare-chested Gutenberg printing his Bible with weight-lifter arms; the other was of Citizen Kane—an archetypical turn-of-the-century newspaper publisher. Then on the west wall were three murals devastating in their devotion to the printed word. By the stairway was Big Moses—a tough two-fisted Moses coming forth with the holy tablets, ready to cram God's stone word down our throats. And the strength of this Moses made me see the scene in a new light—is there anything more hardboiled than the Ten Commandments?

The next mural—above a side door—was a small Norman Rockwell-style scene: a mother reading to her little boy on a grassy knoll. I sent my heart up to that, the only image of motherhood worth considering: a gentle mother reading pirate stories to her son. Wondrously, this woman resembled Sylvia—Sylvia in her calmer moments, like when she read aloud to Lester. I remembered how my own mother had once read to me. We would sit on the slats of my sandbox as she read aloud the same book Sylvia had read to Lester two nights before. And I recalled how my first literary love had not been detective novels. It had been Dr. Seuss. And I could hear the echoing voices of both my mother and Sylvia reading *Hop on Pop*, the book proclaiming the justice due their respective husbands.

My eyes teared. My mother had read Dr. Seuss to me before she found Jesus and I found Chandler and Cain and all those books with beautifully swift titles: *The Big Sleep. The Glass Key. Sleepers East*; all those books about men and cities—the *old* cities, where men were two-fisted and the law was where you bought it. In the old city, you either died by tommy-gun fire or threw in the towel and moved to Eisenhower's suburbs for a slow death of wife and kids. But until one of those ends came, you had your Scotch, your blondes, and your roscoe. And I knew then why I had been so taken with Emily Dickinson: her poems were pared-down and masculine, the predecessors of terse *Black Mask* stories where men were gutshot—"My Life had stood—a Loaded Gun."

I looked back up at the third astounding mural: a monk sat illuminating a manuscript, while outside his window, a man in armor, riding a rearing horse, was plunging his lance into the belly of a bare-chested man wearing transparent breeches. A fellow monk stared out that same window, knowing they were certain to be next. Yet the first monk calmly continued to write —calmly continued to write seconds before death. And wasn't this mural saying that books were the most blessed things on earth; that it was worth dying to read and write, as, of course, men have died throughout history for what they've read and written?

"All these words," Sylvia said, looking up at the murals. "You have no idea how much I've wanted to be able to write something. Just a poem. Anything. What shit a thesis is." She gave a half-sob/half-laugh that hiccuped above our heads up to the ceiling.

I looked across Sylvia's head and saw the naked redhead, painted on the mural ten feet below Moses's foot. She was facing away. The slope of her bare hips and her red hair made her a painting of Sylvia. I wanted to stroke that mural's shoulders, trace both her teres major and minor. I hugged Sylvia tighter. My hands were gripping her waist and she felt my erection. She looked up at me, laughing: "You're a sorrow freak, buddy. You're a sorrow freak for an old woman. You are a Class-A pervert."

Then she pushed her head up and kissed me—a weird biting kiss—almost like a dog—her teeth hit the corner of my mouth, our teeth scraping. Out above her hair, a man on the stairs was taking photographs of us. At first I thought he was a tourist taking snapshots of library lovebirds. Then he lowered his camera and shot me a short vicious smirk, before disappearing down the stairway.

"What's wrong?" Sylvia asked, pushing away.

"There was a guy taking our picture."

Sylvia thought for a moment. "Fuck, that prick already has a lawyer. I bet he hired a detective so he can get custody of Lester!" Then she was running in pursuit. And who else bore the epithet "that prick" better then Mr. Cushman? I hesitated and then followed. I ran down to the first landing and leaned over the balcony. From a beautiful Hitchcockian angle, I watched Sylvia chase the man out the door. Then I ran down the wide marble stairway, plowing into a fat man in a Panama hat with a stack of books. Instinctively I read their spines. He had half-a-dozen books on cannibalism. Obviously he was a holy man like Shem, a man who would eat others rather than munch God's broccoli.

Outside, a small crowd was gathered at 40th and Fifth. I ran over to see a hot dog cart tipped over between the street and the curb, spilling rolling wieners. Sylvia and the library shutterbug were on their knees playing tug of war with the camera strap— Sylvia splashed with mustard, and the man ketchup. Yellow and red. Team colors. My presence distracted Sylvia and the man snapped her face with his palm.

He jumped up and ran to a bus discharging passengers at the corner. He hopped on, swinging the camera by its strap just as the door began shutting. At that moment, a bicyclist zipped down the sidewalk and grabbed the camera just as the door closed. His movement was so graceful, a woman beside me gave a spontaneous clap of glee. The kid pedaled madly into traffic and disappeared. The bus doors reopened with a hydraulic sigh and the private eye stepped out. His mouth hung open.

"Tough tits for you, Sam Spade," Sylvia yelled.

•

We returned to the Chateau to find Ben sitting among the art boxes. He was wrapped in a sheet, and his head had the circumference of a little boy's. Najaf stood scowling behind him, gave a final consideration to his butch cut, then whipped away the sheet. He immediately tensed his face. Babyhead evaporated. Ben became Samuel Beckett.

Sylvia airplaned her palm over her son's head, saying: "Thank god, you finally realized Duane Allman is dead!"

I stared at Ben's haircut and began unconsciously reciting scripture: " 'An angel called Wonderful came to your mother and said, "Do not partake of wine or strong drink or unclean food for you will bear a son. And no razor shall touch his head for he will rescue Israel out of the hands of the Philistines." ' "

•

Later, during the dark dogwatch hours, I awoke to Sylvia sobbing and found her kneeling in front of a flashlight spilling harsh light across her knees and underpants. She wore a ratty T-shirt with a flaked cartoon of a dog on the front. The dots of the dog's eyes had worn away.

Was she on a sorrow-trip about Lester?

I moved closer and caught the smell of the cacti. This was the week when Sylvia started drinking under the volcano—drinking mescal. I didn't see a glass or bottle, but there was a half-eaten orange beside her left calf. Cactus and citrus. I saw bite marks all along her arm, deep enough that a dentist could use them to make caps for her teeth. Sylvia lowered her head to her elbow, and I heard the squish of her mouth as she bit herself again.

I moved my feet. She lowered her arm and pointed the light into my eyes. "Boy," she said. Pause. "Boy."

She was intentionally calling me "Boy." She began a whispered chant of it: "Boy. Boy. Boy . . ."

I cut her off—"Sylvia, did you eat the worm?"—referring to the white agave worm drowned at the bottom of bottles of Mescal. She nodded and rambled: "I saw Emily's bed today . . . But I didn't see it back in Amherst—in the room where she knew the shadows—none of those elephants let me in." The flashlight's spotted beam swept the boxes as she wiped her forehead with her bare bit arm. "Boy, if a pilgrimaging Moslem is denied entrance to Mecca it means he's not worthy in God's eyes. And the Hindus in India worship a god that has an elephant head. They worship a god that has arms, legs, and a massive elephant head. Boy, because I wasn't allowed into Emily's real room it means somebody's god somewhere is telling me something." She held up the half-eaten orange and turned it into a knot of white light. "This means my days are numbered, Boy. Emily signified that my days are numbered."

Sylvia leaned back. Her shoulders suddenly jerked, and she blindly threw the orange. Her target was probably the postcard of Emily Dickinson tacked on the box behind me. But her fruit hit the side of my head.

I stood for a moment, surprised by pain. Then I reached out and gripped the sides of her forehead. With orange juice squishing in my ear, I said: "Sylvia, your days are not numbered because you couldn't get into Emily Dickinson's bedroom. Your days are not numbered. Your days are not numbered."

I not only assumed her days were not numbered, but also that the main content of her speech—the elephant god part—was hallucinatory nonsense. I was familiar only with Mom's Jehovah and knew nothing of Ganesh, the elephant-headed god from India. Then last year—the lit Cooper Union clock glowing midnight—I was stumbling home from a party where powders had been ingested. A bum stopped me on the Bowery. "Buddy, got any change?"

My face was pinpricked and racing, but my coordination was fine, not stoned. I absentmindedly searched my pocket while glancing up. He was an immense figure in an overcoat. And in the streetlight, I saw the elephant trunk hanging down his chest.

This vision humbled the shit out of me, but did Sylvia no good. She was already dead.

Her days had been numbered.

•

The morning after Sylvia plugged me with citrus, she told us all, "I'm leaving New York." I figured she was going to drive the desert, before returning to Husband Town. But she wasn't. She was going to New Orleans. An acquaintance had to leave Loyola on family business, so for six months Sylvia would teach Freshman English to the children of Anne Rice and Professor Longhair.

•

The day before she left, we four were on the F train. Sylvia insisted on giving me this riff about Nathanael West: "In 1940 he and his wife, Eileen, were driving through the desert, heading home to Hollywood. They turned on the radio and heard that their friend F. Scott Fitzgerald was dead. (You have heard of him, right, Orange Boy?) Suddenly, a Pontiac pulled in front of their station wagon. There was a crash. West and his wife got bashed up and died. This happened on Highway 10. And the other car came from Yuma. So this crash involves the road and the town where you and I met." She paused. "The Wests' car had a third passenger who survived. After the crash, this passenger ran in circles around the wreck barking. The third passenger was the Wests' dog—a pointer named Julie." Pause. "In this instance, a car crashed, but a dog survived."

•

W e were taking the subway to Coney Island. Sylvia insisted on seeing the Whales of Passion before she left.

Now, do you remember that specific summer marked by the Death of Elvis, Son of Sam, the Blackout . . . and the Whales of Passion? This was that summer when New Yorkers went whale crazy. For five years, the male killer whales had refused to mate with the females at the New York Aquarium. Whale pimps shipped us Ralph from Ocean World, San Diego. Thus began New York's orca-obsession. Every day the *Post* and *News* did a number about whales. A gray blimp, painted like a beluga, circled the sky. The Mayor made illiterate Moby Dick jokes. Ralph and his harem took everyone's minds off Son of Sam—until the *Post* speculated that since Sam stalked lovebirds, he might go gunning for the amorous whales. An Ahab.

When our subway finally reached Coney Island, I remember I found the aquarium disappointing. I'd pictured the place as having cool wide rooms and huge tanks like in *The Lady from Shanghai*. But the spirit of Orson Welles did not swim in Coney Island. The aquarium was a modest building of dim alcoves filled with small fish tanks—most no larger than an angelfish box in a family rec room.

Sylvia dragged Ben off to check the walruses, and I wandered with Najaf into the fluorescent fish room. As we stood before a box of fluorescent fish, I began a round of genre-talk—having been trying to influence this girl with hardboiled culture after

Sylvia failed with Dickinson. I was explaining that the passive '60s icon Fred MacMurray began in 1944 as an ultra-tough guy in *Double Indemnity*. Najaf was wistful for a moment, then said, "When I was a little girl we used to pick up a Turkish station that broadcast that TV show where he had those three boys."

Standing before a tank labeled "Electric Fish," we both began humming the theme from *My Three Sons*—serenading a tiny compartment of eels, glass fish, and skeleton trout. When we finished, Najaf pressed her cheek against the tank. I did the same. Connected to her by cold glass, I was suddenly so aware of her presence—of her Najafness, if you will—that I found myself saying to myself over and over, "It's her. It's her."

This call from the glass surprised me. A hundred times a week, I would observe aspects of her beauty—walking across the loft wrapped in a sheet; leaning over the sink to wash her hair; wearing a transparent nightgown to play catch with Ben on the roof—but I always observed her aloof.

We pulled away from the glass and were silent. She seemed awkwardly so. A pear-shaped fish, translucent as a light bulb, floated up to her face, and Najaf said: "You know, I have sometimes wondered what sleeping with you would be like and now I think I know."

I was floored. I muttered several nonsense syllables.

She puckered her lips at the floating light bulb, then said: "You would pass all these strange fish into me."

At that moment, Sylvia stomped up, singing, "Goo goo a' joob," and dragged us outside to the large outdoor tank where the lovers floated. My face was flushed, and I stood dumbly considering Ralph the Killer Whale—a hull of black-and-white muscle the size of a Cadillac. As this aquatic Caddy leapt through hoops, both Sylvia and Najaf clapped their hands, Sylvia squealing, "Oh, Lester would love this! Lester would love this!"

Because of her enthusiasm, Sylvia was chosen from the audience to give Ralph a kiss. She leaned over the tank and the whale's head popped out of the water. They kissed. Suddenly, Sylvia turned and stumbled towards us with a pale face, gasping, "Oh my god! The breath! The breath!" We laughed, but she started to gag. "The breath was a smell like puke and rotting meat."

We rushed her to the women's room—a small bunker next to the penguin tank. Najaf went in with Sylvia, then came out alone, saying, "She'll be okay in a minute."

I leaned over a railing and studied the penguins. They resembled molting bowling pins. I glanced up as two men in suits and sunglasses approached Najaf. One handed her an envelope and spoke in French. The other was Moq. He was holding either a thin paperback or a small magazine. I tilted my head. *TV Guide.* He slipped off his sunglasses and looked me over without recognition or emotion, the kind of expression you would use to scan the listings for some dead TV hour like 7:00 a.m. I was *Morning Workout*, *Weather*, or *Frugal Gourmet*.

Najaf opened the envelope and scanned the letter. She began shaking her head. Both men argued at her in French. Ben tensed, sure that he should be protecting his woman. But without turning, Najaf swatted her palm downward at him, and Ben froze like a pointer trained by hand signals.

Soon all three Iranians were shouting. Moq kept jabbing his index finger towards Najaf as if he were punching channels on a TV. The other flicked his wrist as if he were a magician with a pigeon up his sleeve. Then Najaf start crying. They all switched from French to Farsi. People stared. The two Iranians glanced around nervously. Moq used his *TV Guide* to gently steer Najaf towards a large circular building. A sign said it was the *Turtle Tank.*

Ben and I tagged behind. "You guard that exit and I'll guard this one," I said.

Sylvia suddenly walked up. "Why's everybody trying to ditch this incapacitated woman?"

I told her what was going on. She cocked her head and listened to the shouting voices. "Parlez vous la frog?" she asked. The Iranians had switched back to French. Sylvia began translating: "They're telling her she has to move into the embassy . . . It's not safe to live like a whore with the Americans." There was a sudden explosion of male voices shouting. Sylvia said, "Now they're not asking her to come with them. They're insisting. Let's pull a rescue."

Sylvia and I ran into the muggy bunker that housed a circular floor-to-ceiling aquarium, a glowing wall of green soup where sea turtles swam—turtles wide as tables with bald brows and sour beaks. They circled observing us sideways with a remote eye. Beyond the turtles, Moq had clamped Najaf by the shoulder while the other lectured and pointed his finger in her face.

I heard agitated movement behind me and glanced back to see a guy following us. He had a black pirate patch over his right eye. He was pointing a gun.

"Arab assassin!" I flashed. Then: "Son of Sam!" But when he called—"Blessed Jesus, boy! Your time has come!"—I knew he was neither. He was addressing me: Boy.

Why does everyone call me Tarzan's son? I thought.

Then I tuned in. The gunman shouted "Jesus" before "Boy." He was Shem, the man who ate the Lord's beef. Obviously when I had shot him back in California beneath the oranges, my gun's hard salt took out his eye. Now he was the Avenging Angel in a Hathaway Shirt.

•

I introduced Shem as a lunatic in this book, and he was foremost that. But his road to Heaven's meat was marked with pain, and he does deserve compassion. There was a preChrist night years ago, when Shem lay in a motel, pint of Night Train splashed between his ears. He was staring up at my mother's *Hour of the Speckled Bird* blaring from the TV on the wall. Until that moment, Shem had only seen my mother while channel-hopping. But now, he was weeping—watching my mother preach was like the moment he first viewed his daughter's X rays: he couldn't concentrate on the gray ghost egg-shapes in her chest; instead, for the first time in his life he perceived the anatomical perfection of bones. My mother's faith had this same perfection. My mother was a sternum. And she stared down from her side of the screen saying: "My girth is the Holy Spirit ballooning inside. If Christ accepts someone like me—why not you? Why not you?"

My mother nodded stage-right and Shem's stomach bottomed out. He knew Jesus hung off-camera, and the Savior was yanking his wrists out of wood to hold Shem's redeemed little girl. The blood and piss and cancer of the world could roll out of the screen at any moment. He turned away and saw how his life's wreckage had led him to this Licsoll motel room with walls the color of toothpaste. He held up his arm and stared at a stretch of tattoo that marked his wrist to the elbow.

"Why not me?" Shem asked aloud, rising to his knees and lifting the Zenith down to his lap without pulling the plug. He reached for the Gideon in the bedside drawer and placed it on top of the set. He lowered his ear to the Bible to hear my mother preach though the pages. When her program was done, he sat up and flipped the Bible open at random. Matthew 5:29. He cradled the TV and repeated the verse like a mantra: "If thy right eye is an occasion of sin to thee, pluck it out . . ." He droned 5:29 all night above blank TV static. At sunrise, the TV lay alone on the bed giving birth to Yogi Bear. Shem knelt in the bathroom, using a boning knife to flay his tattoo into the tub.

Now seven years later, Shem was standing next to a window of turtles with his scarred arm outstretched wobbling an immense blue revolver. Beside me, Sylvia was shielding her face as if fingers could stop a bullet. I took her hand and turned to run, but suddenly envisioned the Zapruder film that Ben had studied for his assassination class. I saw Kennedy's skull explode. Shem could just blow out the back of our heads! As Sylvia and I began our slow glide through Dallas, Moq and the other Iranian noticed Shem and Shem's gun. The nameless one reached in his jacket, and then there was an explosion that whipped through my skull, transforming into a textual shape in my forehead. I saw the spatial image of the gunshot—a green donut—then I saw the Iranian pounded into the wall.

When the donut disappeared, I started acting like a private eye. I spun towards Shem. His arm was outstretched holding the revolver. I grabbed that arm and pressed flat against him. He was shorter than I remembered. I felt his bones, some sinews. There was stubble on his cheek. I paralleled his position in an intimate fox-trot, our hands joined and outstretched. Did Sylvia have a term for this Arm Language? I felt the heat of his body, and was sure that our penises were rubbing through our pants. I almost released him out of embarrassment, but knew a private eye should ignore the dick and tug harder. So I did. The momentum swinging us in an arc as if we were following numbered dance steps on the floor. The turtles were circling in their tanks as we circled the floor.

Shem intended to pull us in another spin. I tugged harder and started twisting Shem's knuckles like a doorknob. The veins stood out on his wrist. He was wearing a watch with "Christ Is Lord" circling the clock's Roman numerals. I kept squeezing, but he wouldn't drop the gun. His trigger finger curled. He fired.

I heard the gunshot in my teeth. Our arms absorbed the gun's recoil and glass peppered our faces. A green spout of water gushed from a baseball-sized hole in the glass. It sounded peaceful, like a forest brook. Then Shem started struggling again and I poked his patch, my finger dipping in a rim of bone. Shem screamed. Then — perhaps because of my general obsession with the-hand-that-rocks-the-cradle, or because Shem bammed a pleading to God and the Tabernacle of the Speckled Bird — I suddenly saw my mother inside the turtle tank. Submerged, wearing white, she was gently holding the head of a turtle — I slipped backwards to the floor and my mother disappeared and the glass gave. The aquarium exploded in a Niagara of celestial reptiles, glass, and water. I saw each individual turtle clearly as it rode that flood — each immediately retracted its head and limbs. And I saw and knew they were angels. They moved with a speed and grace beyond animal life. Although their bodies had the contours of boulders — I intuited their wings. They were angels. One angel flew upright and slammed Moq in the chest like a punching bag. Before the water hit, my eyes clearly saw Moq's *TV Guide* as it flew. Walter Cronkite was on the cover, the man who forced us to New York to begin with. A burst of water then slammed my chest. While I was growing up in California, I spent teen-time hanging ten on a boogie board, so I knew what to do. I relaxed, went with the wave and tumbled like laundry. I swallowed prehistoric flesh. Those turtles! Bad soup! Abruptly I was beached on my back as the water flowed out through the doorways.

The tank was drained. Sylvia was pulling Najaf up from the muck. Even though turtle-dazed, I lifted my head and appreciated how their wet dresses clung to their hips. I stumbled up and outside into the glare. Ben was lying on wet concrete, the water already steaming from the sun. Several turtles lay on their backs flapping their flippers like babies wanting to be changed.

Sylvia came up and grabbed my hand. "Come on, sweetheart. Are you okay? Let's go."

I hung my mouth open in amazement: Sylvia had called me "sweetheart"! A turtle the size and height of a coffee table began pawing my cuffs. Then Sylvia was yelling—"Wake up, Orange Boy! Snap to! Let's get out of here!" as she slapped my face.

•

We four slipped out of the aquarium and were never part of the investigation of the gunplay, an event first reported in the papers as: "*Son of Sam Spreads Turtle Terror!*" The New York Post interviewed an undistinguished psychiatrist who suggested that Sam had seen humans as bulb-headed reptiles his entire life.

Shem escaped and Moq did too, but his dead partner was identified as an Iranian diplomat. Shem then became a Shiite assassin playing out a jihad among the turtles.

These turtles and angels are tragic in a reptilian way, but they haven't replaced this book's Mythology of Dog—Son of Sam is reaffirmation. Two weeks later, Ben and I would be at Kennedy Airport, walking by an airport bar, when we saw a hushed crowd circled beneath a hanging TV. On the screen a pudgy, startled-looking man was being led in handcuffs by three stony-faced cops through a crowd of reporters. I asked the crowd, "What happened?" Someone answered: "They caught Son of Sam."

The TV said Son of Sam was a postman named David. I could have taken his arrest as just another piece of summer news chowder—i.e. the Blackout, the Death of Elvis, etc.—but the newsman said something that made me swallow my brain: Son of Sam told the police he did what he did because of voices sent into his head. Telepathic voices. Commands sent from a neighbor's backyard. Commands sent by an entity named Sam. Commands sent by a dog.

•

Sylvia soon left for New Orleans, and Najaf proclaimed she was to return to Teheran—her father's city with its flaming minarets seemingly safer than New York. We took her to Kennedy and Ben did not act like a parting lover. He did not beg her to stay. But then Najaf didn't invite him to travel with her. Apparently they both welcomed an excuse to part. Ben drove us to the airport in a shocking candy-apple-red pimpmobile, fuzzy dice hanging from the mirror, explaining, "It's a drive-away car. I'm taking it to L.A."

I asked, "How will you get back? Thumb?" Ben paused and answered, "I'm not coming back." From L.A. he intended to embrace the magnetic north and travel up to Alaska. He would search the icecaps for his childhood night trains, then score a job on the pipeline.

I asked to drive the pimpmobile to the airport. Ben said no. I wasn't covered by the temp auto insurance. "Oh do it," Najaf insisted, nudging me with her suitcase. "You survived the turtles, you'll survive rush-hour traffic."

Ben slid over and I got behind the wheel. The car was Cadillac-huge—and driving was like slicing butter with a grand piano. As I white-knuckled the wheel, navigating us to Queens, Ben halfheartedly asked if I wanted to copilot him to California. I shook my head. If he wanted me he would have gotten the extra insurance.

At the airport, we learned her flight was delayed because of hard rain. We killed time watching skeletons of suitcases slide through the X-ray machines. Najaf told me that I should stay at the loft until the artist returned from Iran—the rent was paid, and she'd left a modest stash behind a particular art-box shaped like a phone booth. Then she said her only words of farewell. A green X ray of a suitcase floated above our heads, and she said: "That's like one of those electric fish."

·

The day before Najaf left, we all took Sylvia to the airport. We waited for her plane and communed "good-bye" with JFK tequila, the closest potion to mescal available at that assassinated president's airport. Sylvia sipped at her plastic glass, wrinkled her nose, then sipped again, as she raved about a book she was reading concerning sailors who had sunk down in diving bells and the changes a neurologist noted to their brains. She had been giving a frown every time the airport intercom interrupted her, until Ben tuned in and said, "Mom! That's the final boarding call for your flight!"

"Oh my god," Sylvia said. "Anyway, I'm reading this book because New Orleans is below sea level and I want to know if my brain is going to be safe."

She glanced to check there was no one behind her, then flung the remaining tequila over her shoulder, yelling: "Wild Nights! Wild Nights! The little bullfighters circle around her!" Then she stood, whipped up her purse and tote bag, and peppered Najaf's olive face with kisses. Najaf sat passively, and slowly tilted her head back as if sitting in warm rain and offered Sylvia her throat.

Ben observed all this standing stiff, shuffling his feet. Sylvia turned and pumped his hand in a military fashion. Then she pulled me over to the entrance ramp, telling the ticket taker, "I'm legally blind. I need my boy, here, to help me to my seat, then he'll get off."

She dragged me onto the boarding snout with it ribbed plastic walls. When we turned a corner, Sylvia stopped, grabbed my shoulder—"Look, I have something more important to tell you —you've heard about James Dean, yes?"

I nodded, puzzled.

"Good for you," Sylvia said. "He's more topical than Emily Dickinson, I guess." She paused and started talking conspiratorially, "Two months after his accident, I read some tabloid saying he wasn't really dead. His wreck left him a disfigured vegetable, and he was hiding in a heavily guarded institution in Sonora." She moved aside for an elderly couple boarding the plane with their aluminum walkers.

"The article was illustrated with a photo of a man looking out of a barred window. A fissure split his face into two knots of muscle. He had no chin. His lower lip dangled down to his collar. But the hair of this poor monster was waved in a James Dean pompadour! And that gave him away. It was too perfect. Pathetically perfect. It would have been more convincing to run a photo of a bald damaged man." She paused, her eyes tearing. "But the photo broke my heart. Not because Dean was dead, but because this poor dogfaced man had missed his one moment of glory. He missed his chance to say, 'I'm James Dean. Give me your love. Give me your pity.' But because of the ineptitude of the fakers, he was denied even this little dish of magic."

A group of businessmen with suitbags bumped between us.

"Orange Boy," Sylvia said softly, "I'm saying this because you can still have your dish of magic . . . and I know no adult ever sat you down to ask that essential question: 'So young man, what do you intend to do with your life?' " She nodded for confirmation. "Well, I'm not going to ask you that one. I'm going to just tell you. You've read enough of those goddamn detective stories. Now sit down and write one."

She backed away from me and laughed, "Now I'm winging to New Orleans. Good-bye."

•

I described that scene to tell you that Sylvia started me writing this book. In bad moments, her influence seems like Sam the Dog's barking backyard instructions. I once joked in a letter that I intended to abandon my hardboiled opus (*Fervent Fisti-cuffs*) to write about her. My working title: *The Big Sylvia*. Sylvia wrote: "Don't you dare! You couldn't handle me. I want Joan Didion. She won't sentimentalize my life. You, on the other hand, will depict me as some millionaire's crazyass daughter who plays the private eye for a sap and then atones by flinging her body on the tracks that run along the levee."

PART FOUR

THE
MERMAID GESTURE

"So, Orange Boy, let me get this straight—your private eye, Bud Crowley, is practicing judo rolls when a gunman bursts into the dojo. Bud jumps out of his roll and kicks the killer's nose into his brain . . . Now, Nureyev, have you ever leapt into a kick out of a roll? Get down on the floor. Try it. That's right—it's impossible."

I held Sylvia's notes against the wheel of my cab and read her comments by streetlight. I refused to believe her observation and the next morning I rolled across the floor of the Chateau, flying into a packing crate called Object #34, and destroying $12,000 worth of box-art. But Sylvia was right. You can't leap out of a roll.

Because the poetic and accurate description of the human body engaged in violence is the consummate goal of hardboiled writing, I was determined to get my fisticuffs right. I studied boxing on TV to observe the piston mechanics of the punch, but these fights were disappointing—the knockout blows never looked like much. I meandered through the channels to study prime-time/ rerun violence. If I could capture the grace of stuntmen combined with the real-life awkwardness of boxing, I'd write astonishing violence. I would be welcome to drink at Hammett's table.

But my television viewing did not lead to drinks with Dash. One morning, while scrutinizing Tarzan's body language on Channel 5, it hit me that it was not Lex Barker swinging vine-to-vine. It was my father.

I turned off the TV and slid out my yellow legal pad. Until that moment, I was able to write by first envisioning Sylvia reading a paperback. Its cover shows a snarling mug clutching two automatics, and the author's name arched above his fedora is mine. I would then scrawl on my pad as if receiving dictation from that already-finished book. But now, post-Tarzan, I imagined a hardcover called *The Life of Orange Boy*, and wrote:

> Although Dad stopped being Tarzan a decade before my birth, his position as Lex Barker's stuntman was always more important to me than his stretch as a detective. I remember having a ferocious argument concerning Tarzan with my peers down at the playground. At sundown, when Dad stumbled by to drag me home for dinner, I convinced him to climb the jungle gym to prove he'd really been the Ape Man. My father chewed his cheeks for a moment, then nodded. He was soon dangling above the sand, but he did not resemble Tarzan. He wore a houndstooth sports-jacket and puce tie the width of a napkin. A critical

eye would note that, although Tarzan's torso was slim as a fish, my father's had the contours of a thumbless boxing glove. My friends began to turn away, several insolently swatting their paddle-balls up and down. Then my father closed his eyes and started to swing. He parted his lips, coughed, and gave the elephant call. At first croak, he sounded like your basic father calling his kid, but as he raised the pitch, his cry almost undulated at the proper Tarzan frequency. Then he paused and took a deep breath. He adjusted his grip and gave the elephant call again. There it was. Caruso never sang a truer tone. For a splendid moment it was obvious: my father was Tarzan. We turned in the direction he was calling and saw the shadows of the herd gathering behind the tract homes. Then my father started swinging more violently. His cry tightened into a shaky bellow. As he hung there twisting his pelvis, the bottom of his shirt slid from his belt, revealing the stout slope of his gut. My father tilted back his head and gave screams of terrifying pain. His hips were slamming the inner bars of the jungle gym, and we all stepped back, fearing the thing would uproot and tip over. Then headlights swept over us as a police cruiser rolled up and Dad stopped screaming. My friends turned and squatted in the sandbox, silently slicing the damp sand with stray shovels. My father dropped from the bars and led me home without a word. He paused on the back porch to tuck in his shirt.

•

From New Orleans, Sylvia sent a blue-pencil edit of my pages with this note: "Although your last attempt resembled a self-conscious University of Iowa story, I was still pleased. Actually, I was touched. Not by your writing—you still go for the cheap shot because you have a modest fluidity with eccentric images. No. I was touched for a personal reason. You provided my definitive image of men: out-of-control crying baby apes. I tell you this because I've always seen you as a spy against your gender. Anyway, at least you are now writing about something you know rather than all that private-eye shit. But don't get a swelled head. Now that you're enlightened subject-wise, we can begin discussing style. Although you are maturing beyond endless streams of declarative sentences, you still have a long way to go to master the subordinate clause. Love, Sylvia."

I was driving my cab when I read this, and ran several lights on Canal Street. Sylvia had missed a major fact: because he was once a detective, whenever I wrote about Dad I was theoretically writing a private-eye story.

I now know I should have run those lights for a more important reason: Sylvia encouraged me to write and finger dadness, but the dad of her target wasn't mine—it was Joshua Cushman. Worse, on her encouragement, I was to write "Call me Orange Boy," while she went and died in a car crash, leaving me lost in the sea foam without even a subordinate clause between me and the great white whale father.

I'll conclude this metaphoric clutter by foreshadowing to a higher irony: Sylvia crashed her car not because of fathers. Or husbands. She crashed because of a woman. A mother. Mine.

•

should tell you why I had a cab to run red lights with. It has
nothing to do with irony. During my first winter alone in New
York (Ben in Alaska, Sylvia in New Orleans, and Najaf who-
knows-where), I was trudging down Broadway in a blizzard and
ended up helping a guy push his cab out of a drift. The guy,
Mossad, owned the cab. He drove it during the day and spent
nights with his family, but wanted his vehicle to make money
'round the clock. His current graveyard driver left empty fifths
under the seat. Knee-deep in snow, he offered me the night
shift. I agreed and within a week I was driving under a full
moon. I passed much of the money to Mossad, but kept half of
my tips and a fifth of the fares.

All went smoothly until a Monday shift marred by two separate
freakouts. I was then racing through Manhattan in a waterlogged
cab, the interior soaked like a convertible left out in the rain.
The seats were sopping. Suds bubbled on the dash. When I
stomped the brake, the pedal spouted like a fountain. Earlier, as
the cab was being pulled through the Mermaid Car Wash, I
rolled down my window—for reasons I'll explain later—and let
jets of water cascade over the wheel. I soon had a fish tank for a
car.

Two hours later, I stopped home at the Chateau just as Ben
Cushman called collect. Instead of a wooden tone, his voice was
rich with a somber emotion. I was so busy placing the emotion
that I almost missed his content. Ben called to tell me his mother
just crashed her car. She crashed it in Texas. And she was dead.

Sylvia Cushman was dead.

Ben told me this using the same strong tone of voice that George Washington probably used to steady his troops as they crossed that wide river of ice.

•

My immediate response to Ben's call was to run back down to my cab and begin blindly racing the streets. As I bumped over the ruts of Fourteenth Street, the cab's shot shocks jarred me from my interstellar mourning. I slowed and saw how the Mermaid's nozzles hadn't washed away Sylvia's postcards which still hung taped above the glove compartment. They were soaked and molded to the curve of the dash—each dispatch another chip in the mosaic of the last months of her New Orleans life. From left to right hung the renowned Emily Dickinson daguerreotype, followed by a Diane Arbus freak (a little moose-lipped hunchback holding a Ping-Pong paddle), and, closest to the passenger door, the SLA portrait of Patty Hearst.

The middle postcard—the Arbus freak—represented Sylvia's mind-set for most of her stay in New Orleans. Like most of her cards, the message was written in microscopic hieroglyphics that could take hours to decipher. All I made out was: ". . . that blazing vehicle fell flaming from the firmament . . ." When I phoned her, Sylvia elaborated: she'd driven out to the swamp to sit in her car and grade papers. Suddenly, a low-flying Piper Cub whined over the tree line—probably flyboys on a drug run—

and disappeared at the same moment a flock of egrets erupted out of the trees. There was abrupt silence. Then a muffled explosion. A black ball of smoke rose from the cypresses. "I suddenly found myself gibbering over and over: 'Every angel is terrifying.' " (Pause). "I'd like to believe that at that moment I was actually channeling Rilke!" (Note: she used the term *channeling* years before it hit supermarket culture.)

As for her second postcard—Patty Hearst hefting her Ingram—I received it two weeks before Sylvia's crash. Other recent images included Annie Oakley, Bonnie Parker, and Emma Peel. These cards contained no messages other than my address, and the congruent symbolism of "women holding guns."

The inevitable Emily Dickinson card had come during Sylvia's first few months in New Orleans, long before the freaks and the gunslingers. During that time, Sylvia mailed me dozens of female icons: Amelia Earhart, Virginia Woolf, and a painting of Joan D'Arc walking in a trance toward an angel. (Sylvia may have also sent women who were not missing, burnt, or drowned, but I can't remember who they may have been. I vaguely remember getting Georgia O'Keeffe holding a cow skull—but then again it may have been a photo of only the skull.)

The ink behind Emily bled from the carwash, but I always copied Sylvia's messages in a notebook, and I can reproduce this one verbatim:

Dear Orange Boy,

The other night I was lying in a humidity-induced stupor. A pile of papers lay on the floor—*write an essay comparing your mother to a fish*—but I was too jelled to read. A small party of mosquitoes gathered on my belly to sup. It took my brain a full minute to telegraph my hand to swat them away. They left a line of welts in the shape of an E.

$E = MC^2$ I think. Then, no: $E =$ Emily.

I lay contemplating Emily, zeroing in on her empty womb. Then I stared up at the ceiling fan and had this vision: a little cone of rubber. It's moist, spongelike. It's permanently filled with spermicide. A woman inserts it. She never needs to remove it. Like a Shell No-Pest Strip for the womb. Now I don't know beans about the pharmaceutical industry, but I wonder if I could make any dough on this vision? I already know the slogan: "Because I could not stop for sperm, it kindly stopped for me."

•

To honor Sylvia's birth control imagery, see my cab as a sperm swimming up Sixth Ave to attempt union with the Thalia Theater on West 96th Street—citadel of comfort. Nearly every afternoon, I went there to view the same movies war-weary G.I.s saw after helping Truman nuke Tokyo Rose; those movies shot at low budget in dark rooms illuminated only by cigarette glow—the noir directors discovering dark images were cheaper to film than images composed of electricity and wood. When the double feature was over, I'd stumble out to the street with my new Mickey Spillane butch cut, squint at the low-hung sun, then buy a single cigarette from the bodega around the corner, and dangle it off my lip Robert Mitchum-style with the world weariness of a nineteen-year-old who had seen it all. I was a hallucination from another decade. I was strictly 1946.

As this hallucination drove his cab uptown, pedestrians stepped off the curb and raised their arms like Nazis. I could have flicked them my *off-duty* light, but my mourning was soured with poison—"Screw 'em . . . let them walk."

I was driving crazed but skillfully up the run of smoking sewers in my cab—milk stool passenger seat flapping in back. I was not driving alone.

The cab had no Plexiglass partition between the seats, so it made me vulnerable to muggers nudging knives to my neck. Then I noticed older cabbies cruising with Dobermans for protection. Although the Taxi and Limousine Commission forbids animal companions, the image of driving through the night with a dog was beautiful. Straight from Eskimo mythology. So I got a dog for protection. I got Lew the German shepherd—Lew the senile German shepherd. Lew, who now twirled in a confused semicircle in my cab, trying to find a dry spot on the back passenger seat drenched from the Mermaid.

I didn't enter the Mermaid just to have soot washed from the cab. I entered nightly to pull Sylvia from New Orleans. I not only read Sylvia's letters in my cab, but it was here I would love her. I would glide the cab through the leather thongs of the Mermaid's opening while motioning Lew into the empty back-seat. The cab would then start its slow slide through the rolling buffers, the water gunning the doors, while white foam spilled down the windows. At that moment, Sylvia was more beautiful than she had ever been. She appeared in my rearview mirror. She always sat behind me in the back, wearing a black strapless evening gown, pearls dripping from her shoulders, her neckline low enough that when she leaned forward to remove her shoes, I viewed the slight weight of her breasts. Not that any of this is exactly what one could view in a rearview mirror. My mirror was a little movie screen. And I was Sylvia's chauffeur—Sylvia's Kato. I pulled her through the cave of the carwash into the cave of my heart. And at my various crested moments in the front seat, I would glance in the mirror and see her eyes looking down at the small book in her lap. The book's edges were gilded and the pages yellowed—not a cheap brittle yellow like old paperbacks but a yellow the tone and texture of antique linen. She was reading Emily, of course. She moved her lips slightly as she read. As irrational as it sounds, each poem appeared to contain the words, "Orange Boy." As she flicked every third or fourth page, she glanced up into the mirror and caught me watching. Her lips closed into a slight smile—a smile at the thought that I could successfully masturbate inside a carwash, the most absurd sexual structure in New York. But her grin never made me self-conscious. After all—I was her Korean chauffeur. Her Occidental mind couldn't comprehend that my Mermaid gesture was the life-affirming counterpart of gunplay from death at the New York Aquarium.

•

The flooded automobile became the totem of both my life and Sylvia's. I park my damp cab and dog beside the Thalia. Inside—on a screen glowing before a dozen slouched *cineasts*—Humphrey Bogart, rumpled angel, stood with swirls of night-fog behind him. This was a blind movie mission, and anything could have been playing—some tedious Antonioni or spaghetti western—but the holy hardboiled projectionists had blessed me. Shining there was *The Big Sleep*, a masterpiece I would eat frame-by-frame like birthday cake.

The shot switched from Bogart to a winch pulling a sedan out of the black surf. This was the early scene where Owen Taylor, a chauffeur, is found drowned off Lido pier. I realized the holy hardboiled projectionists had not chosen this film for comfort. Not only could it be my flooded taxi up there, but based on what Ben told me, the body behind the wheel could be Sylvia's. You see, Sylvia and Owen died the same way:

They drowned inside their automobiles at night.

The significant difference: Taylor's lungs were filled with salt water, while the water in Sylvia's was fresh.

If anyone could drown in a dry brisket like Texas, Sylvia could. At some point during the dead of night, she had the accident— plunging her rental car into an irrigation ditch that cut through the mesquite flats. She stayed a mermaid behind the wheel all night. The next morning a cowboy smelled gasoline on the water and rode his horse along that canal until, up by the ranch-to-market road, he came upon a herd of cattle gathered by the shore, mooing at the trunk of her sedan jutting from the water. Then the cows paused in their mooing, and the cowboy heard it. He'd heard distant spooked-out sounds on these flats before— foghorns, elephants, opera—but always at night, and never sounding this forlorn, this otherworldly that he gripped his saddle horn and went into a trance. A deep moan replied to the cows from beneath that water. The herd bowed their heads, then answered. The cowboy sat hypnotized by this bovine siren call until the highway patrol showed up with "Gasoline" Jackson's wrecker. They towed the Toyota out of the water. The horn had been stuck.

Although fictionalized drama, the drowning of *The Big Sleep*'s Owen Taylor is also important to my plot. Owen was the chauffeur for the Sternwoods, a Los Angeles oil-rich family. Owen was not Korean, however. He was a Hollywood white with a thing for the Sternwoods' youngest daughter, Carmen—who like all prototypical millionaires' daughters was a crazyass. Her particular malaise concerned schizophrenic nymphomania. Owen proves his love on the night she lets herself be drugged by Arthur Geiger, an odious pornographer, who pulls the stoned girl's dress up to her belly, so he can snap photos of her garters and fur. Owen bursts into the bungalow, shoots Geiger, and grabs the roll of film. The next time we see him, he's fish food. This murder is a piece of Hollywood lore. When Howard Hawks, the director, was in the middle of filming *The Big Sleep*, he phoned Raymond Chandler and asked, "There's one thing we can't figure out—who killed Owen Taylor?"

Silence. Chandler sucked his pipe, gave a long sigh, then said, "Damned if I know!"

What no one knows is that now, decades later, Howard Hawks has taken to phoning me. He calls in the middle of the night. I pick up by the third ring. I hold the receiver above my head and try to wake up. Finally, I prop up on an elbow and mutter: "Speak."

"There's one thing we can't figure out," Hawks rasps. "Who killed Sylvia Cushman?"

I stay quiet and hear the swirl of post-midnight traffic down Broadway. A car alarm is whining across the street. Finally, I shake my head. I lower the phone to my lips and sigh, "Damned if I know."

•

You'd think Sylvia's autopsy could have answered Howard Hawk's question. I stop typing for a moment at the thought that Sylvia was sliced open . . . But she was. A stranger held her heart and squeezed it like a sponge to discover a blood-alcohol content of point sixteen—four sheets to the wind in any state in the Union.

But this generated the mystery: what had Sylvia been drinking? One assumes mescal, but there was no bottle of Monte Alban in the car. No monogrammed flask. Nothing rolling at the bottom of the canal. This ranch-to-market road was a shit-kicker's circuit. It was a freak of nature that there was not even an empty George Dickel along the shoulder for fifty miles in either direction. There was only a smattering of honky-tonks within a three-hour radius of the death spot, and the highway patrol failed to turn up a bartender who remembered wetting Sylvia's whistle. Even if they had, if you compute blood-alcohol levels to the driving time of 150 miles, Sylvia would have to have had a stiff sip from a bottle or watering-hole within twenty miles of the spot where the car dunked into oblivion. Even in Texas one does not get crocked by breathing the air. But the deeper mystery is why there were no oranges in her car. Or floating above the wreck. Since orange trees are not native to Texas, the cops should have noticed bright citrus tossed along the road. Unless cows ate the evidence. But then the cops were concerned with more practical mysteries—what woman drives into the heart of Texas wearing only a paisley print sundress and no underwear? And there was no Samsonite suitcase in her wreck, and no motel appeared to be stuck with abandoned luggage. Where was Sylvia's suitcase? And what was she even doing in the Lone Star state to begin with? After a brief investigation, the cops learned Sylvia did not publicly consort with Texans. Loyola claimed she wasn't doing university business.

But the Texans let it all go, chalking these mysteries up to the inherent possibility of freakiness that follows all of us like a crow's shadow. They figured Sylvia looped herself out into alcoholic distress. Instead of passing out naked on some lumpy Wilderado Motel bed, she went driving and pitched the empty bottle of mescal onto the payload of a passing pickup. The canal was just ahead. The blood moon reflected on the water like the ball of a Phillips 76 gasoline sign. Sylvia headed for the beacon wanting to fill her tank, but ended up drowning in that moon like a drunk Haiku poet.

·

R ex Ringer wrote: "Making sense of most human mysteries
is as hopeless as walking into the middle of a play in Iceland
and trying to figure out the plot" (*The Clothes the Corpse
Wore*, 1947).

I agree. For example, what if it had been Sylvia who received a
call telling her I was found drowned inside the Mermaid Car
Wash, my lungs filled with suds? When she flew up to New
York to settle my limited affairs, she would have been confronted
with a number of mysteries implying I had a distressed end.
Whereas Sylvia's end concerned liquor, mine would be a Dog
Trip. Begin with the book I threw out the window (Item 1). It
was a coffee-table book of photographs, although the targeted
consumers don't own coffee tables. It flipped into the bristles
that spun on either side of my cab, the torn pages flipping across
the wet windshield, sticking to glass. See my father's photo of
the 1940s starlet. The naked '40s starlet. And it goes without
saying that the '40s were an era in which an actress revealed
nothing more than her deep cleavage and gams. If any of the
G.I.s who once tacked her nightgown pinup on the walls of their
barracks had seen this shot, the poor chumps would have turned
to pillars of salt. See her pucker-tipped breasts, her twin dorsal
mounds, her pouty lips that once smacked Coop, Ladd, and
Bogey—lips now smacking the snoot of a large black dog.

Consider Item 2: the wet body of the German shepherd lying on
the accelerator of my cab. "And Mrs. Cushman," the coroner
would say, cigar butt between his lips, "the above items may or
may not have anything to do with the fact that the deceased was

found with his trousers around his ankles (Item 3) but consider this, Mrs. Cushman: if this alleged guard dog was supposed to protect the deceased from being mugged, why was the alleged dog not drowned like his master, but found overdosed on tranquilizers . . . over-the-counter human tranquilizers (Item 4)."

Now, this would look bad, the implication being my father's pornographic photograph motivated me to engage in bestial homosexuality with my dog, Lew, whom I had drugged into submission, then attempted to kill in a suicide pact. Yet Sylvia would have clarified the worst of that scenario. Although she'd feel the pain of my death she'd gloss it over like a hard-cookie by cocking her hips, sticking a fist on each one, and saying: "Look, I can't account for the lowering of trousers, but considering the deceased was twenty years old and peaked in hormonal overdrive —who knows?

"As for the photography book—I'm the one who pushed him in the direction of a father hunt. Under my tutoring he began exploring every feeling he ever had about that black-hearted bum who once thrust his own son's fist into a Thanksgiving turkey. But in typical Orange Boy fashion, his father-exploration grew into an obsession. And I'm positive that opening an art book and finding Dad's surveillance shots—published for all the world to see—triggered a mental crisis. But I'm certain this crisis did not motivate Orange Boy to abuse the integrity of his German shepherd. Are you following me?" (The coroner wrinkles his nose. He is.)

"You see, I can explain the dog's drugged condition. Eight months ago, when Orange Boy first started hacking, he was cruising down Broome Street and passed a SoHoite in the street clutching her ears, screaming. In his typical culture-head fashion, he assumed she was a performance artist duplicating a sinister Münch painting. Then he passed a crashed cab, the doors flung open. The driver dangled upside-down from his seat, his face wadded inside-out on his chest like a wet red washcloth. Orange Boy realized this was not a performance piece. This was a fellow cabbie with his head shot off.

"The sight made our young driver reconsider his own mortality in a way that the gunplay at the New York Aquarium had not. He was now hot to get a gun. He went on about how he was going to wrap rubber bands around the grip so his hands wouldn't slip, apparently the only authentic fact he knew about firearms. My immediate response was, 'Kiddo, you are the last person in New York who should own a piece.' Then fate wagged its tail when he saw the 'Please give this dog a home' notice wheatpasted to a lamppost. He adopted Lew from a ska bagpipe band whose visas were up. The mutt's name was Basket—and although Gertrude Stein's Basket was a poodle, at least this naming demonstrates there are a few literate musicians in the world. At any rate, Orange Boy gave the dog a second literary christening by renaming it Lew . . . after Lew Archer . . . the Ross Macdonald private eye who frequently searched for lost fathers.

"Now, the first few shifts with Lew went splendidly. Orange Boy described the animal as possessing the essential 'hangdog' expression. Lew sat in the front passenger seat, carriage erect with snoot in profile, occasionally giving a sad glance with his Emmett Kelly eyes to the passengers in back. But then on the third night, a girl in a blue blouse climbed in and suddenly Lew went berserk, lunging to the backseat with a snarl. The girl scrambled out the door and ran screaming down the street. Orange Boy beat the dog with a rolled up newspaper. Probably *The Soho News*. And then, a few days later, Lew repeated his Hound of the Baskervilles act with another passenger. Another female. This happened five times. Always with women. The sixth time it happened, the passenger yanked off her glasses and made eye-contact with the baying dog, and grunted a single guttural word in German.

"Lew immediately dropped into a curl and placed his snoot between his paws, staring up at the woman, ashamed and confused. 'Eighty-sixth and Lex,' she calmly instructed Orange Boy.

" 'Great dog technique,' our young cabbie remarked, pulling into traffic.

" 'Thank you. I'm a veterinarian.'

" 'Oh really,' he said. A few blocks later he ventured, 'Every once in a while Lew starts howling at women. Do you know why? Is it perfume or something?'

"She slid her glasses back on and said, 'Menstrual blood.'

"Well, here was a problem. Orange Boy couldn't very well screen each female fare as to her monthly condition. He seriously asked me if he should drive according to tidal charts, and I almost said, 'Didn't your mother explain these things to you?' but thought better of it. In the end, he solved the problem on his own without consulting some *How to Raise Your Dog* manual by that Ayatollah of Curs, Vicki Hearne. Since it was the appearance of a dog that discourages muggers, Orange Boy purchased a box of Compoze from a pharmacy. He ground the blue pills up with the bottom of a spoon, then gave Lew's Alpo a light dusting. Lew would then hop into the passenger seat, curl up, and spend Orange Boy's whole shift snapping at the rabbits of his doggy dreams."

•

Two weeks after Sylvia's drowning, I was in a Piedmont plane and its pilot announced our approach to New Orleans International Airport. I pressed my forehead against the window and viewed an immense Daiquiri-colored swamp swirling below. This quaggy soufflé was so abstract I had no idea of our altitude until I saw a tiny cabin the size of a green Monopoly house. As the plane circled, I cast my mind down to that wilderness of alligator and lime—I stand in the reeds as Sylvia floats by in a green funeral of grace. Her body bobs on a small gondola; a pair of 1865 pennies placed on her eyes; lilacs braided in her hair; the original handwritten manuscript of "I could not stop for death" folded beneath her palms. Her shroud is Emily's white dress—the dress denied her by the New York Public Library. A black Labrador trots up and places a tentative paw on the gunwale, before leaping in. The boat tips back and forth as it continues drifting through the skin of lily pads, the dog nobly at the helm guarding Sylvia into eternity.

Sylvia had been correct to suspect my narration of her life and prefer Joan Didion. Beautiful green funeral of grace, indeed!

The fact is that after the Texans were finished with her it would have been impossible to have an Opheliac floating funeral with Egyptian death-dog motif. Then through a bureaucratic mix-up, the Texans cremated Sylvia. And when Texans do the burning, we are not talking a fine sooty ash suitable for ceremonial scattering. We are talking charcoaled bone fragments sent UPS in a cardboard receptacle the size of a shoe box. As Ben held his mother's container in Bloomfield Hills, its rattle instantly triggered a strong memory—he was five years old, sitting at a Saturday matinee. He was jiggling a box of Milk Duds.

•

I trudged stiff-legged from my plane into the New Orleans airport. Ben stood waiting at the gate. He was no longer skinny with junkielike pallor. His skin blazed ivory with ice—an Alaskan suntan. His hair again spilled to his shoulders, and he had a flaming red beard. His body had a taut robustness—as if he just finished gutting an Alaskan grizzly with some pilots back by the cargo ramp. Ben Cushman now stood cross-armed while stewardesses worshipfully pulled little suitcase carts in an eddy around him.

Despite his pioneer look, he was grimacing as if he had just had dental surgery. I hugged him. He felt tight and sinewy beneath his flannel shirt. His body reminded me of Shem's. I pulled back to look him in the eye and asked, "How are you holding up?"

"As well as can be expected," Ben sighed, then shook his head. "Man, a week ago I was in Nome. I can't tell if I'm more freaked over Mom or being back in the land of the Big Mac."

I had flown down to New Orleans to help Ben settle his mother's limited affairs. He led me to a pay phone kiosk, explaining that he had to call the New Orleans lawyer his father had engaged long-distance. We couldn't legally enter Sylvia's apartment unless accompanied by a cop. And the New Orleans police couldn't enter until the Texas Highway Patrol sent them Sylvia's death certificate.

"A death certificate?" I wanted to yell. Sylvia was burnt and urned. What more certification could anyone want? The cops should call Michigan and put Lester Cushman on phone, have that child verify that his mother came home in pieces smaller than his multicolored Leggos.

Now, at the New Orleans airport, Ben walked to the luggage chute shaking his head because both God and the Texas Highway Patrol still hadn't sent Sylvia's death certificate to New Orleans.

"We can't get into Mom's place," he said, "Fucking Texans . . ."

As he spoke, an unintelligible voice blared over the intercom. I was the only one who knew it was Sylvia. I was the only one who discerned her sarcasm singing across the airport: "Where in the hell is Broderick Crawford when you need him?"

·

We navigated to New Orleans in a cab driven by a bayou member of the brethren named Nathan Lowghost. He fit my TV image of a Cajun—dark, mustached, Brill-creamed hair—although Lowghost wouldn't have looked out of place riding the F train to Astoria either. Ben leaned over the seat, pointing, and said, "Bu Dop"—which I misinterpreted as "Be Bop" until Ben then commented on the intricate tattoo of a tiger on Nathan's right forearm. Nathan nodded. Ben told about how many vets he had met in Alaska who'd abandoned the Lower 48 to hump it alone up in King Salmon. As Ben conversed knowledgeably about Vietnam, I recalled Sylvia writing: "Why is Bud Crowley, your private eye, a Vietnam vet? Christ, you were still in diapers during the Tet Offensive! Write about characters you know."

Our cab swam down the narrow streets of the French Quarter. It was dark and raining and the cab's wet windows distorted my view, but I made out grids of light spilling from rows of closed shutters. The cab splashed to a stop, and we lugged our backpacks into the lobby of something called the Gaston Motel on Charles Street—a two-story Moroccan-like building of stucco. It had a Casablanca gunrunner's lobby with a slow-spinning ceiling fan. There were foreign newspapers folded down on chairs. Peter Lorre fanned himself in the corner.

There was no bellhop, so Ben and I carried our own bags down a hall into a courtyard lined with doors like a motel. The rain had abruptly stopped and the sky had the luminous tone of an

Xray. There was the sound of water spilling from the roofs. Ben unlocked our door and we entered a duplex room with a wrought-iron stairway winding between our beds. A crazy joy rose in my chest and I laughed: "We have reached the DNA of your mother's New Orleans."

•

Now see Ben in a bursting T-shirt as he struts out of our room beside Marlon Brando. Together they stride down to a French Quarter pay phone to dial Mr. Cushman's Michigan number. Hear them as they bark into the receiver: "Stella! Father!"

For a small urban sprawl, the French Quarter has an abundance of mythology. Visualize Anne Rice's vampires. Observe Professor Longhair. And my addition to this mythology is: The Meek Son. In reality, the Meek Son does not go to a phone booth. The Meek Son drags our downstairs phone into the downstairs bathroom and shuts the door. He turns on the fan. Then— hear his muffled voice. Judging by his diminutive tone, the Meek Son is being heavily interrogated by Dad—by Mr. Cushman. And the Meek Son answers with respect: "Yes, father. Yes."

I stood in the middle of our room, reflecting how by drowning, Sylvia left both Ben and me at the mercy of our respective pops. To stop her nagging, and write about mine, I had banged out the following:

I was seven years old and watching my father. He was sprawled out on the couch, his head tilted back. I had the sensation he was watching me through his nostrils. I padded over and watched him while absentmindedly wiggling my last baby tooth. He gave a sudden snort and I pulled out the tooth. Then he rolled over and started to really belt out a score of snores.

I took my tooth to his desk, which was covered with caramel-colored folders. An open folder contained photographs of men and women in bed clutching sheets and yelling at the camera. I found the photos boring—my father obviously playing tricks on people trying out beds in department stores. (They were, of course, divorce motel-shots—Dad had taken his private-detective work home with him.)

I shuffled through the large stack of surprised couples, and then came to the pictures of the woman and her dog. The woman was naked. The dog was large and black. They were frisky photos. In several shots, the dog playfully bit her arm. In others, the woman was on her knees and the dog was leaning against her rump, his front paws on her back. They must have been struggling to form a letter of the alphabet. I tried to decode the two figures by reciting my ABCs. At the moment I reached K, my father let out a deep-chested snort. I stopped the alphabet and whipped shut the folder. For no reason at all, I dropped my tooth into Dad's bottle of Scotch.

•

My father's dog pix were first made public, in, of all places, the *Sunday New York Times*. It was a Saturday night and I had braked for dinner, my cab parked two blocks down from the Aristotle Diner, where I was doing honor to my mousaka while reading an article in the *Times* magazine about a scandalous new book called *Hollywood Brutal*. This volume made Kenneth Anger's similar work seem like "Hooray for Hollywood." The new book contained the usual mire of Tinsel Town scandal shots—Robert Mitchum strolling to the pokey on his pot rap, or the ravaged Judy Garland resembling a peat-bog man—but there were hundreds of poisonous photos never seen before, especially in two particularly notorious chapters. The first, "Baby You Can Drive My Car," contained detailed photographs of celebrity car wrecks. James Dean, Jayne Mansfield, Monty Cliff . . .

The other chapter was called "In the Doghouse."

The *Times* interviewed the book's editor, Jill Limehouse—a frail fifty-year-old woman with translucent skin—at the Chateau Maramont where she was holed up, living on celery and vermouth. Four air-conditioners chilled the room and a skin of ice covered the windows. A loaded Pylon lay on the ottoman beside her feet. She was wearing cowboy boots and rubber gloves. She wore the gloves because developing fluid had eaten away her fingertips. ("I no longer have any fingerprints," Jill laughed.) The *Times* asked:

> Don't you feel those photographs of Miss X and her dog are violations of the dead? The woman did make several films considered family classics. "Oh please! No one in Hollywood has any right to privacy. You sell your soul to the public, and then expect to go off and do your doggy business in the dark? But, let me add, I hope you don't believe having sex with a canine is some secret feminine fantasy. It was a pornographic distortion

some studio mogul planted in her head while she was under his desk. And we all know Miss X was not exactly a Madam Curie, was she now? But ironically there is an intense beauty about these photographs. Given what we know about the tragic path her life took, the love between that woman and her dog was probably the most tender she ever had."

This paragraph was illustrated with a cropped photo—a close-up of Miss X's chin and open mouth in the act of frenching a dog snoot. I recognized the position of her jaw. I recognized that dog, that picture. It was a photo I had seen years before on my father's desk.

•

I spent most of that night torpedoing my cab through the neon, squealing in front of every closed bookstore to see if their window display contained a copy of *Hollywood Brutal*. The 54th Street Brentano's did. A sheet of glass hung between me and that book—between me and Sylvia. I say Sylvia because the cover of *Hollywood Brutal* was of an angry woman being lifted into the air by a policeman, her skirt bunched up around her waist. And this angry woman was Sylvia. I studied the cop to see if it was Mr. Cushman. It wasn't. I studied the woman again, and saw how obsessively mistaken I was. The photo was the notorious 1942 shot of Frances Farmer being carried off to the loony bin. But I was correct to have confused the two women. At that moment, Sylvia Cushman and Frances Farmer were driving together through the Texas night screaming at the moon, and debating where to crash their car.

I waited out the sunrise, then the breakfast hour, and at 11:00, Brentano's opened. There was no glass between me and *Hollywood Brutal* now. I not only held my father's photographs, but found him mentioned in Limehouse's foreword. The perfection of those paragraphs was a relief. Once Sylvia read them, she'd see I should abandon trying to write about my father and return to my private eye, Bud Crowley.

But they don't get the *Sunday Times* one night early in Texas. So Sylvia never read about Limehouse. And books are shipped to Texas from New York, so she never read the following passage. She never read these sentences that eliminate any reason for any writer to ever write of my father again.

And that includes Joan Didion.

That includes me.

(From page 10 of *Hollywood Brutal*:)

> Most of the candids in this book that are sexual in nature are from the collection of a self-described "Hollywood peeper," a notorious character who pops up on the peripheries of numerous Hollywood histories. He called himself a "private investigator" but many referred to him as a "visual hatchet man." His alliance was with the studio heads. With erect telephoto lens, he snapped their stars in various unguarded moments, giving the cigar-chomping moguls an arsenal of photographic intimidation to help keep their employees in line. Who was going to buck the system when presented with a photograph of himself violating the Clayton Act with a six-year-old?

I had a martini at Musso & Frank's Grill with the famed portrait photographer 'Sparky' Coots, one of the few citizens who will admit to actually knowing this man:

"The last time I saw him was in 1957. It was at this wild shindig in the hills. I mean, there were bongo drums and people fist-fighting over Adlai Stevenson. It was also the night after Miss X overdosed and died. Down on the patio they had her photo tacked up with black crepe paper strung around it, though to tell you the truth, a lot of guys down there—technical people mostly—were toasting the photo, glad that bitch was dead. It was around 3:00 a.m., things were winding down, when 'Quarts,' the private detective, pulled up, honking the horn of his Porsche ('Quarts' was his self-proclaimed nickname because of his . . . ah . . . um . . . just say because of "the average quantity of his sap.") Anyway, Quarts bounced down the patio steps with this woman shape slung over his shoulder. She was wearing nothing but a sheet. "Nice ass!" I yelled as I passed him on the steps. Now, given the fact a million dollar actress was giving head in the pool, Quarts' entrance with this girl didn't attract much attention at first—but suddenly there was a hush. It was so quiet I heard the traffic in the valley. I turned around to see what was happening. It was then I saw the face of the girl with the nice ass. It was Miss X. I mean, it was her body. That son of a bitch had snuck her out of the morgue in the trunk of his car. Man, I started shaking and went inside. Later . . . I mean, I can't tell you what they did to her . . . I mean, I paced a bit and then had to leave. Quarts was in the driveway hosing off his shoes. I just shook my head and said, 'Christ, man, where are you at?' He was hunched down, the garden hose running at his feet, and he looked up at me with this little sad smile. I mean, it was a real polite sad smile and he said, 'Buddy, you don't understand. I am a pilgrim.' Then he stood and wiped his forehead with his sleeve, saying, 'I follow the older and wiser god—the snake god who swallowed a monkey to shit out this world.' "

•

remembered that when my father thrust my hand inside the Thanksgiving turkey, his smile was also "real polite." His smile was also "sad." And while he held me in the bird, I stood marking time by the number of commercials from the neighbor's TV. Six. Followed by the noise of the football game. During this interim, the turkey became abstract. It was no longer food or meat. The more I stared, the more purple the object became. I could phase out the paler tones of the skin and see nothing but the tissue of purple struggling within. My eyes watered, and as I blinked I beheld a purple-shadowed mountain. A steep path wound up its side where a man in a white robe climbed with a boy. The boy was stooped over and wearing a skirt, his back burdened with kindling.

My father was revealing the demand of fatherhood—he was showing me Abraham climbing the hill to sacrifice Isaac. I closed my eyes and saw the son, now naked, tethered to the altar, father hovering with the blade raised above his boy's bare belly. And my father had a father's rage against Jehovah for demanding this offering. But my father was no Abraham. He was a private detective who got mired down by his rage. So Jehovah crushed him with a hippopotamus in the Rose Bowl parade.

I emerged from Brentano's gripping a *Hollywood Brutal*, intending to rush to a pay phone to call Sylvia collect and tell her about this book. The sunlight falling on Fifth Avenue seemed somber for early afternoon. I jogged to 54th Street and saw the Jersey skyline was iodine. Sunset? I cocked my head sideways to read the watches of the passing shoppers. It was 5:30. I had tranced away the entire day holding *Hollywood Brutal* at the bookstore. I now had forty-five minutes to zip downtown, drug Lew, then rendezvous with Mossad at Fanelli's Bar, where he would give me the cab keys and I would start my shift.

The phone was ringing when I entered the Chateau. I ignored it and cranked open a can of Alpo while Lew sat at my feet in his usual nervous/attentive pose. There is a theory that nervous dogs are nervous because they have no concept of the future. For example, these dogs believe each meal is the last meal they will ever eat. That was certainly Lew's take on reality. With the telephone continually ringing, he choked down his horse meat with desperation while I pulled on my driving jeans. I then picked up Lew's bowl to rinse it, but realized I had no recollection of slipping him his Compoze. What if I rode him undoped? What if I fed him again, but it turned out I'd given him a double dose? I weighed the pros and cons. I intended to drive with my father's book through the Mermaid that night, and wanted no interference. I opened another can and gave my dog his mickey.

Lew tore into his second helping of Alpo so strongly he shoved the bowl around the floor. Being fed twice was a profound experience. This was against all known experience of the world. Had he gained an additional day of life? Had he dreamed his first meal? Or was this second meal the dream? Was he an endless array of dogs infinitely reflected in two mirrors? I draw this out because I did end up doping him twice. We were halfway to the door when he slumped over, curled his spine, and began snoring. The rabbits of his REMs swelled plump and hopped slowly.

•

I lifted and balanced Lew on top of *Hollywood Brutal* to carry them both to my cab. I felt like a Pieta. Then, with book and dog in the crock of my arms, I swiveled a wrist and grabbed my phone. The thing had been ringing relentlessly for at least fifteen minutes.

"Orange Boy! Orange Boy! Where were you?" a voice screamed.

I snapped my answer: "I can't talk right now. I'm late. For work. I gotta get my cab."

She tried to say something, and I just jabbered out, "Goodbye Sylvia! I've gotta carry Lew down to the street! I'll call you later!" But I couldn't maneuver the phone to its hook with Lew in my arms. While I struggled, Sylvia didn't hang up either. She said nothing, but I could hear her phone's hollow woosh on my receiver.

I finally shifted Lew and was about to flop the receiver back on its hook, but realized Sylvia hadn't hung up yet. Raymond Chandler sparked my brain and I sang out: "This is a long goodbye, Sylvia. Farewell. Farewell."

If Sylvia had left her receiver dangling, she now walked back to pick it up and speak. The words she spoke were the last words she ever said to me: "Goodbye Orange Boy. Drive safely. With your dog. And while you're bouncing around town remember the Bible. Remember that quote. I know you can. Remember Matthew 7:6. Remember, Orange Boy. Remember: *Don't give to the dogs what is holy.*"

She hung up before I did.

•

I dedicate Sylvia's words to the memory of Miss X, the Warner Brothers star. She defiantly gave what was holy to her dog, circa 1953. And her dog was a large black Labrador, four years old. My father's shots revealed the surface of that dog's soul manifesting itself on the edges of his body. And this revelation was not some Muybridge frame-by-frame. In Dad's photos the dog is only a black smudge. A living squirt of ink. Without knowing it, my father shot and printed his photos in the grainy style of Robert Frank, the foremost proponent of creating a photograph that draws attention to the fact that it is a photograph. If this dog had been shot in a more traditional style, say in the smooth stationary glory of Edward Weston, the result would have been ridiculous and pornographic. Instead, consider

Miss X—a woman dancing naked with her dog on a patio of cut stones. She is a mist of pointillist specks. We can only approximate her grace and her fleshy beauty. We are viewing a Greek statue in fog. She is Seurat's angel. The Atomized Nude.

In fact, the whole photograph is a sheet of particles. That gnarled cactus just beyond the low wall of the patio could be a sea anemone. Yet regardless of the photo-grain, Miss X's contours clearly hang at the perfect point of ripeness. She is at the pinnacle of her beauty, that last moment of perfection before her muscles finally succumb softly to gravity. Because of this, the singular moment of my father's photograph is more profound than a death mask. Soon Miss X would be ruined by pills. Soon she would never be photographed without sunglasses, scarves, and the protective shadow of a wide-brimmed hat. And soon, of course, she would die of a poorly aimed, self-inflicted gunshot wound and be interred in a closed casket at a modestly attended Hollywood funeral where Buster Keaton, of all people, would be chief pallbearer.

But in the here and now of my father's photographs, Miss X is alive and nothing less than radiant. To this day, the only woman in the flesh I've ever seen as glowed-up as Miss X is Sylvia—Sylvia sipping tea one Sunday morning and reading Emily Dickinson, irrationally using her finger to follow those short lines of verse.

Miss X is not reading poetry to her dog. See her on her hands and knees facing the camera. See her enraptured face! That smile! The strands of her hair across her face—wheat blowing in wind. Her breasts hang as the most obvious, yet truest, of images—fruit. Only a woman who believed she was totally alone would abandon herself so completely. This woman and dog are not posing. And my father's telephoto lens is equal to the eye of God. But these photos not only connect my father to the eye of God, but to the birth of the Age of Surveillance. As he snapped Miss X and her dog, Richard Nixon was staking out a pumpkin patch. But my father caught a greater glory than Alger Hiss. He caught a woman allowing the black dynamo of abandon to enter her beneath the arch and small of her back. See how those black paws press into the mounds of her peachlike haunch! The dog is a black blurred ghost. Black electricity. Yet he is still a dog and to more fully appreciate his love, consider his simple dog brain. A brain the size of a walnut. If we could fly above it, it would resemble a map of the USA composed of six states: a Texas for eating, a California for fucking, a New York for the olfactory center, a Maine for shitting and pissing, a Rhode Island allowing him to fetch and shake hands, and finally an Alaska of love—love for the master or mistress. And on that hot afternoon in 1948, this dog joined California and Alaska by mating his mistress—to him an act as profound as the Louisiana Purchase. He only felt a momentary confusion at the plump smoothness of her rear, a realization she wasn't particularly furry —and where was her tail? But he jerked on, knowing that if Christ did not consider him worthy, he certainly had the holy simplicity of a true seeker, his only desire being the customary piece of postnuptial steak, always offered to him by his lover. She lounged afterwards on the lawn chair, smoking a Lucky Strike, momentarily considering the alphabetical similarity of the Lucky Strike "T-zone" to the T-bone she held in her right hand, which the dog licked and nipped, his whiskers and teeth tickling her fingers, which made her daydream about what John Garfield had smelled like in their close-up, as the sticky dog seed puddled on the plastic bands of the seat beneath her, seed incredibly confused to have swum so far for love to find itself arriving without passport or language in the foreign port of human egg.

As for myself, at that moment, I didn't want be a novelist—I wanted to be a dog. And to be holy. And I was a dog and I was holy. I was that black Hollywood dog as Miss X crouched, alive again. And she was 25 again. And she knelt not in the desert but on the front seat of my cab. I tensed my tail and entered her from the rear. And while doing this, we became the dreams of yet another dog, the one sleeping in the backseat of my cab there inside the Mermaid Car Wash.

Lew.

•

I can now be more discreet or more frank, and in such a dilemma I'll quote my grandfather, forcing him to do my work: "Jesus Christ! There's no decent sex in your book—or should I say 'erotic scenes'? Well, hell's bells, I'll just get to the point: there's no decent screwing in your book, and now you drag us 179 pages to tell how you're jerking off in a carwash. Haven't you learned anything from my books? You can never have your main character masturbate. Besides the fact that the topic is on the level of a character's bathroom habits, it destroys any chance of a reader's respect. Imagine if I had Tim Fontanel pound his pud before he went to have a shootout with some gunsel?"

I offer my grandfather's comments not only because I'm a self-conscious narrator, but as a way of waving a flag to stress there's been an important point to my activities inside the Mermaid Car Wash. They lead to a resurrection from the dead, an activity that Christ had nothing to do with. Sylvia did.

In the carwash, my cab suddenly jerked to a halt. I realized my head had been ringing, but now I heard an orchestra of beating water; the thick bound #6 pages of *Hollywood Brutal* turning with a sound like corn being husked; and the rhythmic thump of my elbow against the car seat. And bathing in the beauty of woman and dog, I jerked my knee up into the radio. There was a crack of static, an electric branch breaking—then a little voice was abruptly singing in my cab—singing from the Twilight Zone because it was impossible to receive radio signals inside the Mermaid. And the singer and song were impossibly absurd: there was Shirley Temple quivering, "Animal crackers in my soup . . ." Oh oh oh bad joke! What oldies station would play this? I quickly flipped off the radio but couldn't help laughing at this synchronicity of woman, pooches, and now Shirley Temple's wildlife song. God only knows how much further irony would have souped my brain were I not suddenly aware that something was missing in the noise texture.

Lew.

He was completely silent. No snoring. No familiar wet chop of his jaws as he tore into the rabbits of Morpheus. I turned and shook my dog. He was still. He was not breathing. I shook him again. His slack body felt insubstantial somehow, his fur just a pup tent. I tried lifting him up, and his head rolled on his limp neck.

He wasn't cold, but felt room-temperature. I tried to will this all away. "My dog is just sleeping," I said. "My dog is playing possum. My dog is lost in prayer." But no. I knew. The mechanics of it were apparent—I had given Lew too much Compoze. It had stopped his heart—my dog had o.d.'d like Lenny Bruce.

Perhaps I could have succeeded where my father failed—venting transcendental rage against Jehovah—if I had been a Jim Thompson-ite and just hoisted my mutt out the window in scorn. Instead I flung *Hollywood Brutal*. The pages of Miss X and her dog were slashed from the book by the buffers and flipped up onto my wet windshield. I couldn't bear Dad's pixs anymore. Were they going to officially haunt me? If Sylvia's skull had been New Mexico, my skull was a Mohave of dogs and women. Should I wear tin dogs on my ears—or a woman's tin haunches? I closed my eyes and stuck my head out the window to let water and soap splash down the side of my head and my shoulders into the cab. The lather rose to the gas and brake pedals. As the suds soaked Lew, he didn't even smell like a wet dog. And as the water continued pouring on to my naked lap, there was nothing to do but cry, "Doggie, doggie, doggie." I opened my eyes. The black-and-white image of Miss X soaked on my windshield. The soap lather had been absorbed by the paper, aging her into a siren Sylvia's age.

•

I drove out of the Mermaid and up Tenth Ave. Streetlights poured green glare on the suds at my feet. My wet trousers were strung around my ankles and hindered pedal-work, so at a red light I slid them off. The driver's seat was cold and wet. It gave me greater understanding of the term "well-digger's ass." I headed uptown until I reached the Cloisters. My radio was cracking with nothing but Spanish. I swung back downtown, deliberately choosing the worst burned-out blocks of Harlem for passage. At every corner, fires roared inside wire trash cans. Stark luminaries. Inside the cab, the soap dried like ash on the dashboard. As I braked for a red light in front of St. John the Divine, a troop of men with stringy beards and conical turbans stepped off the curb. They were halfway across the street when the night sky bleached white, followed by aluminum thunder. In the sudden downpour, the men stopped and held each other's shoulders, laughing. At the next block, I skidded up to some pay phones. Then standing on the sidewalk bare-assed, in a downpour, I dialed Sylvia's New Orleans number. The operator wanted $1.35 for the first three minutes, so I leaned into my cab and grabbed a fistful of fare change. I returned to the open-air pay phone helmet, and sliced my quarters into the slot. Sylvia's number rang. It rang again. Then the line picked up: "Hello. This is Sylvia Cushman's voice, but it's not being generated from Sylvia Cushman's mouth. You're hearing my answering machine. Please give it your message. Then Sylvia Cushman— the whole menu—should get back to you within 24 hours."

I began ranting: "Sylvia! Pick up! Pick up!" until the tape line ran out and the line went dead. I dialed again. I assumed she was home because she had phoned the Chateau earlier. I didn't see the irrationality of this assumption. Three weeks later, when Ben and I would pore over his dead mother's phone bill, I would see that while I had been in Harlem frantically dialing Sylvia in New Orleans—finally ranting a monologue for her into her answering machine—Sylvia was five hundred miles away. She had charged calls from somewhere called Braintree, Texas.

•

"I listened to your message to my mother," Ben said. "I did you a favor. I erased it."

This erased message said:

"This is Orange Boy. I need to talk. Why do you quote the Bible long-distance? Why do you quote about dogs? You know that's not the first time I've heard that quote. When I was ten I heard it. When I was ten I had a dog. A terrier. I named her The Terrier of the Nile because even as a child I longed for Cleopatra. Then the day those astronauts burned up, my dog ran into the street. I heard the squeal of the brakes. Her yipe. I ran outside. I knelt and cradled her. The driver was an old man. He was very upset. My mother ran out and said, 'Go in the house and get this man a glass of water.' I looked up at her and said, 'Mamma, in a minute. You have to say a prayer for my dog. Right now. Right away. So her soul will get to heaven.'

"My mother shook her head. I started crying, 'I want my dog to be up in heaven with Daddy and Davy Crockett.' Then my mother balled her fists and began preaching as if a television camera were rolling: 'Daddy is not in heaven,' she said. 'Davy Crockett is not in heaven,' she said.

"She told me: 'No one is in heaven but Jesus and the angels. Not even Mary is in heaven. Everyone who ever lived is dead in

• 183 •

the ground. On the morning the heavenly trumpets blow, all the dead in Christ will wake as one. You know that. Everyone will rise from the ground to Jesus. And the dead babies who took Christ into their hearts will fly into the arms of their mothers.'

"I started yelling, 'I want The Terrier of the Nile to rise to Jesus, too!'

"And my mother shook her head and leaned her face down into mine. She screamed: 'You know what Jesus said in Matthew 7:6, young man—"Don't give to the dogs what is holy." Now go to the house and get this man a glass of water.'

"And it's not really the point whether Lew my dog is holy or not. He's beyond holiness—he's dead. And I need to talk to you. I need to talk of love—don't laugh—Love! And love has nothing to do with writing, and writing has nothing to with Mom and Dad, and love and writing have nothing to do with smashing dogs in cars. Love is dogs. Do you hear me? And if dogs are love, dogs are holy."

•

dialed Sylvia's number a fourth time, but realized it was crazy calling a recording machine in New Orleans while standing bare-assed at a pay phone on the edge of Harlem. A car with Jersey plates glided up. A rain-wet window rolled down, and a lost-looking fat woman in curlers yelled, "How do we get to the Holland Tunnel?" Then she noticed I had no pants. She gave my penis a long stare—as if she were going to make sure she remembered it if she ever saw it again—and then turned to the driver and began beating his shoulder until their car sped off.

While all this was going on, I realized my pay phone was technologically blessed. The strength of those phone lines was equal to NASA communications that had once been made between Ground Control and the moon. All through the Jersey car commotion, I clearly heard Sylvia's recording over the receiver outstretched in my hand: "Hello. This is Sylvia Cushman's voice . . ."

Sylvia's voice spilled through the rain. And Sylvia's voice spilled over the sidewalk. Her voice spilled around the wet tires of my cab like slush in snow. And her voice spilled through the open cab door, spilling over the wet seats. Sylvia's voice flowed over the body of Lew. My dog. And poured into his ears. Then Lew was suddenly yawning. Then Lew pushed himself up with his front paws. Yawned again. Shook himself off. Circled the wet seat, arching his brow in irritation—"Where's a dry place to sit, goddammit . . ." Lew stared through the open door at me with his somber Abraham Lincoln expression. And as I stood in the rain holding Sylvia's voice, my resurrected dog lifted his head. And began to howl.

•

In New Orleans, the Texans had still not sent Sylvia's death certificate so Ben and I killed an afternoon by touring the St. Louis Cemetery—a Gallic-style above ground bonelot. Baby-bodied cherubim balanced on pillars, possessing chipped faces and missing limbs. The only statue still intact was a stone angel standing with her arm raised in a toast.

Ben crouched in the weeds under a whitewashed obelisk, his position an exact duplicate of Clifford Brown's body language on the cover of *Blue Snow*, rippling his fingers on the valves of his rented coronet. Then he lifted the horn to his mouth and began to blow. But certainly not BeBop. He blew a warped dirge. Although his tone was rusty, he had amazing articulation, attacking each note with sparse no-nonsense Japanese clarity.

Ben repeated one stark riff for twenty-five minutes. Finally, I recognized the tune. He was blowing "Swing Low, Sweet Chariot."

PART FIVE

A STREETCAR NAMED SYLVIA

We stood on her porch. Ben clutched an envelope containing Sylvia's death certificate. Tacked to his mother's door was a green cardboard skull. Halloween had been ten days before. We were unforgivably late trick-or-treaters . . .

This skull was the only thing sinister about Sylvia's. I had always pictured her answering her phone in some Faulkner-gothic hovel—but in reality, she lived in a prefab condo, her unit covered with acrylic stucco swirled like frosting. A crust of sodden *Picaynes* layered the porch.

As we stood before this empty home, the full fact of its emptiness, the full fact of Sylvia's death swept over me. I wanted to raise my hands in Baptist rapture and testify to the congregation that no matter what the specific tragedy of her death meant, at least Sylvia lived her last years in New York peeling oranges and in New Orleans watching airplanes crash—she had not died in Detroit with a husband who gave driving lessons to dogs.

I was part of a small congregation circled on Sylvia's porch. Our leader was a tall dishwater-blonde in her mid-twenties wearing a tweed skirt, her Barbie Doll beauty slightly marred by a braille-like rash on her cheeks. She was the manager of the condos, and beside her stood her associate: a black woman with relaxed hair, also wearing tailored tweed. The third was a black man in knuckle-white running shoes and crisp jogging shorts. Five minutes earlier, he had rolled up to Sylvia's in a big blue Buick with two kids in the back swatting each other with tennis rackets. This was the policeman.

The blonde took out a key ring and stepped to the porch. As she fumbled with the lock, I tasted Ben's current of anxiety. He stood with clenched fists and his "Rock'em Sock'em Robot" jaw. When the lock clicked, the blonde glanced at the cop. He nodded. She shoved the door with her hip. As it swung open, I knew that I didn't want an answer to Sylvia's death to be found inside. But the open door revealed nothing more than a white hallway wall. Ben rushed in, then the cop, then the blonde. I wanted to follow, but sensed some unspoken protocol, and waited. The black woman waited, too. Then as we stood on the porch without speaking, listening to bees drone, my porch-partner made an observation about Sylvia's as perceptive as it was absurd. We were looking into the hall and both noticed a black scuff on the wall two feet from the floor. No mark could be more nondescript. It could have been a shoe-print made when Sylvia lifted her calf to slip on a sling-heeled pump . . . Or the scrape of a furniture leg. And yet, as ambiguous as this mark was, my companion turned to me and dramatically arched an eyebrow, a look saying: "Well. That explains everything—doesn't it?"

At that moment, the trio trooped by the doorway, and as if on cue the black woman and I followed. Inside Sylvia's, there wasn't a trace of Nouveau Suicidal Aberration. She had kept a domicile of normalcy—furniture all chrome and wet-black vinyl. Off-white fabrics, textured like burlap. Coffee table art books everywhere. Sylvia had kept the kind of apartment where you washed the dishes every night.

We gathered in the bedroom—olive shag carpet. Praline wallpaper. A fingerpainting by Lester was framed above the bed—purple handprints on DeKooning swirls. Directly below lay Sylvia's pillow marked with a week-old indentation of New Mexico—her skull.

We formed a semicircle around the blonde. She folded her hands in front of her pelvis and began speaking, staring into the distance as if performing a soliloquy: "Two weeks ago, I received a telephone call from the college. They asked me to check in on your mother because she hadn't reported to work for a week. I knocked and knocked, but no one answered. So I let myself in with my passkey and found your mother on the bed passed out with a bottle of alcohol. I phoned her office. They asked me to check to make sure she was still breathing. I went back and your mother came to the door saying, 'Please, please, please leave me alone.' "

Everyone shuffled, then started toward the door. All except Ben. Without warning, he shot up his hand and shouted: "Wait!" Everyone turned. Ben looked down to the floor. He was as surprised by his shout as we were. He started: "At Mom's funeral, I learned that when she was a teenager she took piano lessons. I never knew that. I thought all my musical genes came from Dad. These two old sisters from Livonia told me how they used to leave their kitchen window open so they could hear her practicing next door. One muggy afternoon, they heard wood snapping and wires whiplashing apart. The humidity had made Mom's piano explode. After that they let Mom practice in their house on their Wurlitzer . . ." The tweed twins and cop listened with strained smiles. "One day Mom asked if she could invite a boy over to hear her play. She phoned half a dozen times from school to make sure the sisters brought some oranges home from the grocery. That afternoon she showed up with some sober-looking kid, tall as a bean pole. He was the captain of the basketball team and was wearing his varsity jacket. He hadn't given it to Mom yet. She made him sit down and then she ran into the kitchen to pick out an orange. Then she sat down at the piano. They told me how she sat with her back perfectly straight and gripped that orange in her right hand. She began playing— playing a Chopin mazurka—the one that only uses the black keys. And she played the right-hand part using the orange."

Ben stopped. Both women looked at the cop, their faces expressionless. Ancient Egyptian portraiture had more expression.

Ben let the twins and the tennis cop out.

•

We walked into the living room, and he began eagle-eyeing the credit-card receipts scattered on the table—American Express would tell him why his mother was dead. Then it hit me—those receipts would reveal Sylvia's trail through Texas. Ben had better detective instincts than I did.

I gave a depressed shrug and said I'd make dinner.

The kitchen counter extended to the middle of the room where a bowl of oranges sat. There was something brown beneath them. Sylvia's mitt? No. I pawed the citrus and found the bowl lined with shrunken dried oranges. I fingered a few and they had the density of Ping-Pong balls.

I started to search for her mitt. If Sylvia had left it behind, it meant she intended to return home from Texas—she'd never deliberately drive into a canal without her glove.

The cupboards were filled with stacks of warped plastic dishware. Either Sylvia ordered her plates from Nevada bomb sites or she had never mastered her dishwasher. I opened that appliance, but it was empty. On the counter above stood three thin glass boxes containing assorted widths of spaghetti. They were a housewife's version of Cornell boxes—postcards were placed in the pasta. Each was of Venus Di Milo. Where was Emily? Sylvia once told me that Joseph Cornell had been a furious Dickinson freak, and had dedicated dozens of his boxes to her poems. I assumed Sylvia's boxes honored his honor.

While I cased the kitchen, Ben did some serious banging: a closet slammed; a chest yanked opened—shoved shut; another closet. Ignoring his noise, I prowled and found the Mescal. Then I checked the refrigerator. Blue light spilled out. Sylvia had installed a tear-shaped Christmas bulb. I smiled. See her wrapped in a kimono raiding the fridge at 3 a.m. See the stalks of blue celery, blue chicken, blue Bud. But no blue glove.

•

After dinner, the phone rings. Ben scrambles from the other room over furniture to dash down the hall and answer in the bedroom. I tiptoe to the door and hear: "No, Dad . . . Yeah, Dad . . . There's nothing here . . . Right . . . Right . . . Right. I'll burn it . . . Right . . . Yeah, he's staying out of the way . . . It's okay."

I lean against the wall pinching my brow.

Ben just agreed to burn his mother's thesis.

•

It was dark. We walked to Lake Ponchartrain in the drizzle, both of us dressed like scarecrows in baggy trench coats and fishing caps we'd found in a closet. Beneath his arm, he carried Sylvia's *Emily* sealed in a freezer bag. He wasn't going to burn it after all. He planned to take it to the shore and sink the pages beneath the water, the way his mother was lost beneath the water in Texas.

"How come you haven't tried to talk me out of this?" he asked.

"Your mother never finished the thing," I said. "Just stashing it away in a closet preserves its unfinished condition. Better to lose it than preserving her failure." I gave a pause. "Whatever . . . there's just no way I'd be the one to sail it away."

"You're not her son," Ben replied.

We reached the top of the levee where a railroad track curved, and beyond—Lake Ponchartrain, a black, flat expanse fading into the mist. Houses stood on ratty wharfs reaching far into the water. We followed the track. We were soon passing through mosquitoes so thick that if we left our mouths open we could inhale our body-weight. For a dozen paces we were swatting and silent, until Ben began laughing at the mosquitos with genuine warmth. Then he choked and cascaded into a crying jag. My first impulse was to hold him, but I just kept walking. He finally said, "At her funeral I stood at the podium. Everyone assumed I was going to read some Dickinson poem. Instead, I read from a draft of Mom's thesis." Ben paused and recited from memory: " '. . . the ache of Emily Dickinson was that no matter how many poems she bore into the world she never had a child, and a child is worth all the poems ever written.' "

At that moment we heard a distant train. We backed away to prepare for the Sylvia Wait. Soon the train was pounding before us. The wheels were really sucking me towards the track, so I turned to Ben, intending to signal him to move further back—but he was crouching, his outstretched arm gripping the thesis like a discus. Suddenly, he whipped his arm—using Arm Language his mother would have died to see—and spun *An Analysis of Spherical Symbolism in the Verse of Emily Dickinson* into an open boxcar.

•

Sylvia had sat on this chair. Sylvia had hung her rain slicker on this hook. Sylvia had played her scratched Phoebe Snow albums on this turntable, the bass cranked down and the treble on maximum. With each object I packed, I felt closer to Sylvia and farther from Ben's pitching stance.

I was so demoned out I started single-handedly humping her furniture aboard Ben's U-Haul, cushioning everything with pillows. Ben watched for a while, then said, "Man, you have to pack these boxes like a Chinese puzzle." I was so tunneled into myself that I cried out in alarm at the sound of his voice. He was standing by the payload holding a loop of rope like a hangman. "Cool out," he said, and then hopped in, too. His weight tilted the cabin and a book box fell. He caught it in midair. "You have to take this seriously," he said, stooping to rearrange my work. I stood, sweat pouring down my face. "You know, I hitched for a while with a guy from Brandeis," he said. "We decided to camp in Denali National Park and check out Mount McKinley. We rode a bus that left us off at the entrance where there was nothing but a wooden post with a ledger hanging from it. We were supposed to sign our names on it, the date we planned on returning, and the phone number of a relative. So we signed the thing and walked straight into the wilderness. I was surprised to discover how freaked I was at all that open space. Our first night out, I lay shaking all night. I saw how cut off from civilization and ambulances we were. But then I started surfing the terror. I mean, if I got appendicitis or something, I'd just open my Swiss Army knife and cut the fucker out. After that night, I loved the seriousness of Alaska. The guy from Brandeis and I once had to throw punches over the best way to climb a cliff—if we miscalculated, and the sun sank, we would freeze to death. I'm telling you this because you have to realize how every action is serious. The samurai say: 'Prepare for your death at every moment.' You have to load this furniture like a samurai, like it was the last action you were ever going to perform."

Ben finished this speech and shoved the final box in place and slit open the back of his hand on a metal hook. The samurai swore and jumped off the trunk, holding his hand over his head to slow the blood. The medicine cabinet was packed in one of the boxes but I tumbled down an entire stack until I found it. I fished out the bandages and followed Ben's trail of blood— samurai corpuscles arguing how to climb mountains—into the bathroom, where he was washing his wound in the sink.

The cut was long but not fatally deep. As his blood swirled down the drain, I had a Fontanelian jolt and said: "Ben, we have to drive that U-Haul to Texas. We have to stop at all the motels within 100 miles of the accident and show your mother's photograph to every desk clerk. We have to show it to every package-store clerk, and show it at every honky-tonk. We have to find out where your mother was staying. We have to find her luggage. We have to take a pilgrimage to the crash site and find out what happened. Something very bad had to have happened out there."

Ben looked up, giving me the visual equivalent of Out Jazz. He slammed the flat of his bleeding hand against the wheat-colored wallpaper and screamed, "Yeah! Something bad happened! My mother died *out there* in a car crash!"

His bandages began to unravel, and in a fury he tried to shake them off, his elbow bumping the wall switch. "And her death has broken my Dad!" he shouted, as both the lights and the bathroom air vent flicked on. The vent sucked in the edge of his bandage, snapping his hand back to the vent. The fan's engine ground to a whine. Ben grunted and with a scream of rage yanked the entire fixture out of the wall, whipping it to the floor in an explosion of plaster and tile. A spark shot out of the hole —an electric champagne cork. This was no longer Out Jazz— this was Stockhausen. Ben crouched, panting, still tied to the fan by his bandage. We were both silent. This was John Cage. Ben slowly stood, dangling the fan as if it were a weapon. He took his free hand and poked my chest, yelling, "Don't you understand anything? It doesn't matter how my mother died. She's fucking dead and Dad is walking around the house holding her earrings!"

I grabbed his wrist to stop him. Then I turned away—face burning—but made eye contact with Ben in the mirror. "Do I have to spell it out?" he said in a softer voice. "I don't want to know what my mother was doing in Texas. At first I thought, 'What if I got here sooner? What if I hadn't hitchhiked across

Wyoming—but taken a Greyhound? If I got here a week sooner would I have saved her life?' Then I realized she knew I was coming."

Ben untangled his hand from the fan. "My mother drove to fucking Texas because she knew I was coming, because the bitch couldn't bear to see me!"

Ben's hand was bleeding again—bad. I worried that a trumpet-playing nerve might be cut. He stuck the hand in a bathtowel and said, "My mother fulfilled her fucking destiny. Now I have to go on and make my own peace with that." Then he started shaking his head. "Man, you better fly back to New York. I'm sorry. You've just read too much Mickey Spillane, or whatever your fucking grandfather is called."

At that moment the doorbell rang and we both hurried down the hall.

A figure had his face pressed to the screen. When he saw us coming, he opened the door and stepped in. He was a kid our age with shoulder-length red hair and a blue bandana, lugging a backpack the size of a small trunk. Behind him, a black guitar case leaned on the porch. The redhead drawled, "Does Sylvia Cushman live here?"

Ben was trying to place him. There was that obvious Willie Nelson vibe—did this redhead have something to do with Sylvia's trip to Texas? Then I had a frightening thought—that red hair! Sylvia had a secret son in Texas!

Was this Ben's half-brother?

Ben and I just nodded at him. Yes, Sylvia Cushman lived here. The redhead reached back out the door and grabbed his guitar case. It was decorated with a Confederate-flag sticker. Without asking, he clomped into the living room. He was taller than both Ben and me, but his hiking boots gave him the three extra inches.

"I'm Jim Ocracoke," he said, peering around the living room. "Is she home?"

Ben and I shot glances at each other. There was no specific thought in my mind that made me say, "No, she's out."

"Will she be back soon?"

"Probably," Ben said.

"Boss!" he exclaimed. Then he leaned backward to remove his backpack. "She said when I got down to New Orleans I should come visit her on the banks of the old Ponchartrain."

That sounded too casual to be the words of a son. Or didn't he know Sylvia was his mother? He leaned his backpack against the wall. Then he turned, tucking in his Lynard Skynard T-shirt.

I said, "Too bad about that plane crash."

"Ronnie Van Zant. What a dude," he said, casing out the empty room. "Sylvia doesn't like a lot of furniture, does she?"

I said, "It's a Zen thing." He eyed my beer, and I asked, "You want something to drink?"

"A Pepsi if you got it," he said.

I went into the empty kitchen. The sink was filled with water and several cans of soda, beer, and a leaking milk carton that had turned the water gray. I picked out a Pepsi and shook it until the top bulged. I walked back into the living room and handed him his soda. I picked up a grease-soaked tub of fried chicken. Hidden within the bones were a few full legs left over from lunch. "Want some?" I asked.

"No thanks," he said. "I'm into macrobiotics. I mean, you know, chickens have consciousness."

"Not after you cook them," Ben said.

Macros didn't drink soda, so Ocracoke was either lying or gastronomically ignorant. But I let that go and asked, "Where'd you meet Sylvia?"

Ocracoke began tapping the lid of the soda and said, "On the entrance ramp to Route 40 outside of Flagstaff. She picked me up and we grooved the road together."

"When?" I asked.

"Last summer," he said. "I was on break from Georgia Tech, comin' back from L.A. When she dropped me off, she said I should crash with her if I got down to the Gulf Coast." He paused. "Where do you dudes know her from?"

"Hitchhiking, too," I said, my face burning in pain. Hadn't I been Sylvia's sole desert hitchhiker? Her only Orange Boy? And she had never mentioned a recent desert drive. She hid her driving from me?

"God, that lady did whirl me around," Ocracoke said, opening the Pepsi. It didn't squirt, just a light loam foamed out. He sipped it and squatted to rummage through one of the pockets in his knapsack.

"Sylvia turned me on to some heavy things," he said, pulling out a skinny paperback. He stayed on his haunches and began thumbing through the book, asking, "You guys ever hear of Emily Dickinson?" Ben and I shook our heads. I crouched to see the cover of his book. It was the Laurel edition of *The Selected Poems of Emily Dickinson*, an edition that went out of print in the mid-'60s. It had cost 65 cents. Ocracoke rubbed his chin like a scholar. "She's this poet that lived like a hundred years ago. Wow. Now this will blow your minds: '*No rack can torture me because my soul's at liberty.*' "

He took another sip of his Pepsi, then knelt to open his guitar case. Ben and I leaned against opposite walls watching. The inside of the case was lined with royal-blue felt marked with the indentations of the strings. The guitar itself looked new—the wood the color of dry sand. He pulled out the instrument, and began the fussy mechanics of tuning it. When he was satisfied, he began strumming a chord, and after a few false croaks, sang: *"This is my letter to the world/That never wrote to me/That simple news that Nature told/With tender majesty."*

I shuffled my feet. His Wonder-Bread interpretation of Emily was a travesty, but he made it worse by next flat-picking a bluesy song about the narrator driving down the road with a redheaded woman. She peels an orange. She throws the skin out the windwing. The refrain: *"Love to watch your hands on my wheel, baby. Love to watch you suck that orange."*

He abruptly stopped singing. He looked up at us. "Let me ask you guys something. Is this, like, a commune?"

Ben and I stayed silent. "No," I finally said.

He began noodling his guitar again. He looked into the carpet and said, "Look, man—I don't want to take your space, but you guys should hike out of here. I mean, Sylvia and me, well, we had a thing last summer, you know?" He stopped picking, shook his head, and grinned. "I mean, I know she's old and everything, but you don't know what it's like to stomp the peddle on the edge of a bluff while this boss old lady is going down on you."

I took a step forward from the wall, thinking, "Why have I stepped from the wall?" Perhaps I was about to do a dance, a very Latin-macho tango, although no observer would have commented, "Ah! Look! Rudolph Valentino!"—especially after I took three steps from the wall and kicked Jim Ocracoke square in the face.

To an observer, the motion of my leg would have appeared as a simple punt, but I have to tell you that I felt Ocracoke's nose cartilage through the worn rubber toe of my tennis shoe. Whenever my memory replays this afternoon, I always see it from the visual angle of a witness looking in through Sylvia's front window. In reality there was no witness, although the living room's tri-paned bay bubble was large and the front sidewalk only six feet from the house. Since no one passed by, I use author's liberties to place an old Spaniard shuffling down this sidewalk with his cane. He's wearing a black hat. He pushes the brim up as he mops his face with a handkerchief. Then he hears Ocracoke's cry. Two beats later—a horrible, horrible sound that makes the old man grab his chest. This old man is Segovia. He's just heard the smash of guitar wood, the last quiver of pulled strings—and he believes that Death's black angels are coming for him again. But when the old man presses his face to Sylvia's window, he smiles in relief. There are no black angels inside—just a young acrobat hopping on one leg, his foot stuck in the sound hole of a cheap guitar. Ocracoke's. As Ben twirls his arms for balance, I grab his side so he can shake the damn guitar off his boot. The thing flies into the wall and bangs out a final anguished chord.

Now we have a different witness. See the fat beer-bellied Bavarian in his mangy leather jacket. As of this writing, Rainer Werner Fassbinder is dead, but he outlived Sylvia, and he had been one of her idols in the Chateau days. See us as he sees us—three strapping boys, all in T-shirts, the one with long red hair holding his hands to his nose.

Because Ben and I spent all morning humping boxes together, we were as attuned as ballet partners. Ocracoke was too distracted by his nose to immediately understand what was happening when Ben and I both began beating him—not with our fists, of course, but with Sylvia's unpacked objects, objects I'll name later. And with each of our smacks to the redhead, our witness —appreciating the erotic possibilities of this primitive punishment—beat his own arm in the air, panting, "Ja. Ja. Ja."

And as Ben beat away, I myself did not pant, "Ja. Ja. Ja." I laughed as I recalled a particular painting hanging in The Met —a medieval triptych of the Crucifixion whose first panel depicts the scourging of Christ. I recalled the sneer of the petty bureaucrat whipping the Germanic Christ. And now, here was Ben beating Ocracoke, the only difference being that Ben was no bureaucrat beating a state's displeasure into a Messiah. Ben was forcing any love Ocracoke felt for Sylvia to rise above this kid's disrespect. Perhaps there is a bakery term that describes beating a mixture to make the sediment rise. Or a winery term. But simply put—Ben was smacking sweet holy love into Ocracoke's ass. I felt the current and grabbed Ben's arm to say something that wouldn't have been out of place in some New York group-therapy session, some meeting place far from Freud and closer to psychobabble. I said, "Ben, I loved your mother. But I haven't felt that I could express my pain here because it would interfere with yours."

He looked down at me, panting. I'd never seen anything—man or dog—pant like that before. His arm shook. He dropped his book. His arm was jammed with electricity. General Electric

Arm Language. He held his vibrating hand up to his face and closed his eyes and said, "I know. I know that."

He then ran to Ocracoke's guitar and snatched it up. Several strings were still attached to the neck. In fury, Ben took a rocker's position and madly strummed the thing with his vibrating hand. Because most of the guitar's soundboard was smashed, Ben's strumming was more percussive clicking than full-bodied power chords. As Ben tortured that guitar, I wished I could have placed Sylvia as the witness at the window. I won't immediately name the new witness, because his presence will seem hopelessly kitsch, not tragic. But I remember getting home late one night during that infamous Blackout/Son of Sam summer, and finding Sylvia sitting with her head in her arms at the kitchen table. I assumed she was stoned and drummed my fingers on the table, saying in that particularly snotty voice that only 18-year-olds can master, "Hey! Wake up! Elvis Presley just died on the potty tonight!" And Sylvia raised her head. Her eyes were the color of Mercurochrome, her entire face wet. And even then it didn't occur to me that she was weeping about Elvis. I had never seen *Jail House Rock*. To me, Elvis was only a fat Las Vegas lounge act. Dean Martin's brother. I didn't understand that Elvis had only swelled up like Emily Dickinson. I couldn't see that Sylvia's youth had, in fact, "died on the potty" that night. She was crying for Elvis the way she had cried in 1955 for that deformed boy faked as James Dean.

And now in New Orleans, Ben, her son, began furiously strumming a broken guitar, possessed with the same snake of energy and joy that had been darting through the ages—or at least since the 1950s—and this snake swallowed Sylvia's son whole, even as it had once swallowed Elvis himself, who now—unseen by *The National Enquirer*—stood at the window witnessing Ben wail his Kaddish with the same incredible energy of *Jailhouse Rock*, strumming and screaming: "My mother is dead! My mother is dead! And I'm so angry! And I'm so ashamed."

Ben sang this over the atonal chug-chug of the guitar while he jumped on the carpet and our final witness replaced Elvis at the window.

You probably wouldn't have recognized her, this centenarian—but she is Frances Steloff, the founder of the Gotham Book Mart, the most renowned bookstore in New York, the woman who first promoted James Joyce in this country so long ago. Why is she here? Because—although we are not using Joyce (or Henry Miller for that matter)—we are beating Ocracoke with Sylvia's books. Ben had taken a thick Abrams on O'Keeffe and hit the redhead on the shoulders. As he arched backwards, I slapped his belly with a smaller hardcover. And I assure you (as I later assured Frances) that the boy wasn't being hurt as much as scared shitless by the thumps and muffled smacks of our tomes against his torso. Remember, books can bruise, but they don't break the skin. If you are a parent—I hear the experts are recommending corporal punishment again . . . consider raising a book against your child—perhaps even this one! But let me confess: I wasn't paying attention to titles I used. I'd like to joke that I was using *Against Interpretation* but it was more likely something innocuous like a thesaurus. Yet when my heart was no longer into beating Ocracoke, I became a librarian, and ran to Sylvia's book box to search for a more suitable weapon—a weapon Sylvia could get behind.

When I found the title I wanted, I rushed back to Ocracoke and took whopping swings of The *Collected Poems of Emily Dickinson* to finish slapping him into sainthood. Slapping him into the higher faith of Sylvia. Slapping him into a Holy Orange Boy.

PART SIX

TAR PITS

walked with Fassbinder to the Ponchartrain. We discussed
Fritz Lang, the film director who fled Hitler to Hollywood and
invented film noir. Fassbinder asked if I'd ever seen the 1919
silent film *The Cabinet of Dr. Caligari*—Lang wrote the script.
"Of course!" I said, and told the story how after his trials, Fatty
Arbuckle cloistered himself in his mansion, watching *Caligari*
over and over. Arbuckle believed that deep inside his fat, a thin
man was sleepwalking.

Fassbinder smiled, and told me how Lang had been originally
scheduled to direct *Caligari*—". . . but the producer gave it to
another. Lang's original title had been *The Cabinet of Dr. California.*"

We returned to the houses. These streets were lined with trees,
and above the blowing leaves filtered the sound of a trumpet.

Ben. I stopped in astonishment. He had transcended the confused pain of his mother's death and blew with the humble out-of-tune quality of a child first learning to play the instrument. There was a brief silence, then he began diddling arpeggios, those monotonous little herdings of notes up and down the scale. Ben's deliberately clumsy tone made his playing sound humble, as if God had asked Glenn Gould to play the piano, and Gould used his elbows—signifying how pointless his talent was. Then I looked up and beyond the trees saw the lit window of a second-story apartment. A little boy stood blowing his trumpet behind a music stand. These were the arpeggios of an innocent.

Fassbinder left, and I walked alone to Sylvia's. In the setting sun, I saw that the U-Haul was gone, nothing left on the pavement but a little valentine of oil. I ran inside. Ben was gone. Ocracoke was gone. The only backpack left on the floor was mine. Sylvia's house was empty except for Ben's trumpet smashed in the bathtub, the bell beaten flat—Daffy Duck lips.

When I rechecked the kitchen, I found an envelope with three hundred dollars in traveler's checks along with this note in Ben's scrawl: "Catch a flight back to New York."

I walked to the front porch. A mailman whistled up. "Late delivery," I remarked. "Folks like to get their mail after the sun goes down," he said and handed me Sylvia's, stuffed inside a rolled *The New Yorker*. A dog pranced by. When she saw I gripped the basic contour of a rolled-up newspaper, she slunk away, glancing over her shoulder. I swatted *The New Yorker* against my free palm, then left Sylvia's—just leaving the front door open. To this day, surely her apartment has remained the way I left it, and when you finish this book, you'll tour Sylvia's like Emily Dickinson's home—Sylvia's door perpetually left open, her windows, too—the carpet below rotting from rain. And as you wander through the empty rooms you won't find plastic runners, or plastic-coated furniture, or a fat white dress sleeved in plastic. Sylvia's condo stays empty of artifacts. Except, lean in the bathroom. Look in the bathtub. Ben's Daffy Duck trumpet lies in a police evidence bag.

•

I bought myself an automobile at the Billups Station down the street—behind the pumps sat a dozen junkers with prices soaped on the windows. I still had a lot of New York dough, so my financial resources were pushing $450. There was one vehicle in this range—a dented 1969 Oldsmobile with "$350" soaped on the windshield. If that car had the ability of self-reflection, it would have seen itself as a piece of modern sculpture, a masterpiece of color and texture with its faded green paint job the color of lime chiffon, its hood of burnished metal reflecting the color spectrum like an oil slick. The car would also see that the dwarfs of irony had rubbed their paws on its bumper leaving this sticker: HONK IF YOU LOVE JESUS. The car would also feel its wound—the under-edge of the vehicle a continuous tear of rust the texture of fried chicken. Raymond Chandler once carped about Ross Macdonald's writing style, complaining that Macdonald described an auto as "acned with rust" instead of the less pretentious "spotted with rust."

Neither seems the height of descriptive language. Looking at my Olds I considered my addition to literature: Shake 'n Baked with rust.

This car begged me to drive it to give meaning to its existence, the way a dog can survive without us, but needs us for purpose. And I didn't choose this vehicle for transportation as much as I chose it to be my companion. And it was. The car became my companion for a short portion of this story the same way Lew the German shepherd was. Which reminds me—let me tell what happened to Lew after he was resurrected by Sylvia's voice. It bears nothing to the story, yet I won't leave loose ends.

I donated Lew to The Beacon, a hotel for the blind on 23rd Street. At this moment he's trotting beside some angel-faced blind girl, teaching her to cane.

I remember as I left the hotel, an ice cream truck pulled up jingling its song. The blind were soon clustered at the curb calling out their requests. I looked over my shoulder and saw Lew sitting calmly at the doors, watching. It was then I understood how Sylvia could leave Lester in Michigan, leave the child in paternal limbo. As for me, I decided I'd get over Lew the same way Sam Spade got over Brigid O'Shaugnessy. And then I reached for ice cream.

•

slept in my new Olds beside the levee. The next morning I
navigated northwest out of New Orleans, trying to give myself
over to the car's herky-jerky steering. At first I thought it was
my poor driving that generated all those honks, until I figured
out that so far fifteen people signaled that they too loved Jesus. I
passed a clump of hitchhikers and yearned to see Ocracoke
standing with outstretched thumb—but I assumed he was now
hitching and combusting in some firmament, then calling out
for Sylvia and reigniting at the glory of her name.

By noon, I needed a reading fix and pulled out Sylvia's mail-roll
to get *The New Yorker*, figuring I'd make do with one of those
stories that read as if the last page-and-a-half had been removed
(when I passed a Stuckey's, I'd buy a Travis McGee). As I fiddled
with the rubber band, an envelope flipped up into the draft. I
caught it against the wheel. It only took one glance at the return
address to begin bughouse driving—tailgating dangerous semis,
flipping my signals on and off.

Sylvia had just received an envelope from the Tabernacle of the
Speckled Bird.

When I calmed, I used my teeth to tear open the stamped side,
and shook out four pages of official church stationery. Sylvia had
just received a letter from my mother.

I swerved. I got horn-smears from traffic. The blood drained
from my lips and you could have done the dishes with my face.
The fact that Sylvia and my mother corresponded seemed as

potentially apocalyptic as blindly shooting two uranium atoms at each other, equal to Samuel Allison's trying to smash atoms in an abandoned squash court located directly beneath the football field of the University of Chicago in 1941. If he had succeeded, Chicago would have been blown flatter than a flounder. My mother's correspondence blew my spirit flatter than a flounder.

•

Dear Mrs. Cushman,

In these days, I do not have the time or strength to answer the hundreds of letters that are sent to Me. However, My secretary showed Me your letter and I knew the Holy Ghost had guided your hand to write Me. I am sitting at My doctor's and he is pumping holy honey into My blood. This process takes one hour and I will use this time to dictate My reply.

I will get to the point. Dear woman, it is never too late to wash your hands of Satan. You opened your heart to Me, telling Me of the Satanic Influence of your husband. How My heart is with you! On television, I do not wear My own painful past on My sleeve, so you might not know what I am about to tell you: My late husband also hunched in Satan's shadow. I was a silly girl when I married him. By society's lax standards, I would have been considered an innocent. But let me tell you, had My husband and I crashed together in an auto accident, Satan would have pulled us both down to Hell by our ankles. I was as damned as My husband was because I had not yet had a Personal Experience with Jesus. And I believe Jesus allowed Me a godless marriage as a reference for later life, much as He has allowed your godless marriage for you.

Know that every husband, even a God-fearing one, is an

instrument of Satan. I cannot state this strongly enough. Because you are a married woman, I will get to the point—the human male organ is Satan's thing. Now, do not cast this letter down and think that I am one of those poor women terrified of sexual intercourse!

Remember, in Genesis 1:26 God said, *"Let Us make man in Our image, after Our likeness . . ."* But read in Matthew 1:20, *"Be not afraid to take Mary as your wife, for what is conceived in her is from the Holy Spirit."* Now, if man is made in God's image, why did our Lord impregnate the Virgin Mary using the Holy Spirit? Also, Jesus was a man, but Scriptures clearly tell us He did not exercise man's option to copulate like a dog. As for women—even though the Holy Lord did not need an organ to give child, the Female Opening is still a blessed thing. There is no other way for the child to have exit from the Mother. Now, let Me jump ahead to the Rapture and to further explain My point. Just several short years after 1985 (when I open the glove compartment of Our Holy Mercury and give the world the Third Book of the Bible), the Great Satanic Beast will walk the Earth. And as Revelations 13:16 says, *"The beast will compel all, the small and the great, the rich and poor, the freeman and the slave, to have a mark put on their right hands or on their foreheads . . . Let him who has the mind for it calculate the number of the beast, for it is a man's number, and his number is 666."* Many viewers write Me pleading, "Oh help. We do not have the mind for it. We cannot calculate the number of the beast. What does it mean?" I tell them and I will tell you.

These numbers are a perversion of the Six Tiers of Heaven. I will explain: After Rapture, all females will be resurrected at the child-rearing ages. Small babies and young girls will blossom into womanhood as they are pulled into heaven. The wombs of the elderly will become fecund. A cluster of angels will dress us in beautiful white wedding gowns, and place delicate white veils woven of diamonds on our heads. We will become the Brides of Jesus. We will kneel before Him and He shall rain a Shower of Gold upon us and our fruit will become ripe with His Daughters.

As we go through our gestation period, all resurrected Christian men will appear before our Savior. Jesus shall raise His hand and the men's bodies shall be smoothed over. I don't mean castration as if these men were gelded stallions, I mean a painless smoothing over like a knife smoothing frosting on a cake. Oh what joy these men will feel! To be finally free of the flesh that made them seek out those abominations of flesh, and made them kneel before women, and sometimes provoke such a frenzy that they could even copulate with each other. And what simple joy they will feel to be able to calmly sit and contemplate the clouds, the breeze. And in that peace, the Men of Jesus will get Seeds of Light.

After this Transformation, we Brides of Jesus will give birth to the Daughters of Jesus. And when our Daughters reach the age of 16, the Christian men will rain golden seed upon the girls. Our Daughters will then give birth to the second generation of Angels. The eternal population of Heaven will now be complete!

God will now divide Heaven into Six Tiers: The Holy Trinity will sit and rule from the First and highest Tier. The Angels, such as Michael, shall sit on the Second Tier, close within earshot of their Masters. The Brides of Jesus will live on the Third Tier. We will be the closest members of humanity to God. Below us, on the Fourth Tier, the Daughters of Jesus will wait on us, their Mothers. The men of Jesus will live on the Fifth Tier. There they will happily toil, growing grain and tending sheep. And finally, the second generation of Angels will live on the Sixth Tier. They will be the watchguards over the barrier between Heaven and the damned, who will swim forever in the stink pits of Hell.

Now, Heaven will have elevators and such, so we can visit

each Tier. But it is important to realize there are Tiers and you are assured a high position in our Heavenly Reward. As a Bride of Jesus, you will be the closest to the hem of His gown. Closer than you can imagine.

And so, please take care, use the wisdom I have blessed down to you wisely, and continue to watch Me on television.

Sincerely Yours In
Jesus Our Lord, Amen—

•

finished the letter and pulled off the road beside a billboard mysteriously proclaiming "Best Boudin!" I got out of the car and watched the red children's-hour light sweep across the swamp—the terrain itself reminding me of 1967 *Newsweek* photos of Vietnam. As the traffic whizzed behind me, I was consumed with a sadness that was classic like Greek tragedy. To me, if a woman begged relief from my mother, then that woman was so irrevocably hopeless that she would be better off dead. Yes! A woman would be better off dead than to stuff my mother in her belfry . . .

In short, it was a blessing that Sylvia Cushman was dead.

With cold fear noodling my guts, I started wigwagging down the highway. You see, I realized: despite Sylvia's craziness in regard to my mother, I was the one who actually slid screaming out from the woman's womb, and thus her crazy genes would always be a trellis between us. It felt as if at any minute Mom's snakes would crawl up that lattice to eat my roses . . .

I whipped into the parking lot of the Hungry Cajun—which proved to be a glorified Howard Johnson's with Tabasco sauce splashed on everything, even the coffee.

Before I paid, I asked a waitress, "What's 'boudin'?"

Why honey, she said, blood sausage. It's good.

•

Around midnight, I came upon a pulsating string of police lights. A roadblock. As I approached, my stomach twisted with a premonition that Ben's U-Haul had become a twisted wreck—an irrational fear since the northbound route to Michigan was miles behind me.

As it turned out, a derailed train had spilled noxious chemicals in the swamp, and traffic was being routed off I-10 to a county two-lane. I followed the detour through a grove of cyprus draped in moss. In my high-beams, it was like driving through a tunnel of Brillo pads. I yawned and fuzzed-out at a fork in the road, and went straight instead of left. As I slowed, searching for a spot to make a U-turn, my headlights illuminated a large white slab radiating from the shoulder—a pure geometrical object of luminosity. Lot's wife. A pillar of salt. It was Sylvia Cushman's refrigerator.

•

slammed my brakes and fishtailed off the road, smashing my rear against a nut tree. I sat, pecans raining on the roof. I opened my door. My legs were rubber—Cabbie's Polio. Using the side of the car for support, I staggered to my car's now rumpled tail, then stumbled fifty feet down the gravel to the refrigerator. Sound was a peculiar sensation. For hours there had been nothing in my head but tire music, but now I heard the chant of nocturnal insects, the shuffling of my sneakers. Only a hangnail moon hung above the trees and the terrain was dark. The shoulder followed an incline which sloped into a black expanse—wetlands—a surface reflecting rippling slivers of moonlight while flecks of flame flickered. The swamp was crowded with smokers tossing away their butts? Nope. The flare of fire-flies.

I approached the back of the icebox—the landlord's Frigidaire that Ben and I had packed up to steal. I circled to its door, shaking. Was Ben's body stuffed inside?

I yanked open the door. It was empty. The swift jerk of my arm made me lose my balance and slide down the bank, flailing my arms. I leapt from the incline and landed ankle-deep in cool ooze. I regained my balance and saw the silhouettes of furniture among the black-bladed ferns.

I climbed back up the hill and shook the muck off my shoes. I ran to my car, then backed down the shoulder, parking so the headlights spilled across the swamp. The frogs went silent. In the bleached glare, I saw Sylvia's chairs and Sylvia's bookcase and Sylvia's reading lamps tipped down among the ferns—Henri Rousseau meets *Better Homes and Gardens*. I slid a second time down the hill and sloshed to one of Sylvia's fake-Bauhaus chairs. I plopped down, causing the chair to sink deeper into the mud. I leaned my neck on the headrest and saw funnels of moths at the headlights. There were several passing cars, but no one stopped.

How comforting it must have been for Sherlock Holmes to saw a fiddle while contemplating a mystery. I sang a Talking Heads song, but only came up with two possibilities of what happened: (1) Ben was shanghaied; or (2) Ben totally flipped and abandoned his mother's furniture to the alligators. In both cases, Ben was heading for Texas. Ben lied when he stated he didn't care about the details of his mother's death. It had always been his intention to travel to Texas. He had just been waiting for an excuse to jettison me so he could make the journey alone.

I trudged a second time up to the shoulder. I pressed my palms to the side of the refrigerator, then shoved, and the thing tumbled over the ridge, hitting the muck with a sodden fart. I then drove the car back along the shoulder, the passing fan of the headlights revealing a billboard plastered with the inevitable: "Best Boudin!" I parked behind the sign and crawled into the immense backseat—the cushions easily six feet long, the sprawl of a queen-size bed. No wonder children had been conceived in these cars. I stretched out, but slept only in spurts, jerking awake every time those damn disembodied faces peered through the back window, now beaded with my condensed breath.

It was a bird cry that irrevocably woke me. It was still dark, but the bird kept yammering until it finally cried the sun out of the swamp. I opened the back door and sat halfway out, holding my head. I was just getting old enough to feel the need for coffee.

When the daylight finally hit, everything became relentless green. Back in the swamp, Sylvia's furniture had sunk deeper among the flora and slime—only the heads of a few chairs and the tops of the bookshelves remained. I examined the cuneiform of the various tire treads that marked the ridge, but I wasn't detective enough to read the text. I saw Sylvia's books floating in the green gruel, and slid down the ridge to retrieve them. Some of them we had used to beat Ocracoke. Most were too waterlogged to be saved. Farewell *Emma*. Farewell *Jane Eyre*. Farewell *Mrs. Dalloway*.

I was setting the few salvageable ones open on the backseat to dry, when I heard a car pull up—the opposite side of the billboard. I froze. A door slammed. Below the sign was a rotted wooden latticework, where I knelt and peeked at the blue car parked twenty feet away, its engine ticking. The driver stood farther down the shoulder. Sweat marked the spine of his mustard polo shirt, and he kept raising his hands up to his face. Ah, he was holding a camera. A reporter? He turned in profile for a moment, then slid down the hill. He had a nondescript face and a nondescript haircut, yet he looked vaguely familiar. When he disappeared, I ran up to his car. Michigan plates. I tried to open the driver's door as quickly and quietly as possible, all the while darting my eyes back and forth to the embankment. I leaned over the front seat, which was littered with MacDonald's bags, a

Louisiana road map, and some cassette tapes. I glanced at the tape labels—not music but lectures: *How to Win Friends and Influence People*. A tube of hemorrhoid medicine lay half-curled on top of the dash. I leaned farther into the car and opened the glove compartment.

What I found made me shake with excitement. I felt like I did when I explored the Cushmans' bedroom and discovered Sylvia's vanilla-colored vibrator. I was excited, and also grateful—the gratitude concerning the affirmation that people actually owned such devices. Now, here in this glove compartment, I found a gun. A revolver. Big chrome. Its fat grip pink and green— rapped with rubber bands—ribbed like a lizard belly.

I heard movement and stashed the gun back in the dash. I softly clicked closed the door. The stranger's head was in view. He seemed deep in thought. I crouched. Trapped! If I dashed back to the billboard he'd spot me. He crunched toward the car so I scuttled stooped to the grille. The car swayed as he climbed in. I continued scuttling clockwise to the passenger side, then stopped. I studied the front tire. As soon as it rolled, forward I'd jump down the embankment so I wouldn't be spotted in the rearview mirror. But then the car swayed toward me. Was he leaning to open the passenger door? No. He must be getting his gun from the glove compartment . . . The car rocked again and I heard his shuffle on the gravel. Then silence. I glanced under the car and saw his muddy brown loafers. Was he poised with his gun —his hands firmly on the rubber-banded grip? I envisioned him slinking around the car—us playing ring-around-the-rosey. I waited and waited. He just stood there. I finally darted my head up to the passenger window.

He was facing the road. His pants were loosened. And he was applying his medicine. I only mention this because the sight of his indignity was why I recognized him. The last time I saw him, he was in New York. His face was smeared with ketchup. He was the guy Sylvia spat "tough tits Sam Spade!" to. And whether his tits were tough or not, I assumed this private detective still worked for Joshua Cushman. He was surely trying to hunt Ben down. And me.

I ducked as he turned. The car rocked again. Then abruptly the engine caught and the car drove away. I forgot to roll. The car sailed down the road and I just stayed kneeling with my mouth hanging open. When he was out of sight, I stood and raced for my Olds. The detective was heading the wrong way and I didn't want to wait for his return. I started my car and tore back down the detour. I didn't stop checking my rearview mirror until I was whizzing down a causeway that led to Texas.

•

This road passed through more intense Vietnamese terrain—rice paddies stretching to the flat horizon. I tried reading Sylvia's books while I drove, but too many had pages stuck together. By midmorning, the car had gotten so warm the wet books began to smell. When the pages were completely dry and contracted, the books began crinkling in the backseat as if someone were reading. I reached behind me and stacked them all on the front seat. When I was rolling along the long concrete curve that spans Lake Charles, I began pitching Sylvia's books out the window, whipping my arm with the same precision that in 1953 soldiers on their way to Korea had used to furiously throw their copies of *Dark Legs of Death*, the Rex Ringer book where my grandfather killed off Trixie. For fifteen books she had never undressed, but now in Chapter 7, just as she unbuttoned her blouse and was about to slide it down her ice-white shoulders to finally finally finally reveal the fruit of her breasts, she was shot by a jealous dwarf.

•

I now became a dark-driven Huck Finn, my somber soul my Nigger Jim, leadfooting it through a swamp-pancake geography, driving dazed, drunk on driving—mumbling to myself. Half a day passed before it hit me that my car had penetrated Texas. The pickups still had gun racks but their license plates changed from white to black and this philosophy inflamed their bumpers: COWBOY HATS ARE LIKE HEMORRHOIDS/SOONER OR LATER EVERY ASSHOLE GETS ONE.

For the next two days, I drove down a two-lane so flat I could have rolled a bowling ball beside my car. And the supine geography began whitewashing my mind—nothing was real. I stared at my brow in the rearview mirror, wondering, "Is that me? Is that me?" Bugs hit the windshield and exploded into raindrops.

With the next dawn, the sky turned translucent green as a funnel cloud crossed the highway. It was distant. Unreal. A black intestine between God and Texas. Thirty seconds later a cow fell and bounced on the blacktop. I swerved and kept going.

By 4:00, a string of water glared on the horizon. Ten minutes later, I braked at the shore's shoulder, but miscalculated my speed, hurling my chest into the wheel. When the dust settled, I climbed out. The ground instantly wobbled up and down. I had been driving so long that anything stationary was visually overwhelming. I knelt in the road until I regained my balance. Then I staggered to the water. The black-and-white-striped road wickets were sheared off along the left lane. The air smelled faintly of manure, but I saw no livestock. I stood and stared into the brown water. This was the canal where Sylvia had drowned.

I contemplated the surface but that didn't get me anywhere—no woman's hand came up holding a sword or typewriter. This spot seemed such a nondescript place to die. I felt no psychic fallout. Then a cattle truck lumbered up the road, and as it got closer, I saw the gridded payload was filled with mice—mice the size of children. The truck passed. The driver waved. And here was Sylvia's little joke: The truck was loaded with kangaroos.

·

That image would be gratuitously surreal if I didn't leap ahead to tell you that down the road was Pattullo's Ostrich Farm. Later, a gas jockey explained to me that many Texans were raising Australian livestock. That gave me a new hypothesis about Sylvia's crash: Sylvia is driving in the dark, lost, the overhead light lit as she tries to steer and unscramble the road map spread open beside her. Ahead of her appear the taillights of a slow-moving truck. Suddenly, her headlights reflect dozens of luminous eyes. The clouds part and in the moonlight, Sylvia sees the truck is full of kangaroos. She leans her forehead against the wheel as she laughs Emily's: *I am the only kangaroo among the beauties.* Sylvia is charmed out of her mind. She follows the truck, this moonlight mirage. Then clouds cover the sky. The road curves. She's going too fast. Her hood is slicing through the black water.

And as for the canal glaring below me, I stripped and jumped in. The water was no colder than a swimming pool. The water tasted dank, so I didn't open my eyes. This canal was supposedly shallow, but the pressure was strong in my ears. I frog-kicked down until my palms pressed jelly. This was the zero-center of fecundity—not so much a "shit hole"—but the birthplace of germs . . . no, not germs—microscopic life, as if a paramecium from this water could sprout gills and warp into a fish, then grow stubby legs and crawl out of the water and wander until it had reconstituted itself into a thick-browed version of Sylvia—Sylvia hunched over with dangling breasts and a tail and possessing the mind of a bright monkey, some warped Darwinian cycle starting all over in the empire of Willie Nelson and 'roos.

I felt an object in the muck and grabbed it, kicking up to the surface. I treaded water with one arm and with the other held up a baseball mitt. Several weeks in the canal has discolored it to the tone of a rotting banana.

I crawled out of the canal with the blackened mitt, and leaned naked against the car. The metal was hot, but didn't burn. I contemplated the slipper my drowned Cinderella had left behind. It was waterlogged and barely held its shape. But God damn! This mitt had once slipped over the fingers of Sylvia's left hand! I put the mitt against my forehead. I placed the mitt to my lips, but it tasted rank—a big batch of hepatitis. I lowered it and slid my penis under its tongue like a Fidrych codpiece. I was no necrobaseballist—I just wanted to communicate with Sylvia however possible.

I ended up whipping the mitt over a barbed wire fence.

Then I got dressed and drove away.

•

Oh forbid that any lost and weary traveler washes ashore in Braintree! Its metropolitan area consists of an abandoned gas pump, and one lone phone booth with gray dusty glass—the booth where Sylvia spoke her last message to me concerning dogs and the holy.

See the remainder of the local scenery—a handful of shotgun shacks scattered beyond the lip of a gravel pit. A green battered statue of some rebel saint. An armadillo squashed into a wedge at the curb. A pack of dogs chasing something in a distant tire yard.

I drove up and down the farm roads searching for some sign of Sylvia. What would have brought her out here? I wasn't sure what to look for. A billboard with an inadvertent reference to Emily? A motel with a turquoise kidney that Sylvia did a string of breast strokes across?

I spread my road map beside me but it was incomprehensible here. I just steered towards the sunset, passing nothing but fields of grasshopper pumps. The only human I saw was an old man plowing a field with a tractor outfitted with a shotgun rack. As the sun slipped down, I topped the crest of a hill and saw hints of civilization—on the other side of a black river stood a mall. Floating above one of the roofs was an illuminated pizza. My road shadowed the river and I drove searching for a bridge. A one-eyed pickup sped by, almost running me off the road. A bottle was thrown. A voice screamed a sentiment that I assumed was generated by my Louisiana plates: "Go back home, coonass!"

The road I was speeding down was soon pitch dark. This coonass only blinked for a moment, but suddenly a figure was scorched in my headlights, standing smack on the yellow line. I swerved, slamming on my brakes. Footsteps. Knuckles on the window. I rolled down the glass. An Arab stood there. He was gripping a small machine gun. He leaned in and calmly demanded, "Where is the pizza, boy?"

•

I'll add one of those bullet-division marks, because there's no smooth way to explain an Arab with a machine gun demanding pizza. I sat in total confusion, until I recognized him. Najaf's uncle's bodyguard. The TV freak. Moq. As I recognized him, he was squinting, trying to recognize me.

"Moq," I said. "I'm here for Najaf."

And as I spoke her name, I knew Najaf was about to reenter my life as if this moment were a chapter in a book I was writing. But then, this is a chapter in a book I'm writing. As I sat behind the wheel, I postulated: Najaf never went Swiss-side. For some geo-political reason, her father had her hiding down in this godforsaken place. This was why Sylvia came to Texas—the two were palling around.

My moment of clarity expanded to the present: Moq knew my arrival was only good for trouble and he was coolly considering shooting me. Ah, but I was born the fortunate traveler—another pair of headlights appeared in the opposite lane.

Moq turned, then shook his fist, "You're late, boy!"

The lights were glaring in my eyes. This new vehicle looked like a pickup. A pudgy silhouette walked into the headlights—a sow-faced kid holding a pizza box. Moq took it with one hand and struggled in his jeans for his wallet while the pizza draped dangerously out—grease-box, soft clock. Moq paid and walked over to the passenger side, then climbed in uninvited. The other driver stood in the pool of light counting the money. When he finished, he yelled, "Try tipping you sumbitch maybe you git it sooner!"

The Arab placed the pizza box between us and stuck his head out his window, yelling in impeccable Americanese: "Fuck you, pin dick! Your prick is covered with shit from fucking your mother up the ass!"

The driver wedged his upper body into the open window of his vehicle, and jerked back into the light holding a ridiculously small rifle. Reflexively, I had my car zooming in reverse. There was a flash, and simultaneously my windshield frosted into a sheet of cracked glass. The shot sounded like the bang of a ball in a bowling alley. The shooter's vehicle backed and sped off. Moq began hooting, slapping his knee.

I turned. "Did I miss something?"

The Arab wiped his eyes and said, "I love that guy." Then he jiggled through another giggle. Finally he said, "One day one of us will die—but it will be him." He held his machine gun up and sang, "Bang. Bang. Shoot. Shoot." Then he added, "This is the only pizza for fifty miles. Of course it's not as good as Famous Original Ray's."

I stuck my head out my window and drove forward. At this point getting the windshield rocksalted was par for the course. Even Alice eventually stopped saying "Curiouser and curiouser," and just played a mean game of flamingo croquet. Near the curve of the road was a chainlink gate. The Arab wedged the pizza on top of the dash—a welcome smell! Will he offer me a slice?— and jumped out of the car. The Arab unlocked the gate, then waved me forward. I drove through. He relocked the gate and climbed back in. I bumped us down a rutted road surrounded by the black silhouettes of oil derricks. Soon the air was filled with a double smell of burning rubber and a distinct animal stink. That killed it for the pizza.

As I drove I was erect, erect with excitement—I was driving into the solution of this mystery. I was entering the City of Knowledge. We were slowly driving toward a ridge, glowing faintly. At first, boulders obscured the view, but then I saw a two-story farmhouse and barn surrounded by four tall arc lights. The farm was lit as bright as a night game in a baseball field. As the car wound down the hill, I saw the farm was surrounded with what looked like little wandering pillows. By the barn, a Cadillac was parked—an older opulent model—and in the center of the yard stood a single scrubby tree, its leaves bleached in white glare. An animal smell made my eyes water. When we got closer, I saw the pillows were, in fact, chickens—hundreds of chickens.

No City of Knowledge . . . just the Locus of Poultry.

•

S hould I narrate chronologically like Tim Fontanel? That private eye would have tossed the farmhouse with the logical progression of a Chesty Morgan striptease. He would surely remark on the schizophrenic housekeeping—some rooms clean as a whistle; others a wreck. He'd go to the kitchen and note the peeling weeping-willow wallpaper, yellow stains, cabinets sagging, a tin sink crammed with petrified plates of food. He'd enter the long hallway—as spit-polished as a bowling lane. To the right: Moq hunched over a plastic tray lapping pizza, glazing at something laugh-tracked on TV.

Tim turns to the first floor bathroom. It has a porcelain sink and tub rounded like melons, giving the room an intimate, private feeling. The room is messy, however: hundreds of dried droplets on the mirror, crusty floor. A single tooth lies in the sink. Although recognition is impossible for Tim, I will know this tooth. It's Sylvia's. I recognized her filling.

I walked upstairs and found books lining the second-floor hallway. They were the same authors as in Sylvia's New Orleans library, but they were not battered *a la Ocracoke*. Their endpapers and deckles had been scribbled on with crayons—many signed by Lester. These books were from Sylvia's old Michigan library.

The upstairs bathroom was wet and mildewy. Another wonderful old tub squatted there on polyp feet. Above the empty toilet-paper dispenser someone had traced their palm with a black Magic-marker. Below they wrote: The Arab Hand.

Next door was Moq's room—Spartan, clean; a mat, a pile of folded clothes, and taped to the wall—a photo of a general at a podium, the Shah behind him. Below this photo, a footlocker. I opened it. Inside was a complete arsenal—guns, knives, and bombs casually tossed together like playthings in a toybox. For the first time in my life I held a hand grenade. Oh, angry fruit! There were also several James Bondish pistols—elegantly black, gleaming like porcelain. No rubber bands around their grips.

I admit that I've surely exhibited cultural bias, even racism, in my picture of Moq. What kind of Arab was he? What was his childhood like? Had he ever been a hashish boy? Was he even a Moslem? The only intimate insight I had into this man—who, the next morning, was literally to have his head blown off, thus making his character traits irrelevant—was the fact that beside his bed mat were stacks of *TV Guide*. On each page he had noted his viewing strategies with numbers, underlines, and arrows.

•

On the other side of the upstairs bathroom was room that gave off a female vibe. I entered whispering, "Najaf. Najaf." The room was empty. I saw a narrow nun's bed, the sheets deliberately twisted into knots. Sitting on a simple wooden table was a plump porcelain water pitcher shaped like a woman's hips, glowing softly in the spotlights pouring through the window. Somewhere a clock or time bomb ticked.

•

I kept walking in and out of Sylvia's room, taking it in a little at a time. The door was in the middle of the room. Everything to the right was sane—the collected works of George Eliot in a neat row along the wall; a boom box surrounded by Deutsch-grammophone tapes—mostly Mahler. But to the left—the Arab Hand, the psychic debris: a strange formation of mescal bottles filled with curled pages of Dickinson; a pliers caked black with blood; the carpet crusted with caramel vomit. And even more bad details—a scoop in the wall level with what I approximated would have been a woman's forehead. And in the middle of this room stood a large television attached to a videotape machine. VCRs were just entering the market, and this was a clunky spooling videotape recorder, probably part of an uninstalled security system since several flat-bodied closed-circuit cameras sat in a coil of cables on the floor. I turned the TV on and tried to get the videotape to spin. I was so involved in this fiddling that I wasn't really surprised when an image abruptly flared on the screen: Mother.

This video image encompassed more than just her show—within the circumference of the TV screen was a secondary TV screen. Someone had taped my mother's show by pointing one of the surveillance cameras at the television itself. The sound had been recorded by condenser mike, so it had a compressed, claustrophobic quality. I also made this observation: When one watches television, one ceases to "see" the dial, the volume button, the antenna, etc. Yet, not only did I now notice the dials and antenna on the inner television, but it also drew my attention to the dials and antennas on the outer "real" television itself. This Magritte camerawork made it appear that my mother was broadcasting from the deeper psyche of the TV itself: my mother slouched on a slablike throne, looking as wasted as a leaking beach toy, propped up by three large sickle-moon crutches, chanting, "Jesus, Jesus, Jesus," as wailing women walked up bundling babies. With a new camera angle, I noted the first cameraman was a small boy peering through his viewfinder on tiptoes. Then a new shot and my mother is burying her face in baby bellies as if they were slices of watermelon. She rocks back and forth grunting until each baby begins to cry. The camera then scans the audience: women with bouffants raising their arms enraptured; men pinching the tops of their noses, weeping. A dignified Chicano solemnly steps up, holding a little limp girl to his chest. The child's legs dangle. Her Mary Janes shine.

Beneath her curls, her neck hangs so bent there's no mistaking that this child is dead. My mother grabs that little girl and then rocks back and forth, puckering her lips into the girl's ear. Whispering. Suddenly—an abrupt peal of a dissonant organ. The little girl's arm begins a palsied spasm. Gasps from the audience. The girl's legs begin jerking. The camera zooms as her eyelids flicker open in terror. The little girl begins wailing and waving her arms.

My mother was, is, raising the dead. In the background, men are carrying plates of meat.

•

I waited by the downstairs TV room for a commercial, then stuck my head in the door and asked Moq where Najaf was. With his mouth full of pizza, he mumbled, "Out by the Cadillac."

Outside, the chickens were circling the Caddy with their goofy mechanical strut. Under a stark tree, I saw the figure that had been standing here all along. Not that I could have readily recognized Najaf—she was wearing a stained white hooded robe. Tim Fontanel would say, "From the back, she resembled a Druid searching for a laundromat." Najaf's carriage was frail. She turned slowly and registered me with dead eyes. Then she squinted, trying to place me. Here was the once healthy girl who'd played catch on a Manhattan roof, now as bleached as a silent-film heroine—Mary Pickford trapped on an ice floe. I walked up and hugged her. She slumped in my arms, all sharp pelvis and scapula. Her robe was a ratty terry-cloth poolrobe stained with blood and dirt. I pulled back and she greeted me in perfect Sylvianese: "Fish Boy."

I smiled, then Najaf sobbed, "Help me" and pointed behind her.

A picnic table stood beneath the tree, the wood weathered the color of dirty water. A few white leaves lay on the tabletop, as well as an open book. Sitting in the middle of the book was a large lizard flicking its tongue, the thing in question olive green with a horned brow and a body dotted with nubs. It watched me sideways like one of those parrot-headed turtles. Then I registered the obvious. The book. See the red ribbon, the double columns of tiny type. The lizard was perched on an open Bible. Here was the root of a common medieval *symboli*—Satan as snake as St. George's dragon. Najaf sunk to her knees and gripped my leg, pleading, "Please, please get my Bible back."

Somewhere Sylvia was surely asking: "Where is Alan Funt when you need him?"

I had been blocking an additional item found in the farmhouse, and I've duplicated my denial by withholding this same info from you. Up in Najaf's room, in her closet, were clumped piles of shoes—girl's shoes; some female foot slips into a sandle, a pump, or a mule. This is not an unusual find. Girls wear shoes. But on the sole of each shoe was written in marker: *Look at My feet. It is I myself. Touch me and see; for a ghost does not have flesh and bones. Luke 24:36.*

Out among the chickens, Najaf was barefoot. I walked to the table. The lizard arched, puffed up its head—its tongue going about eight flicks a second. As I reached out to swat the animal away, I saw the line of milky jelly glistening. This lizard had laid eggs in the crack of the Bible. In the *Book of Joshua*—(Oh, what irony!) There was something so disgusting about the lizard's filament that I gagged. There was a stick under my shoe. I reached down—several chickens going for my wrist—and picked it up. Then I stuck the end of the branch under the cover of the Bible. With a jerk, I flipped the book closed. The lizard streaked off the table, the chickens immediately swarming around it in complicated Busby Berkeley patterns. A hen emerged with the reptile awkwardly in her beak—while the other poultry gave agitated clucks. I turned to Najaf and asked a question that made sense at the moment: "Chickens have consciousness?"

Hugging the Bible, Najaf crawled atop the picnic table. She was weeping, but her tears seemed infected—the wetness circling her eyes thick as egg whites.

"Hey, come on," I said. "Are you okay?"

She didn't answer.

With the sincerity of the confused, I said: "Tell me what plane you really caught at JFK."

She knelt, wiped her face with her sleeve, tilted her head back and began cackling until her position made her choke. She fell to her ass and hugged her knees. The bottom of her robe gaped open. "It doesn't surprise me that you showed up," she said when she finished coughing. "It took you long enough to find our hideout."

Her legs were spread. I looked away and asked, "Hideout from what?"

"Satan," she said, rising to her feet. "And the usual death squads."

I kept another item from you until I reintroduced Najaf. Up in the bedroom, beside the bed, was a little nightstand littered with pharmaceutical containers. Inexplicability, the labels stated they were estrogen pills—for horses. Now Najaf pulled a similar container from her robe, and shook several mint-colored pills the size of gumballs into her palm, and popped them in her mouth. Her neck heaved as she choked them down. She looked up, her eyes flaring with their original spark, as she said: "Oh you poor boy. I can tell! You want me to be lucid!"

She paused and wiped her face with her sleeve, then asked, "Do you know, in Kentucky there is a coal bed 2000 feet deep?" She paused, letting the full implication of this question sink in. She then asked, "Do you know how much original dead vegetable material it takes to create a coal bed 2000 feet deep?"

"I don't know, Najaf. How much?"

"Dead vegetable material several miles high."

I said nothing. She beamed. "Well, what do you think creates miles of dead vegetables?"

"I don't know, Najaf."

"A great flood!" she laughed, clapping her hands. "There were giants on the earth in those days, and the sons of God cohabited with the daughters of men, who bore them children. God saw that human wickedness was growing out of bounds and washed it away. Everything is now so obvious—everywhere you look, you can see the truth of the Bible and the truth of the Lord and the truth of the flood. And it is a good, good thing."

Then, giggling, she jumped to her feet, letting her robe slide down. She swayed naked above me. The arc lights washed her ribs electric. She put her palms above her head and began wiggling her hips. Words were scrawled in Magic Marker inside her armpits. I made out: "Christ is Lord." With a demonic grin, she began jerking her hips as if spinning a hula hoop. In her own way, Najaf was using nudity to Spillanifie me from the truth.

Najaf stopped wiggling and jumped off the table. The poultry clucked away. She put one hand on her hip, and pointed at me, yelling, "Jesus doesn't say it's a sin to want to visit Graceland. No! No! No! Jesus just says, 'Why on Dad's great earth would you want to?' "

I pinched the bridge of my nose and then held my forehead. Then I lowered my hand and slugged her in the stomach.

I'd never punched anyone before. The Arm Language was alien, but somehow wonderful—her stomach a drumskin of meat. She fell on her seat, then lunged forward, gagging, holding her waist. After she caught her breath, she looked up and sneered, "You punch like a girl."

That was such a Sylvian response I didn't know whether to laugh or cry. Najaf leaned back, lying completely on her back and extending her arms above her head. "So that's what's really important to you, Fish Boy? You want to know what Sylvia was doing out here? The big truth? You want the big truth?"

Yes. I wanted the Big Truth.

•

Najaf slid her robe back on, and I followed her up a slope of dried weeds. Najaf climbed as if her bare feet had no feeling. She reminded me of Sylvia pounding shoeless across an Arizona parking lot lugging a volume of Emily Dickinson. At the top of the hill, the moonlight revealed the silhouettes of two horses. One snorted. In the middle of this field sat a large crate shaped like those suburban structures used to store trash cans. Najaf opened the lid and leaned in. As I walked over, she pulled out two gas masks.

was no Roy Rogers, but my grandfather once kept a nag in the orchard, and I learned to gallop under citrus. Najaf rode ahead of me. It was still dark and I wondered if our horses had night-vision like cats. They had no trouble trotting down a trail that to my eyes was only distinguishable as a faint gray ribbon winding through the dark. After about fifteen minutes, the skyline flamed, and in the sunrise, I saw the surrounding cowboy terrain—the sagebrush and chocolate boulders. We rode up to a plateau of grasshopper jacks and junked Studebakers—the rusted shells riddled with bullet holes. There was a pungent odor in the air that resembled road tar, only stronger. My eyes stung and it was difficult breathing. Najaf stopped her horse, and handed me a gas mask.

I strapped it on. My breathing was immediately amplified and moistened my face. I had no peripheral vision. I was suddenly a kid strapping on a Huckleberry Hound Halloween mask. Najaf slipped on the other mask and twisted a small valve under the chin-canister. I did the same. Instant warm, stale air. I got dizzy.

We rode an hour to reach the edge of the plateau. Below spread a large lake filled with black water. When the sun gleamed off its surface, it resembled a vast lake of tar. We rode down to the shore. It was, in fact, a vast lake of tar.

Parts of the surface gently bubbled around islands hardened into crusts. Although there was nothing appetizing about this geology, the crusts had the exact texture of Betty Crocker brownies. Beyond this first tar lake was a smaller one. Several bodies of cattle lay on the slick surface, their hides fantastically bloated into big blue-gray bubbles of fur. Hamburger balloons.

We rode farther to a crater ringed by oblong boulders. Little Stonehenge. At the bottom was a black surface the size of a supermarket parking lot. As our horses picked their way down the incline, mine seemed sure of itself, so I just gripped the saddle horn and shut my eyes. When I opened them, we were down at the shore. I saw the surface of this tar pit was dry. Najaf jumped off her horse and tethered its reins to a lone car bumper twisted on the shore. She walked up, then tugged my reins. My horse abruptly stopped and I tumbled over its head onto my shoulder. I stared up at the animal's belly, while willing away possible bone damage. The horse suddenly reared and displayed his horseshoes. These shoes were actually nailed into the horse's pulp! Did a blacksmith nail Christ to the dogwood?

I stood and felt creaky. Najaf pointed across the black lake. I stepped in that direction and the skin of tar gave slightly, like a wrestling mat. I took a deep breath and fogged up my gas mask. I started walking. My shoes left indentations on the surface— Hell's equivalent of walking on water. A dozen paces in, my foot squished through the skin into hot tar and I leapt back, the black gruel sizzling my sneaker, melting the sole. In the middle of the tar, something glinted. Glass. I moved closer. A huge Mason jar was embedded upright in the tar. The glass was gritted with dust, and for some reason I misread the bit of raised text as: MAN-SON. This Manson jar was large enough to hold a motel-size King James, but there was no Gospel inside. Instead—folded sheets of paper. Covered with ink, with writing. I knelt before this Manson, knees pushing the mat of tar. There were two similar indentations beside the jug. — Sylvia's knee-prints as she knelt and read. The lid was hot. I had to use my sleeve to unscrew it and remove the folded wedge of paper inside—the three sheets of stationary marked with the logo of Cushman's car company, folded into thirds. The paper was not crinkled or dogged, but the paper was hot. I'd never read text from hot paper. I've left *The Baby in the Ice Box* on a dash all day during the Dog Days of high 90s—but the pages were never this fevered. These pages were truly *parchment*. Toast.

I was convinced that Sylvia would kneel and read this letter through her gas mask. I knelt and read this letter through my gas mask.

•

Dear Sylvia,

Remember how you used to joke that my heart was black? Do you remember the night we watched the *Huntley-Brinkley Report* and they told how Christiaan Barnard had transplanted a woman's heart into a man? We joked about whose heart I had. You said Joseph Stalin and I said Louie Armstrong, and then we made love. I wanted to conceive a child, but you got on your knees and showed where to enter you. We'd never done this before. I had to reach around and feel that I really was in the other place. Suddenly you pushed me away and couldn't help it and relieved yourself on the sheets. You've said you can't remember what happened next, but you know what happened next. You know that I was so full of love that anything you did was beautiful. I held the thing because it came from inside you.

Remember when you held my head at the Mayo Clinic? We'd just received another hopeless diagnosis and you wept over my ears. Don't ever forget how accurately they hear. They hear you at this very moment! They hear you opening the front door. They hear you throwing the newspaper on the couch. They can hear with such accuracy that you used to keep me up at night with the sound of food digesting in your stomach. Even now, from hundreds of miles away, I hear everything you do. *I hear you!*

Go back to that Huntley-Brinkley night. Know this secret—I put your thing in a Baggie and hid it in the freezer. And every time you left to drive some desert, I took it out and held it and said, "Come home! Come home! Come home, bitch!" And now, I take it out again and hold it and say the same thing.

Then I go to the boy. I make the boy say it too—say it to heal himself. But what a tragedy—at best he'll only be healed in a partial manner.

What do you think causes the boy to get sick? To swell up? Do you really think he has allergies! Maybe he swells because of his neglectful mother's driving? Or maybe the boy is allergic to Mother's Emily Dickinson? Oh, roll your eyes! But when you're not out driving, you are dragging your New England white trash carrion through our home. What a dilemma for the boy! He swells to get mom's attention, then he stays swollen to keep mama at bay. Poor little spud! Don't you think our boy would be better off raised as a mutt—a little dog driving for Father!

But don't think you can ever drive away from us. There is no happiness beyond my home and no happiness beyond me. But I don't need to chase after you. Anything you try to get, you will ruin on your own by yourself. Just know that I and the boy are sitting here. Both holding your frozen stink. Both using it to listen to you. Both hearing your every move. We are listening to you. Listening! Listening! Listening!

I am your husband,   Joshua

•

Najaf was leading her horse up from the tar pit. Her shoulders suddenly crumpled and she leaned on the horse weeping. She pounded the saddle several times, and the horse jerked its feet, confused by this command. "Every day Sylvia would come out and kneel in the tar and read that letter through her gasmask," Najaf wailed. "Then she'd come back and push Moq out of his chair and watch TV over and over. 'Let me watch too!' I'd scream, and finally Sylvia showed me the big woman in the TV. We started watching her day and night. When we took the pills, we saw we were sinners. The big woman told us how badly we needed Jesus. We needed Jesus at dawn, but we needed him worse at night. We were thirsty for Jesus. Jesus was our bread. Jesus was our anchor, our root, our roof. We had Jesus in the light. We had Jesus as a bird, and Jesus on our tongue. At first we only spoke of Jesus, then we only spoke to him . . ." Najaf suddenly coughed. She bent at the waist, then shot up and choked out a completely skinned apple. I stood open-mouthed at the gastronomic possibility of this. I was not phased by the overt biblical symbolism of the fruit, only confused by the practical meaning of its presence.

"Jesus wasn't making us happy," Najaf cried. "But he wasn't making us sad. Jesus was trying to get through to us on the television. Jesus was in all that light. We looked hard for him. On many days we were very very happy. But then Sylvia would go reading. She'd come out to the tar and read." Najaf stopped. She did a little circle, then whipped around and started screaming. "All that woman did was read! All Sylvia did was read! Then she went off driving and doesn't read anymore!"

PART SEVEN

PERU

give you warning. Here is the dark stomach of this book.

•

The above being said, the dark stomach begins as I stand in Texas watching a blind snake skinning itself beneath a telephone pole. My eyes shift up and follow the wires to the horizon. Najaf has just unstrapped the saddles and I hear her hosing down the horses. When she finishes, we walk down the ridge toward the barn.

Moq lay belly-down in the chicken yard with his chin on the edge of the trough. A crow perched on his crown. Poe Yoga. I saw the hole, wide as a coffee cup, in the back of his head. Chickens had pecked his trousers into an intricate pattern of black and gray threads. He clutched his small hairdryer gun in an outstretched hand. Apparently, he'd gone down shooting—fifty feet away, the body of my Olds was drilled. The crow suddenly cawed, then dipped its beak deep into Moq's wound and flapped off with a morsel of his thoughts.

Obviously, we'd been found by enemies of Najaf's father.

The farmhouse windows were open. A gust flapped a curtain. The motion made me grab Najaf's waist and yank her behind the barn.

"Where are the keys to your Cadillac?" I asked.

Najaf's lower lip quivered "Moq?" She dug in her pockets for her pills. I shook her shoulders and asked her again.

"In the kitchen," she whimpered.

"In the kitchen?" I yelled. "You think they're in the kitchen? By the soufflé pans or by the jars of mango chutney? Where in the fucking kitchen?"

She shrugged and I reflexively raised my arm. I actually was about to slap her! But then I thought, "Why shouldn't she freak out?" I touched her cheek. There was a pitchfork against the wall and I grabbed it. Najaf crouched behind the Cadillac while I zoned myself into a *Seven Samurai* state, trying to make peace with the fact that I was going to dart across the chicken yard into the farmhouse and probably get clipped by some Iranian terrorist before I even reached the back door.

Toshiro Mifune I wasn't, but I did achieve the dog-chasing-the-ball headspace you get when you blindly cut for a freeway exit across three lanes of traffic. I ran holding the pitchfork like a rifle, scattering the chickens, until I reached the wall of the house, and hugged against it, panting, not wanting to enter. I looked up and saw that a gunman only had to lean out of an upstairs window and casually pop me off—so I hopped into the kitchen. Silence. No, not quite. I could barely make out Najaf's ticking bedside clock.

The kitchen didn't have a lot of jabbing room, so I raised my pitchfork upright—*American Gothic*—and searched the counters for a key ring. I saw an old electric can opener, stray bottle tops, a spoon, pizza box . . . no keys. My back was to a door. Later I learned it led down to a cellar filled with bushels of sprouted potatoes. Had I thought of it, I could have easily flicked the bolt and locked the door when I first entered the kitchen. But as Tim Fontanel says, "Baby, hindsight is just looking at the world through your asshole." I ignored that door until I heard its hinges. The kitchen air turned dank. And then I was just helpless prey, a seal pup belly-down on the floe as the polar bear smashes up from below—too late! too late!—a fat belly bumped my back, a hairy arm grabbed my chest, and then something incomprehensible—a wet sponge being pressed over my nose and mouth. It smelled like bug spray and burned my skin. My lungs turned inside out. Oh, the tingling at the back of my head! My brain cells felt like leaves from a tree . . . A flock of moths covered the branches. They flew away. My brain was bare. I was asleep. Good night, my friends, good night.

Black Mask writers prove their mettle by describing their hero coming around after being conked, sapped, or drugged. The first thing these gumshoes want are belts of Scotch, followed by a tumble with a blonde, although in the past decade, the conceptually real detectives of revisionists spend a week moaning in bed.

I came out of wherever I was remembering a line from a book. Not Chandler or Spillane . . . but finally finally finally my grandfather. Rex Ringer:

> Fontanel opened his eyes and mumbled, "Gimme a fistful of aspirin and will somebody please feed that damn elephant some peanuts and make him stop bawling?"

There was a blind man tapping his way across the floor next to my head. My arms were stretched above my head as if frozen in mid-dive. Obviously the blind man would stop tapping if I completed my jackknife and hit water. I opened my eyes. Above: vibrating white. A sheet of Antarctica. I had never Melvillized white before—but above me stretched a higher horror of the stuff: a ceiling. In the center hung a light with a hexagonal shade of frosted glass, also white. There were about eight inches between the ceiling and the rim of the shade. I moved my eyes too fast and got airsick. But I couldn't vomit. Something blocked my throat. In addition to never Melvillizing white, I had never eaten a couch cushion—but I instinctively knew my mouth was stuffed with foam rubber. Tape wound from the nape of my neck around my mouth and chin. When I moved my head, it pulled my hair. Above my head, my hands were duct-taped to a bedpost. I turned to the left. When the room stopped gyrating, I saw the blind man with the cane was Najaf's alarm clock ticking 4:35.

Then I heard footsteps. A man entered. I felt confusion mixed with relief. He wasn't some ragged ayatollah in a turban. No. It was large hairy Mr. Cushman—Joshua Cushman wearing duck pants and a navy-blue polo shirt that didn't quite reach his belt, revealing a hairy ring of belly. A little alligator leapt in joy across his chest. His arms were wet and matted with his black hair. He strolled over to the bed and leaned on the mattress and grinned into my face. His breath smelled of cigarettes. Inexplicably I felt concern. Mr. Cushman didn't smoke. Sylvia's death had driven him into the arms of nicotine.

"Hello, tiny friend," he rasped. He lowered his head as if to kiss me and slipped his lips to my ear. "You little babyshit buttfucking homo," he whispered. "I'm going to knead your kidney into pudding." With that, he dug his fingers into my side and squeezed.

Welcome to my bad times.

•

Later, Mr. Cushman stood above me, hand to his chin— posed like Jack Benny. For some reason, the tips of his fingers were purple. "You should be punished," he rasped. His forehead alternately rippled with scowls, then arches of pain. "Look at this—I'll never dial a phone again." He held up his hands. Buttons of purple skin covered each finger. He must have done this by digging into the concrete garage floor when I honked him down in Bloomfield Hills. That's why I was gagged—I couldn't yell into his ears and resmash his delicate ear snails.

"Now," Mr. Cushman said, "We need to think of a way for you to tell me where Sylvia is."

I thought: *Someone stole her ashes? Ben?*

Cushman cracked his knuckles—wincing at the sound—and arched his hands above my torso—oh, let me make this book's third reference to Glenn Gould!—then Najaf walked by the doorway.

She had been wandering down the hall. She wore a black cocktail dress and pearls. Cushman would tell me that he dressed her this way. He wanted Najaf to dress like Sylvia.

Najaf.

The girl would have been a piece of slinky perfection, except her jaw was wrapped with black electrical tape. And she was wringing wet. Dripping.

Cushman noticed her and croaked, "Oh my! Honey! I thought you'd left your body."

Najaf furrowed her brow in confusion. Mr. Cushman strode over and took her hand, "Come on. Let's do Ophelia some more. And you can tell me where my wife is."

The first Mr. Cushman literary reference!

He led Najaf out and I heard them enter next door. The wall knocked where the bathtub was. There were splashes. Above these noises, I just barely made out Mr. Cushman murmuring in creepy Karloff monotone: "Come on, little mermaid. Tell me where Sylvia is. Tell me. Tell me. Tell me."

Oh my god! Mr. Cushman believed Sylvia was alive! You know as well as I do that the woman was flecks of ash and bone chips, but to her husband, she was a whole woman still wearing her baggy Diane Keaton slacks. Mr. Cushman had lost it. He was a man without instincts. Let me tell you—the instant Ben had phoned me, I felt the certainty of his mother's death in my bones. This certainty slapped me as hard as if someone had led me to her slab and lifted the sheet.

Sylvia Cushman was dead.

Sylvia Cushman was dead.

She was dead.

And instead of being righteous and writing a book about his wife, Mr. Cushman was trying to resurrect Sylvia with fear and pain. Our fear and pain.

There was sudden silence. Then a frantic thumping. As Najaf was pushed beneath the water, I knew neurons of fear sharked through her brain forcing out her chemical debris. I believed that when Najaf opened her eyes, her vision would be clear.

As for myself, I started to pray.

To Christ.

Then I considered, "There are no atheists in foxholes." I banged my headboard in time with the beats next door. I'd be damned if my last function on earth would be sending SOSs out into the firmament! The third time my skull whacked wood, I had an escape plan. At first I envisioned this plan as one devised by Harry Houdini or Dutch Cretzer. But then I knew it was Rube Goldberg (and please remember, Mr. Goldberg is dead and thus beyond ridiculousness):

(A) I'm taped to the bed. (B) I set the alarm clock with my feet. When Mr. Cushman enters the room to do me harm (C) the alarm goes off. (D) The sound of the alarm rips through Cushman's ears, and (E) he doubles over screaming. At this point (F) I lift my legs and (G) lock them around his neck.

I curled and clamped the alarm clock between my sneakers, flipping it to the bed. The alarm was set for 8:00. It was now 4:45.

Thumps and dunks.

How could I guess when Cushman would come? How much of whatever he was going to do could I take? What time should I set the alarm for? While I attempted the impossible task of estimating this, I used the toe of my left shoe to force off my right shoe. That was not easy. The shoe jammed on my right heel. Then I used the toe of my left shoe to slide down my sock. I used my bare right big toe and its neighbor to twirl the tiny dial to reset the alarm . . . As I write this, I have to stand for a moment and jog in place. Oh the tediousness of that long-ago attempt . . . Recently, I passed a SoHo restaurant where an armless man sat at the window eating sushi with his feet. On *Johnny Carson*, I once saw an armless Korean girl bow a cello using her toes . . . Oh sweet god! Bare feet should be used to dance or stomp wine, not manipulate chopsticks or bow cellos! And certainly not to diddle a clock trying to set the alarm. And it was only a growing black rage that gave me the patience to set that fucking dial for several fucking increments before 5 o'fucking o'clock—now nine fucking minutes away.

Next, I studied the room. Where to hide my sonic bomb? If I left it on the nightstand, Cushman could just switch it off. If I lay on it, my body would muffle the ringing. Then I saw the spot.

I balanced the clock on the arches of my feet, and attempted to kick it up into the light shade on the ceiling. Each time I missed, the clock fell to the bed. The impact switched off the alarm. I had to again flip the tiny lever back on with my toes. I had to balance the timepiece back on the arches of my feet and try another kick. On the third miss, the clock almost flew to the floor. By the seventh try, I became confused. What was this exercise I was doing? What was this object? Those numbers? Those clock hands—arrows from Cupid? I was on stage. The clock was a skull. It took me dozens of tries to clunk Yorick inside glass.

I was successful, but I went numb. What a mistake! I should have set the alarm to go off immediately! The continual ringing would be a barrier of noise. Cushman wouldn't enter the room, just cower in the hallway. Of course, I'd still be taped to the bed —a Mexican standoff. But then, Cushman had shot Moq. What would stop him from reaching in through the door and blasting away? Besides, the alarm had probably switched off when the clock hit the glass. Oh, Rube Goldberg! How could I have imagined strangling Cushman in a leg lock? I did not have the John Irving thighs of a wrestler.

I began shaking and my teeth chattered. Then I realized— beneath my gag, my teeth could chatter! Although the chunk of foam inside my mouth was too large to swallow, I could chew it into smaller, swallowable pieces. I could then use my blunt tongue to push the tape from my lips. Then I would sing for Cushman! How I would sing! Maneuvering the wad with my tongue, I started nibbling at the foam with my molars, swallow- ing the granules I worked off. Gumshoe Tim Fontanel leaned over my bed and wisecracked, "It needs steak sauce."

And then Mr. Cushman stormed into the room.

His face and shirt were soaking. He stomped towards the bed. I was not prepared for him. Wasn't I five years old? Time for my nap!

I can't describe the next five minutes detail-by-detail. Later in this chapter I'll reveal the transcendence behind pain—but not now. Just know that Cushman didn't slap or hit me. He yanked my jeans down my kicking legs.

He then began insulting me.

But not about anything I'd done.

He insulted my penis.

He went on and on.

I was beyond humiliation, and took his sputterings in stride. I only jerked in fear when he began a tirade that made no sense: "You fucking Jiminey Cricket Carter peanut-pecker piddling Honda-fuckhead Toyota-fuckhead Tokyo-fuckhead. We oughtta strap you down deep in a well so good American people can do mileage tests around you, and good Americans can beep their horns, and good Americans can smash their dogs into you."

He then squeezed my taped chin and asked, "Are you right- or left-handed?"

I concentrated on this question.

I had forgotten.

And in my circumstances I suddenly saw the face of the Lord and my Lord was Mr. Cushman. I would do anything to please him. I would be right-handed if he wanted. I would be ambidextrous. I would write with my toes. I would take my blunt tongue and write letters of respect across his Arab Hand. But then he was gripping a large knife and lunging out—I pulled my jaw out of my head, trying to call: "Don't Dad! Dad! Dad! Dad! Dad!"

Mr. Cushman cut my bonds.

He dragged me off the bed by the back of my T-shirt. He slid me cross the floor. Why couldn't I put my pants back on? I looked up at the ceiling light and saw the face of the clock behind the frosted glass. Should it have meaning for me? It didn't. It was 5 o'clock. I was suddenly relieved and began thinking: "Good. The worst is over. Now we are going to go downstairs and watch Walter Cronkite."

•

We went downstairs. We did not go and watch Cronkite.

•

Mr. Cushman dragged me into the kitchen. He hoisted me up by the shoulders and slammed me onto the table. He picked up a roll of silver duct tape and shoved me down on my back. He bent my right leg at the knee and, using his teeth to rip the tape, taped my calf to the table leg. He taped my left calf to the other leg. He then jammed my arms down and taped my elbows around the third and fourth table legs. I was spread-eagled. I was tabled. He dragged my table to the stove. I struggled to cover myself.

A teakettle and a pan sat on the back burners of the stove. The front burners were empty. Cushman fiddled with the knobs and I smelled gas. "Shit," he rasped. He fished a matchbook out of his pocket—Big Boy balancing a burger on the cover. Cushman lit the pilot light. Circles of blue flame swooshed under the burners. Big Blue Halo. I remembered the time Sylvia had lit a sherry glass of mescal, then blew the blue flame out singing, "Happy birthday to me . . ." before drinking the hot glass of cactus.

Cushman found a big tin spoon and placed it on a burner. He watched the metal turn black. Then he turned, saying: "Now I want to know where Sylvia is. You know, don't you? She's run off and stole my son. My trumpet son. I want to know where they are. I want to know where she took Ben."

He picked up the spoon.

•

Priests, in particular, have rhapsodized on the martyrdom of saints—eyes plucked, breasts hacked—horrible mutilation as love-proof for God. But why does God need this proof?

On the other hand, would Theresa have wanted the Lord to stop her injury, stop her offering? Don't you know that she lovingly cupped each breast to the blade? That she did so with the same grace as the Chinese poet who presented his severed hands to his emperor? "What is your pain but joy to funnel up into the master?" she asked me. "Considering our vast history of saintly pain, what does your little burning matter, your little offering here on this Texas table?"

Before I could answer, Mr. Cushman was done with what he was doing and tossed the spoon into the sink. To this day I only eat at restaurants—never in kitchens. That sizzle.

Cushman left. I was making the table bounce up and down. The ceiling creaked above me. I bounced all over the kitchen. Tears streamed down my face as I tried yelling through my taped jaw. Then I lay there snorting, trying to breathe through my nose. That's when I saw the flames and—oh my!—can you imagine the beauty of those flames? A back burner was still lit! A lovely little lick of flame danced beneath the teakettle. A gentle hiss of water. On the kettle's spout was plugged a little whistle in the shape of a bird. The whistle was blue plastic. The bird was a sparrow. Can you foresee this miraculous cause-and-effect? The water heats and the water boils and the water steams and the steam flows through the sparrow's throat and it sings a shrill sweet song that tears through Cushman's ears, the shear sharpness triggering a stroke.

And who made this faint baby's breath of gas? Had Cushman accidently twisted it on? No. Sylvia had done it. The ghost of Sylvia. Sylvia had done it out of love.

Then footsteps. Mr. Cushman back in the kitchen cradling a hefty shotgun in the crook of his arm and clutching a writing tablet in the other. A raw red fish started flipping in my stomach. Cushman set the tablet on the table. He reached into his pocket and pulled out a fat black Magic Marker. He took the cap off with his teeth, and then tore the tape off my right hand and stuck the marker in my fist.

He moved to the head of the table to lift me up, straining my neck and leaning the back of my crown against his belly. He then whispered, "Okay, little Proust! Tell me where Sylvia is."

My hand was shaking. I couldn't write!

The kettle was doing vague water rumblings. A distant train. Taped to this table, I had to be Scheherazade for Mr. Cushman. *One Thousand and One Orange Boys*. I tried moving the marker. But my nerves were so ravaged. The marker skid around in jags and scribbles.

"There, there," Mr. Cushman said, patting my shoulder—the touch of a father whose boy just struck out at Little League. "Calm down. Take a deep breath. Just write where Sylvia is."

My hand steadied. I tried again. I gripped the marker tight—an ink stain expanded into a black kidney. I couldn't remember how to write! I didn't know my ABCs. I tried to visualize pages from books I knew. Nothing. Cushman tapped my shoulder, whispering, "Got writer's block, little peter? Don't let me rush you. Just tell me where Sylvia is." He lowered his head so I felt his nose on my crown. "Just tell me where Sylvia is or I'll dig your eyeballs out and roll them up your asshole, you Jap sedan."

Suddenly a *Webster's* worth of language tumbled back into my head. Suddenly, I was reluctantly thankful for my bout of lingo-amnesia because I now knew the story I must write—Cushman had hallucinated a detective novel where Sylvia was still alive.

Only it lacked the final chapter. So I would splice together several Rex Ringer plots about women who faked their deaths by putting the body of another into their car and staging a fake crash off a cliff into the ocean.

But then the water on the stove began to dance louder. I'd better hurry if I wanted to write this story before the boiling. Then I heard another sound: The gentle grind of car wheels rolling over gravel.

Cushman heard the auto and jumped. He crouched by the window to peek out. Through the screen, I saw a blue car roll into the yard, the chickens flapping out of its path with agitated clucks. Mr. Cushman grabbed his shotgun and stood flush against the wall to the right of the door. The sedan stopped. Dust swirled. The driver opened his door. He stood up and squinted. It was Mr. Cushman's Private Detective, the man I had seen at the swamp with Sylvia's refrigerator. Would he rescue me? I had to think. This was not a film noir world where private eyes were shady crooks. Nor was this a Raymond Chandler world where they were Christ figures. Private eyes were just working stiffs. And working stiffs were the guys who discovered abandoned refrigerators. And working stiffs wouldn't stand for torture.

I would rather write for him than Cushman! Let this man be my editor!

Cushman was fidgeting with his rifle. He hadn't seen the face of the intruder yet. I worked my jaws trying to shout a warning to the Detective and began waving my free hand, but the Detective was busy kicking the chickens in his path. Mr. Cushman gave me a scowl and made an impatient arm gesture for me to be still.

Was he crazy?

At this moment the teakettle went off.

It screamed a shrill whistle. O' radiant song of steam! The infant cry of the Industrial Revolution! A cloud of anger was shooting from the spout. But Mr. Cushman did not collapse. He stood gritting his teeth, popping his neck tendons while the sound pounded through his ears. His eyes bulged. The whistle pitched higher into a shriek. His little ear snails were surely twisted now! But Cushman endured. Cushman stood fast. Cushman did not betray his position.

The Private Detective stared through the door. He heard the whistle, but what could he see? He was looking into the dim mesh of a screen door. Was it too dark to make me out? Here on the table? But if he could, how was he reading that sight—a boy with no pants taped to a table, waving his hand. What would you think?

Then Cushman cocked the rifle. A gun cock is a distinct sound. The Detective heard it and braced. Maybe I've depicted this man in comic light—his sloppy tango with Sylvia, his hemorrhoids—and maybe he was good at his job or maybe he was inept, but for one sacred moment he became the avatar of private eyes. With smooth precision, he slid his hand beneath his jacket. And he whipped out his revolver. The sun poured down upon it. It was a holy object of deliverance, its grip gloriously wrapped with a rainbow of rubber bands.

That was the moment Cushman leapt up. He swung the shotgun up to his shoulder and fired, blowing out the screen door and driving the iron beetles of God over the heads of the poultry into the Detective's chest.

Then the sound of his own gunfire hit Cushman's eardrums. He fell to the floor, and began humping the tiles, holding his fists to his skull, bawling in donkey cadence. Outside, the Detective had been knocked to the ground and was lying there quivering on his back. His chest smoked. The cleared chickens began cautiously returning, clucking with their Egyptian headshakes. I, myself, began wiggling and shimmied the table across the floor toward Cushman. I was going to tip my table on him. The teakettle kept shaking metal-against-metal on the stove and I snorted through my nose trying to breathe. Just as I reached him, he stood. With a simple movement, the man shoved my table back across the room, then stepped outside. The chickens scattered. He rubbed his chin while considering the Detective: "I told you you were fired and I told you to go home to Dearborn. Now look what's happened to you!" The Detective was just mouthing, "Please. Please. Please." Cushman picked up the Detective's revolver and bent down. I heard the shots. Cushman rose and pitched the gun across the yard using Sylvia's fluid grace. Cushman stomped back into the kitchen, grabbed the steaming kettle, and threw it across the room. He used his own clunky Arm Language. Still whimpering about his ears, he stopped and studied his palm. Maybe he burned it on the kettle? He looked down and touched my shoulder, saying, "Be very quiet now. Be very very quiet."

Cushman hoisted himself onto the counter. He seemed to sit for hours. I just lay trying to be still. Then Cushman was breathing over me. I was looking up into his nostrils from an outrageous *Citizen Kane* deep-focus angle. He began whispering: "Let me tell you something, little pecker. I can out-Gandhi anybody in this neighborhood, but you cross me and your ass is grass." He chuckled, "You see, I see things as they are." He thumped his chest. "I see very clearly my place in the world. I paid the trump of my devils years ago." He fingered my forehead. "I found my place in the world driving down from the V.A. Hospital in Alameda. The Pacific Coast Highway was fogged in, so I cut inland through Cholame. I came to a crossroads where three girls were standing on the shoulder, weeping. They were holding flowers and photographs. One of the girls flagged me down and asked for a lift back to L.A. I asked her what happened. She started crying and told me James Dean had died. I didn't know James Dean from Joe Blow. He'd only been in one picture, and who gives a shit about John Steinbeck? Anyway, I asked, 'Why are you crying?' and she told me she was weeping because this boy had been robbed of his future. Robbed of a glorious future *by* a teenager. Some kid cut in front of Dean's car—a *frontal fifty-mile egg-crack with one bag of meat*. And as Sylvia told me this I joined her crying. I was crying for myself. I was crying because my car wreck robbed me of my lips. I was crying because of my ears. I was robbed of my glorious future. Sylvia thought I was weeping over James Dean. And do you know what I said to her? It just came out. I said, 'If you put my cock in your mouth

I will do anything you say.' And she thought a moment and said, 'Will you prevent this from ever happening again?' And I said yes. And she put on lipstick and then slid my cock in her mouth. And do you think girls did that back then? They certainly didn't. And maybe it sounds crazy to you, but I said yes to her promise. Ha! Let me tell you there are stranger promises made in this world, baby boy, let me tell you that. And when we drove down to L.A. she made me write all that I promised to do on paper and we mailed it. Shit, you know we mailed it to the North Pole? Seriously. Do you know why? I'll tell you why. In those days the United States Post Office had pride in their work. They maintained dead-letter offices all over the world. They didn't throw a scrap of mail away. We knew the post office would keep my promise forever."

Mr. Cushman paused to rummage in his pockets and pinched out a packet of Winstons. "You will never understand what that woman meant to me!" Cushman rode a cigarette between his lips and mumbled, "At Cholame, Sylvia had been on vacation with her family. It was a year later in Madison when we met again. She reminded me of my promise. She told me that on that first day in the car she had seen my greatness." Cushman lowered the cigarette and I saw the worm of ash grow. I squeezed my eyes shut just before it fell. It dropped on my eyelid. Hot insect! I shook my head, then winked the remaining ash away. When I opened my eyes again, Cushman was casually leaning against the stove with his legs crossed. "She always saw my greatness. I was her Albert Schweitzer. If the fucking Ubangis had cars, ida gone to save them. If the fucking Eskimos had cars, ida gone to save them—ah, you don't have a faintest idea what

I'm talking about—do you? Do you know I've kept my promise? You think I'm some corporate lackey? Let me quote you something . . ."

Mr. Cushman closed his eyes and raised his burning cigarette. He looked like a parody of a coffeehouse beatnik as he recited reverently:

"The Cadillac fin
bore an uncanny resemblance
to the tail
of the stegosaurus.
A thirteen-year-old Chicago boy,
trying to catch a fly ball
on a summer day
in 1961,
had run into a 1961
Cadillac
fin,
which pierced his heart."

Finished, Cushman opened his eyes, owling them and laughing: "You know what that is? I bet you don't. It's pure poetry. *Unsafe at Any Speed*. God, I love that book. If Ralph Nader had a pussy, I'd get on my knees and kiss it."

He stomped up and squeezed my chin. "You dumb little prick —you think that's a contradiction? That I give honor to Nader? This just illustrates what a tiny turd your mind is, boy. I do my duty to save lives. I save the little children from the intentions of Detroit. I save the little children so they grow up to become doctors. I save the little children so they grow up to be ballplay-ers. They grow up to be mothers." He looked up at the ceiling with watery eyes, then bounced his face down to mine, grabbing my hair with a snarl: "And they grow up to become pygmy-pricked Jiminy Cricket Carters like you."

He slammed my forehead back down and spit: "You made me shoot that fellow out there! But do you think that bothers me? No! Do you think I just shot him because I paid him five thousand dollars to find Sylvia and he did nothing but drive around this Panhandle with his thumb up his ass? Huh? Do you? Answer me! No. He didn't have to die for money. You know why I killed him? Because he drives a fucking Nip sedan —a fucking Nip sedan with a body frame as thick as an anchovy can and an eggshell gas tank." Cushman pointed out the door. "That man out there was driving a deathmobile. That man out there was going to eat it sooner or later. I just shot him to accelerate the inevitable desire of the Nippon auto industry."

Mr. Cushman took a drag on his cigarette, then poked my chest as if he were firing a missile. "Man, I'm sick of this conversa-tion."

Abruptly, he whipped up a big knife. Big knife. Cushman placed the blade under my chin—serrated ridge—and whispered, "You ever read the Bible, boy?" I nodded my head like there was no tomorrow. *Give me that old-time religion.* "You know the story of Abraham? I would never sacrifice my son." He started snort-ing and appeared transfixed by the motion of the blade. Then he peered down in my face and asked, "And whose son are you? What poor son of a bitch ended up with you as his offspring? Wally Cox? I bet your dad is a little shrimp like Wally Cox."

I knew his intention and whipped my writing hand between my legs. He struggled with my wrist and dropped the knife. As he stooped to pick it up, I grabbed the tablet from the counter. Cushman stood, extending the blade. I grabbed the marker. I began scribbling, scribbling in automatic writing. Cushman held his head sideways to read: "Because I çould not stop for death, it kindly stopped for me."

He laughed, "Oh, you bet! It's going to stop you with kindness!" Then I was furiously scribbling: "Mr. Cushman! With respect! I have the map. The map is in the bedroom."

"What map?"

I wrote: "I know where Ben and Sylvia are. They are in Peru."

Peru?

I had no idea why I wrote what I wrote. Then I realized *Peru* was true inspiration. I had become a human conduit of something amorphously holy, like a jazz musician jamming. Sylvia once told me how W. B. Yeats's wife took dictation from ghosts —automatic writing. When Yeats asked, *Why are you writing me?* the ghosts used his wife to reply: *"To give you metaphors for poetry."*

Sylvia was a ghost, but *Peru* was only a word—no poem. But what was I to do with it? Cushman lunged out with his knife, and before I could react, he used three simple strokes to cut me from the table. I automatically shot my hands between my legs to make sure everything was there. Mr. Cushman watched me fumbling, without expression. He picked up his shotgun and said, "All right, Captain Kidd. Lead me to this map of Peru."

Neither foot had feeling. I wobbled splay-legged so my burntness would not rub my thighs. I shuffled in this pitiful manner to the stairs, feeling worse than a low thing. Monkey Boy hobbles down the hallway. Monkey Boy grips the banister of the stairs. And as I began pulling myself up those stairs, the impossible happened: Monkey Boy fell asleep. I was still climbing the stairs, but just dimmed-out like a driver asleep at the wheel. I was just a sleepy boy going upstairs to bed. I was being followed by my Father. Followed by Dad. And Dad was going to put me to bed. Dad was going to tuck me in. Dad was going to crack the window and flick on the nightlight butterfly globe. Dad was going to tousle my head. Dad was going to say, "Good game, son. Sleep tight." And I would say, "We learned about Peru today in school. Can we go there on vacation?" "We'll see," Dad would laugh. "We'll see. Now go to sleep."

Then Dad rams the shotgun in the small of my back and barks some command . . . I was instantly in the present, climbing the final step to the upper hallway with Cushman following. I turned my head. Inside the open bathroom door, bare feet floated in the tub. Then Najaf raised her head from the tub and stared. She had the kind of expression Joan Didion must have after writing a perfect brittle sentence. Najaf was now as redeemed by pain as a saint, a pain that not only cleared her mind but blessed her with vision. She now saw an affinity between Cushman and her own father: two torturers with savagely hurt hearts encompassing a calm center of love. For Cushman, she knew it would only take days for him to finally feel his true center. She saw this task taking five years for her father. (And I'll tell you that her vision would be confirmed as far as her father was concerned. He now lives out his exile building Shaker chairs.)

As for Cushman, he began muttering, "Goddamn that bitch. I wondered where this was." Why was he cursing Najaf? I turned and saw Cushman sliding a volume out from one of Sylvia's book stacks. The book was slender and lacked a dust jacket. I wanted to ask him what he was reading, but my jaw was still taped. And seeing this book reminded me who I was the way a boulder reminds a geologist that he is a geologist. I was a lover of books. My identity in place, I was suddenly practical. Peru— the geographic location—wasn't Sylvia's point to me. The statement, "Upstairs I have a map" was. I should lead Cushman upstairs into Moq's room. Moq has a footlocker. I open the lid of that box with the pretext of getting my "map from Peru." I then grab one of Moq's guns, its handle exquisitely wrapped in rubber bands of gold. After I pull the trigger and pull the trigger, I rip the tape off my mouth.

So I followed Sylvia's inspiration, and led Cushman into Moq's room. But this was Najaf's room—I turned right instead of left! My legs started shaking. I had to get us across the hall to Moq's. I could have simply turned and pointed into the right room, but I reasoned that it would be a mistake to show lack of confidence to Cushman. Instead I elaborately studied Najaf's room. Making a big show of looking puzzled. I turned to him, and motioned my hands like blades, chopping them up and down. Cushman tightened on the gun and looked confused. Then he got it. I was using my hands to designate a box, the box that should be present in this room.

There was only one place where such a box could be kept—beneath the bed, that narrow bed with duct tape still wrapped on the headpost, that bed that would never beat against the wall in love. I decided to make a play of reaching beneath the bed so Cushman would continue to believe in my sincerity. When I didn't find the box, I would lead him into the other bedroom and pick up Moq's gun.

"Get your fucking map," Cushman whispered.

I shuffled to Najaf's bed and sank to my knees. Supporting my body with my left hand, I stuck my right under the bed. Abruptly, in this position, I began to tremble. The shaking became uncontrollable. Then my history ran home to me like a lost Great Dane. And this homecoming was so inappropriate—I was in the middle of trying to rescue myself! This was no psychiatrist session that New Yorkers go to. I was trying to invoke Hammett, not Freud!

What I remembered was how my mother would stand at the foot of my bed while I knelt to recite some new prayer she had penned. As I knelt at Cushman's feet, those thousands of prayers returned: my mother never having me pray for my salvation—instead having me pray for her and her church; I prayed for my mother's continued high stature in life; I prayed for the success-

ful healing of her followers; I prayed for the souls of her mission-
aries swallowed in a Turkish earthquake; I prayed night after
night, six hours at a pop, for her beloved icon, Richard Nixon
—my mother knew that these prayers erased that six-minute
segment of tape. But the most consistent topic of prayer had
concerned my father. At first I assumed I should pray that before
he died he had asked Jesus into his heart. But my mother told
me to pray for his eternal burning—Dad was an infinitely vari-
able piece of meat and my prayers the recipes for his cooking. I
prayed that his liver be roasted. I prayed his eyes melt into jelly.
I prayed his tongue be blackened, then charred. On the night I
refused to go on, my mother clenched the back of my neck and
pushed my head into my mattress, screaming, "Pray that he
sizzle, boy! Pray that he sizzle!"

And now, kneeling below Cushman, I realized that the verbal
energy I had directed out the top of my head was still stuck there
—all my mother's prayers, all those ridiculous words to Jesus—
stuck in my brain pocket, an internal gasket like that slight
detour at the beginning of the large intestine where deposits can
collect for years—a middle-aged man pooping out the plastic
toy soldier he had swallowed as a boy. And as I knelt below
Cushman, my head was so leaden with stale prayer that my
forehead fell to the bed.

Cushman comprehended the resigned state of my body. It was
too late for me to go Charlie Chaplin-ing around the room,
motioning in sign language about boxes and maps and Peru.
Cushman knew that I had been lying. But strangely enough, the
fact I knew I had been lying felt more important.

Cushman gave a disgusted grunt. We were so attuned that I understood his grunt as clearly as if he had just given a sermon. He was going to do it now.

"Fuck the noise," Mr. Cushman rasped. "I'm going to enjoy this."

He tapped me on the back with the gun. "Get like a doggie," he said. "Show me your candy ass."

I moved my elbows off the bed, and knelt on all fours, resting my chin on the mattress. It smelled sour. I shuddered when he rested the barrel on the nape of my neck. The metal was hot. And this skullheat sent me into a mental movie theater—not the Thalia Theater, that Edward Hopper vision of urban loneliness—but to a modern theater, a tetraplex with a bowling-lane-length popcorn bar and twelve screens playing new Hollywood product. I swung through the revolving door toward the lobby, but as I pressed against my wedge of glass, I knew this lobby was the Lobby of Humiliation. If I entered I would be reduced. I would be a rodent welcoming the fuck of the gun. And I wanted the nobility of a dog. So I kept pushing the spinning glass and circled back outside. And out of that lobby, I felt a fresh burst of rage. Out there I raged at Cushman for attempting to reduce me. Out there I proclaimed: "It is my brain that is Lord. Let my power swallow him."

The shotgun tensed as he slowly squeezed the double trigger . . .

and then I was born again

. . . the sound hit me as if I had ears all along my spine. It swirled up my backroot and blossomed in my head. Not that the sound was particularly loud. It was just so startling and metallic. God, it would be murder to wake up to that sound every morning.

You see, the alarm clock I had kicked up into the ceiling light went off. It rang late, but it rang!

The alarm had an especially brittle quality. The clock vibrated madly against the glass shade. According to my original plan, this sound should have incapacitated Cushman. It didn't. But when the alarm rang, he reacted like a man at a skeet shoot— jerking the shotgun to his shoulder and blowing out the ceiling light. I rolled to my back and covered my face at that burst of plaster. When I opened my eyes I saw the dark blue eye of the sky. He'd blown a hole in the roof. Cushman himself was belly-down, wailing, hugging his elbows over his ears. This was the second time today he'd shotgunned his little brain snails. Above his head, electric sparks rained from the exposed wires that laced the ceiling. I leaned against the bed and watched Cushman mewing on the floor, the sparks flaring around him. Blue dandelions.

He began wiggling for his shotgun. I scrambled up, but Cushman crawled there first, rolling his gut over the gun stock, protecting it with his weight. I straddled his back. It was like roughhousing with Dad. *Hop on Pop*. I ripped the duct tape off my mouth. My lips and chin were raw. I spit out the foam rubber. I rode Cushman's back, breathing heavily through my mouth. I heard distant music in my ears. I heard my mother's theme song. I heard "The Great Speckled Bird." A song first performed by Roy Acuff and his Crazy Tennesseans in 1943. I tried to sing. My voice was hoarse and cracked. I hugged Cushman's back with my knees and reached beneath him for the gun. He was still blubbering, but brought his belly down to pin my forearms with his weight. As I struggled for leverage, I realized I was positioned as if I were trying to greek him. I was embarrassed! I should explain my intentions!

Then I grabbed the knife handle in his belt.

My nose pressed the nape of his neck, so I lowered my humming lips in his ear. I studied the folds of that fleshy petal. It occurred to me that auditory canals were the tunneled passages men should worship in love. I nuzzled my lips deep into Cushman's pastry. Then I opened my mouth and sang: *What a beautiful thought I am having!*

Oh, this song was shattering into his ear! I took a deep breath, inhaling over the rut of his auricle, letting the sound of sucking air hurricane down his canal. Then I continued: *Concerning the great speckled bird!*

He beat his chin against the floor as he frog-kicked his legs. He contracted his gut, and I yanked the knife out from under him. The blue hole of the ceiling reflected in the blade. Cushman suddenly hoisted himself up with one arm and reached around for me with his other. "I am the monkey on your back!" I called out and sliced the knife between his thumb and pointer. I was amazed at the tactile experience of hand on blade against hand bones. It reminded me of a night in New York that Sylvia made us Cornish hens, and I went at my bird with the only clean cutlery in the loft—a butter knife.

Cushman made an "Ay yi yi yi" sound, an ugly mariachi cry, and a spiral of blood hit a falling electrical spark, sizzling into a flaming loop—*O sweet song of blood and electricity!*

I pushed down on the small of his back. He tumbled sideways, and I performed the following act with great concentration: I put the tip of the hunting knife in his left ear. Giving a final holler of Hallelujah!, I used the weight of my body to jam the blade in up to the hilt. I used the weight of my belly to press patiently forward, forcing the knife to bisect his skull. And this slicing was slow. Tedious. But I had patience and noticed little details. For example, Mr. Cushman had shaved his right wrist so his Timex would not pull his arm hair. It was 5:45. Cushman had only been at me for 70 minutes. I remembered writing Sylvia: "I'll phone you on your birthday at 11 p.m." When I called two hours late, she laughed, "Well, Emily Dickinson didn't learn to tell time until she was fifteen." Cushman's index finger started quivering as if he were dialing a phone. He was placing a person-to-person to Sylvia, but it was nobody's birthday. When she answered, he pleaded, "Please meet me. Please forgive me." His book lay several feet beyond his hand. Keeping one fist around the knife grip, I grabbed the book with my free fingertips. The spine said, *Thurber's Dogs.* I wondered if it was a first edition. With my free hand I flipped the book open at random and placed it, face up, under Cushman's outstretched hand: one page of text and a full-page line drawing was of a man sitting in an armchair firing a gun into heaven. A startled basset hound peeked out from behind the chair. Then I read the text beside this drawing.

It was a description of a small dog dragging a chest of drawers with his teeth. I was startled by this writing. There was more seething hardboiled energy in Thurber's description than in any private-eye novel I had read. Then I felt a tension release on my knife and my literary considerations ended. I rolled off Cushman. I stood and shook my legs.

His skull blossomed open.

But no thinking cauliflower slid out. No. Do you know someone who is a surgeon? Confront them with this question: Why have you doctors hidden the truth from us? The contents of intense men's skulls are different from yours and mine! The inside of Cushman's head was divided into pigeonholes, and in each compartment appeared a shimmering image, paper-thin, yet three-dimensional like a hologram. And each brief flutter depicted car chrome and slit skin: Monty Cliff's cheek on the wheel. Jackson Pollock's tree-trunk splatter. Tom Mix dying by auto not horse. And there were additional images that weren't strictly car wrecks—poet Frank O'Hara on a darkened beach— what's that roar? The wings of angels? No! No! It's a dune-buggy! And within those images floated smaller postage-stamp visions —anonymous car wrecks. Joe and Joanne Sixpack: bang and crash. And near the top of Cushman's spine burned a tiny image no larger than a birdhouse hole. There I saw myself—straw-headed lad tooling my grandfather's Pontiac out among the oranges, skidding into the tree and anointing my vehicle with fruit.

spent an additional five minutes alone with Cushman's body. And I made communion—but not divine. It started with a Poe vision—a homicidal orangutan climbing through a window a là "The Murders in the Rue Morgue." But the ape was Cushman—*his blood turns no bread to fishes!* Then I knew the sacred heart that flamed inside his monkey business. I knew that the truest expression of God's love was elevating us above the apes. I saw a science chart of a monkey strolling into an ape into Piltdown man into Fred Flintstone into a modern flat-gutted lifeguard. And superimposed on that chart was Sylvia Cushman. She danced from child in tutu to teen pounding piano with orange to woman spread-eagled in the Wilderado Motel to a now big-bellied nude with the lazy softness of a Renoir. Then I saw Sylvia lost in death—lost "out there" somewhere. And "out there" felt like an eternally empty movie house showing *The Glass Key*. I saw that Mr. Cushman in his own way had tried to resurrect Sylvia with his love. Yes, love. There's no other term for it. But his love was ugly, not worthy of forgiveness. He had just wanted his second chance like Peter—who denied Christ three cockcrows' worth, but was then given another chance to go preach the gospel, an offer sealed with a gift of a vast blanket composed of mammals, reptiles, and birds, and the offer from God: "Rise, Peter, rise and eat."

rose and stepped away from Cushman's head.

So much for his second chance. So much for forgiveness.

And now I'll write the truest statement in this book: I can't perform forgiveness; I do not forgive my mother; I do not forgive my father. And yet, I'm the only one who can translate Sylvia's message of *Peru*. To learn the meaning, follow me into the Thalia Theater. The film noir shining across the screen is from 1947: *Dark Passage*. It is a work of love between Humphrey Bogart and Lauren Bacall. On the screen, Bogart is staring down at the brain-battered corpse of his best friend. Bogie shakes his head, then sadly says this apparent nonsequitur:

> "Poor guy.
> All he ever wanted to do
> was play the trumpet.
> And go to Peru."

A CONCLUSION

TOWER RECORDS

For years, I've lived in New York. Tonight, I'm standing on my roof ten stories above Broadway and East Fourth. There's enough L.A-style smog in the air that the moonrise is the color of a cantaloupe. I'm up here with my dog. She sits panting with expectation. Her ginger fur is lightly striped like some dogged mutant of jungle cat. I start swinging my hands, encouraging her to take advantage of a dip in temperature to exercise. She barks, and then begins racing around the roof, scuttling along a horizon of asbestos and night sky.

My dog is a bull terrier. My dog is a pit bull. And she isn't named after some film noir dame. No Gloria Graham the Dog (*The Big Heat*). No Martha Vickers the Dog (*The Big Sleep*). See me leaning on the parapet, surrounded by a twinkling skyline, clapping my hands to encourage my dog with the usual doggy expectations:

Sylvia, sit!

Sylvia, heel!

No, Sylvia!

Bad Sylvia! Good Sylvia!

•

Across the street stands the Tower Records building. I live down in a second-floor loft that's parallel to the windows of Tower's upper jazz section. Earlier that evening, I stood at my window watching serious neohipsters purchase Miles Davis—and simultaneously played fetch with Sylvia. I'd toss a paperback and she'd leap, catch it in midair, then her momentum would slide her across the floor while she worried the book with terrific thrusts of her neck.

I was pitching: *The Only Dame Among the Kangaroos*. By Rex Ringer. His last novel.

•

The night I finally returned to my grandfather's orchard in California, he plied me with Scotch and taped the story of the two years I was "missing in action" (his words). The next morning, he said that since he used Scotch, not mescal, my story was his—mystically speaking. He sat down and in four weeks typed out a private-eye novel about Sylvia. The result didn't follow my more psychotic digressions, but I had become Tim Fontanel. I was two-fisted instead of neurotic and allowed to sleep with half-a-dozen well-endowed women. My grandfather ended his book not with the cleaving of Cushman's head, but with an epilogue called "Frankenstein's Cadillac"—Tim Fontanel tossing the body of a dead auto executive into the trunk of a Cadillac. He and his Iranian moll drive it to a gas station, and park beside the ice bunker. Tim packs his trunk with ice, covering the body. Then they race to Los Angeles where he intends to have this corpse resurrected with a bolt of psychic electricity from a controversial faith healer.

Of all his chapters, my grandfather was the closest to actuality in this one: Tim and I drove across the Mohave—Najaf in the back —to find Los Angeles aflame. Najaf looked up from her lizarded Bible and said, "Volcano Town."

It was. Smoke smudged the mountain lines. The foothills were dotted with brushfires burning in concentrated funnels of smoke like plane crashes. These fires had even reached Pomona—my mother's Tabernacle appearing under a sheen of orange smoke. We could still, however, make out the dome. It was now blue. (It had been many colors before—lemon, blood red, even chartreuse. Once a year, Christ appeared and revealed his beating heart to my mother. Lying within his holy muscle was always an egg. My mother would then order the Tabernacle's dome to be repainted the color of the eggshell. Judging by this current hue, Christ's heart had recently held the egg of a robin.)

We headed for the dome down San Vincent Street, a quiet boulevard of pink bungalows with fences of palm-arch cinder blocks. Because our air conditioner was going full blast, we were sonically insulated within the car, and when the events began, they happened outside us in a pantomime: Those small girls running down the street, swarming down the sidewalks. The girls—Hispanic—all wearing white dresses; all puffed sleeves and ruffles. Was this the circumference of some renegade birthday party? We slowed and the girls surrounded the car, their mouths open O's. They pulled out Bibles and began methodically slamming the hood and windows of the Caddy. The car rocked as the slap of Bible against metal thumped into our air-conditioned isolation. The talking drums of Jesus had arrived.

A mob of adults followed, running towards us. Two police helicopters insected into view, shadowing this stampede. As they surged around the car, I saw that the mob was clutching small bodies—children. Dead children.

Najaf suddenly leaned over the seat, shouting, "He that disobeys the Son will not see life but God's wrath remains upon him."

Then she was scrambling out of the car and elbowing her way among the girls to begin slamming her Bible against the Caddy with the others. As this Bible thumping grew louder, I flicked on the radio. At the Thalia, I'd seen a Cocteau film in which Orpheus receives poetry from Hades over his car radio. But on our radio—just cracks of static. Then a woman's voice telling us: Big rains were coming. Her voice telling us: There were riots in Teheran. Her voice telling us: My mother had died of heart failure that morning, her heart clogged with honey. At this moment, a circle of the faithful were barricaded inside her church with her body. A mob hacked at the front door with axes. The mob intended to rush in and chop off my mother's hands. They intended to press these severed palms to the lips of their dead children whom they brought to be resurrected.

•

A decade later, a mob gathers daily in front of Tower Records—an army of panhandlers circling the revolving doors. I recognize their faces. This is their beat. As the customers push in and out of the building, they give aggressive riffs: "How can you buy records when I'm starving? You think Madonna don't get enough to eat? She got enough. Me! Me! Me! I don't get enough!"

When I head toward those doors, they change their chant: "Hey, Orange Boy! Who you gonna resurrect in there? There ain't nobody dead in Tower Records. You ain't gonna do nothing for Sylvia in Tower Records. 'Sides, you didn't even resurrect her husband, did you? Your mama died so yous had to burn the dude. You drove your car to Joshua Tree desert. You hauled Cushman out of the ice and waited till the sun dried him. Then you poured the gasoline—man!—then you lit him at his mouth. You made that dude a fire-eater. You made that dude a reference. He was—what's her name?—Joan. Yea. He was Joan of Arc. He was Gram Parsons. When his pelvis combusted, he sat up and became the monk who burned himself in Saigon. And Cushman's heart was last to flame, but it didn't shape itself like no Statue of Liberty torch. His heart was a pyramid with an eyeball at the top just like the one on American money—which you're gonna give us cuz we're not dead! And we're not rich burnable honkies. And this is New York, not some desert. Now give us your advance . . ."

I shoulder past into Tower. Symbolically, it makes no sense that a record store, not a bookstore, is the final vortex of this novel. But it is. Every Wednesday, I search here for Ben the only way I know how. The weekly incoming shipment is unpacked and I search for a new recording with Ben Cushman on the credits. I start with Hooley Ahola and it always takes three hours to reach Chester Zardis.

Earlier this evening, I headed to Tower to do my monthly search and found it circled by nymphets squeezed into spandex and flak jackets that said: Missing Mommy rules OK! They were clutching makeup kits. No—CD cases. This was an autograph party. I walked to a window and saw a tangled-hair brat pack sitting at a table sucking Buds. Their arms were crisscrossed with leather straps studded with gleaming thorns. Just as I was about to turn, the fourth Missing Mommy turned toward the window. He swung his apoplectic hair out of his face and yawned. He saw me staring and stuck out his tongue.

I couldn't breathe. I knew him.

I returned to Tower when I assumed the group had returned to their hotel. I flipped through the Missing Mommy slot and read the credits of a CD called *The Hairy Purse*. The lead guitarist was Lester Cushman.

I'd always envisioned Lester left in a never-never-land of five-year-olds, fingerpainting toadstools with Wendy. I studied his photo. Although he had the musical genre's usual sneer, it was his eyes that must have made the girls in the spandex go moist. They were the eyes of the eternal five-year-old. Here was a boy who would make you do the mud shark, but afterward offer you a palm-full of M&Ms while you watched Bugs Bunny on his VCR. I bought *The Hairy Purse* and opened it. My heart broke reading the lyrics. Torment had Ping-Ponged Lester through these years, and he was now making a probable six-figure income snaking out at Sylvia with antiMom death chants and longing: "Mother had me/Didn't have no daughter/But she ran away/and hid beneath the water."

He did no songs about Dad.

•

At midnight, I was leaning against the parapet of my roof, feeling ironic and jaded, feeling like Fritz Lang when he said, "See you tomorrow" to his Nazi friends, then secretly fled Berlin to Hollywood, where he would spend two weeks filming take after take of Lee Marvin throwing hot coffee into Gloria Graham's face.

I crouched on my roof at canine level. I began shaking my fist, encouraging my dog to really let go: "Come on, Sylvia, you bitch—run run run!"

She dashed faster and faster across the black asbestos in beautiful tight circles, her little pig body taut, filled with the mad joy of running, and to my mind, the mad joy of being Sylvia. At that moment, I stood and glanced across the street.

On the roof of the Tower Records building, I saw Sylvia Cushman.

She stood on a moonlit patio staring, faintly enveloped in a diaphanous gown. She was heavier than I remembered. The moonlight made her body look as if it were sculpted of chalk. With her extra weight, she resembled a nude from a Romantic painting, from a time when it was beautiful for a woman's belly to slope out from her breast, the weight adding extra contours to the pelvis.

Then her body arched as she swung her arm in a swift pitch. The only big women who have such grace perform opera at Lincoln Center. Sylvia threw something across the street to a lower roof next to my building. Surely it was an orange.

I had to turn away. My mind was like an overdone drawing twirled on an Etch-a-Sketch. It had to be shaken upside down and erased. I had to clear myself to make sure it really was Sylvia standing there—standing on the roof of Tower Records pitching citrus.

I turned and looked again. The patio was empty. But a single orange slowly sailed through the air. I was stunned, was unconsciously hunching my wrists as if I had palsy. The orange continued its arc. I heard Sylvia the dog still running her circle. I heard her panting. I heard her paws. And then abruptly, for no reason at all, Sylvia the dog sailed into view—leaping through the air in perfect form: both sets of paws extended outward—as she leapt over the edge of the roof's parapet, leaping for Sylvia's orange.

For an instant, we made eye contact: A glisten of moonlight on the dog's opal eye; crazy tongue giving a final ripple; two perked ears slicing the air. Then my dog was gone. Then the dog was gone.

I froze. It was a sheer ten-story drop to East Fourth Street. No ledges. No balconies. I stood very still, the traffic noise accordioning through my ears. Then I stretched over the parapet and looked down.

And there was no dog down there.

No dog at all.